Honor Thy Father and Mother

Filial Responsibility in Jewish Law and Ethics

THE LIBRARY OF JEWISH LAW AND ETHICS

EDITED BY NORMAN LAMM

Jakob and Erna Michael professor of Jewish philosophy

Yeshiva University

Honor Thy Father and Mother

Filial Responsibility in Jewish Law and Ethics

by Gerald Blidstein

KTAV PUBLISHING HOUSE, INC.

New York

1975

Library of Congress Cataloging in Publication Data

Blidstein, Gerald J
  Honor thy father and mother.

  (The Library of Jewish law and ethics)
  Includes bibliographical references and index.
  1. Commandments, Ten—Parents. 2. Ethics, Jewish.
3. Parent and child (Jewish law) I. Title.
BM523.5.R4B55   296.3'85   75-38808
ISBN 0-87068-251-2

MANUFACTURED IN THE UNITED STATES OF AMERICA

for
my father ז״ל
and
my mother תלחי״א

CONTENTS

Editor's Foreword

It is with great pleasure that we welcome the appearance of Dr. Gerald Blidstein's volume on the fifth commandment. This is the first fruit of Ktav's *Library of Jewish Law and Ethics,* and it is a happy omen indeed for the other works in this series, some already in advanced stages of preparation.

The authors' broad erudition, his careful scholarship, and his fine analytical skills have been felicitously combined in his focus on a theme which, to my knowledge, has never before been treated at such length and depth.

I am confident that the specialists will value the scholarly attainments of the author, and that the general academic community will warmly welcome this volume on a theme that is always timely.

Norman Lamm

October 15, 1975

Acknowledgements

This study was sponsored by the Rogozin Institute for Ethics and Human Values (Yeshiva University), of which I was a Fellow for the years 1966–1969. I am grateful to the institute and its administrators for the opportunity granted me. I especially wish to thank Professor Isadore Twersky for his encouragement and counsel.

Introduction

Kibbud av ve'aim, the honoring of father and mother, is an enduring element of the Jewish ethos. True, none of the authoritative documents of Judaism dwell extensively on the motif or details of filial responsibility. The Bible devotes but few sentences to the duties of a son, and the Talmud compresses its discussion to a few pages; the major codes are similarly terse in their presentation. But the quantitative test is a deceptive one. The meagre extent of instruction in filial responsibility is far less important than the intensity of that instruction. The depth and power of a teaching are crucial: these determine its importance and influence.

The intensity of *kibbud av* must not be sought in biblical statements, declarative sentences simply considered. It lies elsewhere: in the patriarchal narratives that presuppose the graceful subordination and loyal service of children to parents; in the power and meaningfulness of God's self-description as "father" of his people Israel; in the strategic location of filial piety in the Ten Commandments, where it is the first of the "social commands" and indeed the *only* positive demand in the Decalogue made upon man in society. The intensity of *kibbud av* is not to be found in extensive dialectical interpretation in the Talmud but rather in the context and stress of its teaching: man must honor his parents as he honors God, for all three share in his creation; indeed, one tanna taught that the responsibility in the case of parents is even greater. *Kibbud av* is called the most difficult of God's commands, probably because of the infinite responsibility of the task. Characteristically, the Mishnah lists "*kibbud av,* the doing of *hesed* (acts of lovingkindness) and bringing peace between man and his fellow" as the three acts "whose fruit is enjoyed in this world and whose stock remains for the world to come"—one is first surprised by the specificity of *kibbud av,* then instructed by it. This Mishnah is the first statement of Torah found in the *siddur,* and is thus the first teaching encountered by the Jew every day.

What is *kibbud av ve'aim?* The terminology is itself instructive. "The honoring of father and mother" does not discriminate between the parents—each is inherently entitled to the same measure and timbre of honor as the other. And if "father" precedes "mother" in Exodus 20:12, the order is reversed in Leviticus 19:3. Judaism is quite nonpatriarchal here. Terminology is revealing in another way, too: we do not speak of "parental power," as in the Roman *patria potestas,* or even of "parental authority," as is common in modern discussions, but of the task and action of the son who honors. Jewish law is characteristically framed in terms of responsibility rather than right, and this distinction is especially apt here. The ethos of filial responsibility is simply not grasped if it is seen as filial adjustment to parental rights or submission to parental authority. The son or daughter does not, ideally, respond to demands made of him or her but is responsible for a pattern and process of *kibbud.* The temper is active, not submissive.

What is *kibbud?* It is clearly rooted in *k-b-d,* that which is heavy and weighty. To honor a parent, then, means to make him a person of moment, to express your knowledge of him as a person of worth. But despite good intentions, this vague vocabulary is too easily dissipated in the rough-and-tumble of life. The tradition rigorously specifies a concrete foundation. Using biblical terminology, it constructs a typology of *morah* (reverence) and *kibbud* (honorful service). *Morah* requires that the son not sit in his father's place or speak before him or even contradict him: father and mother are to be treated with the reverence naturally expressed for a superior. *Kibbud* requires that the son personally attend to his parent's needs, that he wash and dress him, and in short perform the service of a personal body-servant. Service, too, is an expression of worth, both as symbolic gesture and as the satisfaction of actual need.

The direct and personal quality of *kibbud* ought not to be ignored. Though the earlier rabbinic sources declare that a son must both serve his parent and provide for him, the Babylonian Talmud concluded that financial provision is not necessarily a filial (as contrasted with a social) responsibility. Clearly, the act of personal service in which the son gives physically of himself in a direct way is seen as the archetype of *kibbud.* Practically, though, Jewish law always expects a son to provide for the support of a poor parent. The scope, source, and enforceability of the obligation may have been matters for disagreement among the jurists, but the existence of the responsibility itself was not disputed.

Both *morah* and *kibbud* are expressions of inner personal valuation; they are not behavioristic roles. The objective act reflects, ideally, an emotional truth. In the absence of an inner conviction of parental worth, a jettisoning of the objective responsibilities is still not permitted; that would be false to the Jewish understanding of law and morality. But, at the same time, it is clear that the masters of the tradition knew well that more than formal obedience and service were necessary to carry out the requirement of *kibbud av,* and that the obligations alone, unfructified by inner vitality, grow sterile and even become impossible to maintain.

These responsibilities are certainly not placed only upon the young or even primarily upon them. Imperatives are categorical, not calendrical. Both the filial potential for meaningful service and the corresponding parental need grow, in fact, as the son becomes an adult. And the ego suppression required in *morah* is similarly much more rigorous and demanding in maturity than in childhood. Neither *kibbud* nor *morah* is a pattern of youth but of a lifetime. Indeed, it is possible that a pedagogy of *kibbud av* for the young is impossible in a society that rejects it for adults.

This volume is an attempt, then, to describe and interpret the Jewish teaching on filial responsibility. What is the nature and scope of this responsibility? What meanings does the tradition discover in it? What problems arise within this ethos, and how are they tackled?

* * * * * * * * * * * * * * * *

Let me warn the reader of two possible misapprehensions: First, concerning the apparent wealth of specific guidelines and norms presented in this study, the discerning reader will note actually a paucity of materials. In fact, both Talmud and codes are extremely chary of discussion and regulation of the filial relationship. The attentive reader will note that entire conceptual structures are extrapolated out of single talmudic statements; that medieval commentators rarely broach totally new areas of the topic; that codifiers barely go beyond the talmudic sources themselves; that we rely heavily on the responsa literature because rabbis ruled in matters of filial responsibility only when asked, and even then the number of such questions is always very small. The Talmud clearly left many obvious dilemmas undiscussed, and subsequent teachers did not rush in to fill the void. I assume that all this is deliberate, that the rabbis realized the unique quality of each relationship and did not hasten to issue generalized rules; that they perceived the sensitive nature of the relationship and the limited effectiveness of legislation in this area.

Second (and this misapprehension is related to the first), it should be obvious that a survey of normative materials on an aspect of the family does not presume to capture the family as a lived experience. This is not primarily due to the limited nature of my topic, but to the kinds of materials I survey: no family, after all, lives its life—ambivalent and crisis-strewn as it may be—as an expression of what *ought* to be done as found in a code, though some may keep an eye cocked in that direction. "Take the family— . . . for a true insight into its life, would it be sufficient simply to enumerate the articles of any family law?" (Marc Bloch, *The Historian's Craft,* p. 148.) This is true even if one utilizes a much broader concept of "family law" than that doubtless intended by Bloch. Thus, the reader should not expect a description of the Jewish family—I undertake to be neither its historian nor its biographer—and he should not construct a description from this study. I describe and analyze some norms that helped form the concept of what a family ought to be, on the one hand, and that expressed and reflected Jewish family ideals and realities, on the other.

* * * * * * * * * *

It is difficult to assess the sociological impact of these teachings throughout history. To what degree, and in what ways, were parents honored? How central was the maintenance of parental worth in eighth-century Babylon or twelfth-century Spain or sixteenth-century Poland? My analysis is conceptual, not historical: I have considered the historical milieu of my sources, but have not analyzed them as a means of learning about the actual practice of filial piety in various eras and places. I am quite sure that the very sources here isolated for a conceptual treatment could be put to excellent use by the historian-sociologist. But until that is done, we cannot claim to know much about the concrete fulfillment of filial responsibilities.

How much of the teaching seeped down to the people? Certainly, most were unaware of the subtle distinctions discussed by eminent authorities, nor do we know to what degree the most obvious teachings were accepted by the people. Yet we must also realize that the bulk of the teachings and discussions considered in this study are halakhic, that is to say, they deal with specific, concrete problems and set forth the way Jews ought to pursue. There are answers to questions actually asked and considerations of situations likely to arise, as well as articulation of general principles and formulation of general norms. Halakhic thought, itself, proceeds through a vigorous dialectic combining modes of discourse associated with both ethics and law: the quest for guidance based on a profoundly internalized system of values, on the one hand, and the lucid pursuit of argument and precedent, on the other. Taken at face value, we find in the Halakhah a—perhaps, the—characteristic expression of the Jewish ethos upon life's varied issues.

Due to the unique appropriation of Torah by the Jewish people, the principles and rulings hammered out by moralists and jurists deserve to be taken at more than face value. For these teachings were not turned to by specialists in law alone; they were the companions and heritage of the entire folk. Nor were they appealed to only when the specific situation discussed had to be confronted in real life; they were the staple of spiritual and intellectual nourishment, constantly studied and repeatedly heard. The devoted attention to the most singular of cases brought with it echoes of the full range of teachings and reinforced the commitment to the whole. The teachings, then, are much more than an expression of the Jewish ethos. In reality, they were a pedagogy that molded a people, a "tree of life."

I
The Significance of Filial Responsibility

The fifth statement of the Decalogue commands, "Honor thy father and mother, that thy days be long upon the land which the Lord thy God gives thee." The responsibility of children to parents has ever been central to the Jewish ethos: its very inclusion in the Revelation at Sinai testifies to its significance, as does its strategic place in the Ten Commandments—it is the first of the commands directed to man as social being. And since that crucial defining moment, the thread of filial piety has been woven firmly into the tapestry of Jewish life.

Why is it assigned so central a role, and why has Jewish tradition consistently stressed its virtue and preciousness? Alternately: what are the sources of parental authority? What compels the filial response? It is of course true that filial responsibility, the duty of the younger generation to esteem and care for the older, meets a real social need—the physical preservation of the older generation and the transmission of its values. But Judaism does not stress the instrumental role of filial responsibility in conserving society, seeing in *kibbud av* rather a shaping, directing value that contributes to the meaning of life in society.

Jewish reflection upon filial responsibility focused on these dimensions of significance: (a) parents are creators, and the recognition of human creators forms a continuum with the recognition of God the creator; (b) the ethical value of gratitude is first encountered in filial thankfulness towards those who gave one being and sustenance; (c) the structures of authority essential to human life are dependent upon the model of filial piety; (d) filial piety is a "natural" component of the humanity of man and his culture.

I.
Parents and God—Creators and Creator

The common biblical metaphor describes God as father, a loving and responsible father who demands and deserves the filial honor and reverence of both the individual and the people. God is father to Israel, whom he creates and redeems; he is father to the widow and orphan,

1

whom he protects and defends.[1] And when Israel betrays God or ignores Him, He is portrayed as a father despised by his children: "If then I be a father, where is my honor?" demanded Malachi in the name of the Lord.[2] Throughout, God reveals himself in the human image of paternity, an image that carries with it resonances of care and love, and expectations of reverence and service; but the Bible does not suggest that the parent shares in the divine work of creation or that honor rendered a parent implies honor of the ultimate Creator, too.

The first hint at this idea in a Hebrew source may be contained in an ambiguous phrase of Ben-Sira (c. 250 B.C.E.):

> He who honors his father will be long of days,
> He who honors his mother bestows it upon God.   (3:5)

This may be identical with the later rabbinic teaching that he who honors parents, honors God. But another translation of the Hebrew is possible: "He who honors his mother will be repaid by God"—an interpretation that would constitute an apt parallel to the first half of the sentence. And the statement, moreover, may refer, not to the common creative quality of God and parent, but to the assertion that opens the chapter: "God set the honor of the father upon children, and the law of the mother he strengthened upon children."[3] One acknowledges the authority and imperative of God, then, by honoring parents, as He required. In any case, the structure of these opening chapters of Ben-Sira is significant and characteristic: Chapters 1 and 2 interweave the virtues of wisdom and the fear of God, and Chapter 3 follows immediately with its claim for the honor and reverence of parents, apparently second only to the fear of God itself.[4] The Jewish Sibyl, too, described the ideal righteous man as one who "honors the ruler of the world alone, . . . and after him, his parents."[5] This same evaluation is found in Josephus (fl. 70 C.E.) as well, while Philo (fl. 30 C.E.) says, "Honor . . . next to God thy father and thy mother. . . ."[6]

In talmudic tradition parents share with God the labor of producing life and the grandeur and honor of that achievement. The rabbis call parents "partners" with God in the creation of a man. "There are three partners in a man: God, his father, and his mother."[7] The "partnership" of God and the parent does not point to a dualistic vision of man, with God the creator and possessor of the spiritual soul and parents the creators of the earthly body. Rather, both God and parents work hand-in-hand in the intricate achievement of creating life. God is involved not with the creation of Adam alone but with the creation of each human being—each man is wondrously formed in the womb by God.

This idea is basically biblical, of course:

> Your hands have framed me and fashioned me. . . .
> You have clothed me with skin and flesh,
> And knit me together with bones and sinews.
> You have granted me life. . . .
>
> (Job 10:8–12)

> For you have made my inward parts,
> You have knit me together in my mother's womb.
> I will give thanks to you, for
> I am fearfully and wondrously made.
>
> (Psalms 139:13–14)

"Knowledge of biological process in the growth of the embryo did not preclude its ascription to divine activity."[8] The wondrous, that which caused astonishment and reflection, is the work of God; life—in any of its manifestations—must come from God: "If all the people in the world came together to create a single mosquito and give him life, they could not do it."[9] And a *baraita* explains the "partnership" of God and man, thus:

> God gives to the child spirit and soul, beauty of features, the powers of sight and hearing and speech and walking, and intelligence. When a man dies, God takes his share and leaves the parents' share before them. The parents cry, . . . saying, "so long as your share was mixed with ours, ours was safe from the worms and maggots, but now that you have taken your share, ours is flung to the worms and maggots."[10]

Here the rabbis do discriminate (for good didactic purposes) between the divine share and the human contribution. God is responsible for the animation of life in all its manifestations—mobility, perception, beauty, vitality (it is interesting to note the rabbinic estimation of beauty as the work of God and as allied to life); man provides the physical basis. The thrust of the teaching of a divine-human partnership was the reflection upon the wonder of creation, in which man acted with God, and the seriousness which this reflection endowed filial responsibilities; for not only does the parent thrill to his partnership, the son must also be in awe of it.

It is stated, [a] "Honor your father and your mother" (Exodus 20:12), and it is also stated, "Honor the Lord with thy substance" (Proverbs 3:9)—Scripture equates the honoring of parents with the honoring of the Lord. It is stated, "You shall fear every man his mother and his father" (Leviticus 19:3), and it is also stated, "You shall fear the Lord" (Deuteronomy 6:13)—Scripture equates the fear of parents with the fear of the Lord. It is stated, "He who curses his father or his mother shall be put to death" (Exodus 21:17), and it is also stated, "Whoever curses his God shall bear his sin. And he who blasphemes the name of the Lord shall be put to death" (Leviticus 24:15–16)—Scripture equates cursing of parents with blasphemy against the Lord. . . . [b] All this is properly so, because the three [God, father, and mother] are partners [in the creation of] a man.

[c] The rabbis taught: There are three partners [in the creation of] a man—the Lord, his father, and his mother. [d] When a man honors his father and his mother, the Lord says, "I reckon it as though I abided with them and they honored me." . . . When a man pains his parents, the Lord says, "I have done wisely not to abide with them, for if I did, they would pain me."[11]

The parallel respect owed parents and God is based, in the final analysis, upon both the biblical verses marshaled so adroitly and the perception of partnership at the close; this perception sensitizes the rabbis to biblical nuances and mobilizes scriptural warrant. With this parallel firmly impressed, the honor and reverence of parents becomes a basis of the Jewish ethos, as weighty as the honor and reverence of God; indeed, God Himself, as it were, is honored or dishonored in man's relationship with his parents: honor shown them is for that reason shown God, for it acknowledges as valid and binding His claim as well.[12] The human relationship takes on added urgency because it is patterned on and reveals the divine; and God is brought close as He is assimilated to the warmth and immediacy of the family. The impact of this teaching on the Jewish filial ethos must not be underestimated; it vigorously animated the successful pedagogy of filial responsibility and haunted its failures. The parent was endowed with archetypal seriousness, and life within the family was charged with near-numinous significance and meaning. "When R. Joseph heard his mother's footsteps he would say, 'Let me rise before the divine presence [Shekhina].'" [13]

Though R. Joseph may have risen before his mother because he sensed her personal godliness, it was the parent's sharing the work of creation with God that provided the thrust for the earlier teachings. Creatorhood demands certain responses of the created. Doubtless, one senses here the ethical motif of gratitude owed to all benefactors and certainly to those who grant life itself. But the response demanded by the rabbis seems to issue from a deeper, more primordial recognition, one in which the physical fact implies a world of value. Creation was the unique act of "He who spoke and the world became"; the Creator is good and great in the act of creating, and all subsequent human creativeness shares in this goodness. When man recognizes his creatureliness before his parent, he recognizes the ultimate creatureliness, and the ultimate Creator, as well.

For by acknowledging parents, man admits that he is not the source of his own being, that he owes existence itself to forces beyond his own personal reality. This can remain a most abstract, intellectual perception, to be sure; it is difficult to jar the certain sensation of self-sufficiency. But the religious consciousness demands the awareness of a greater source of reality beyond. The issue of origins, then, is paradigmatic of the choice between radical self-centeredness and acknowledgment of the Other.

It must be understood, however, that the focus of these teachings is man and not God. The fundamental instruction concerns man's responsibilities toward his parents, not toward God. And though parental worth is derived from their sharing the work of creation with God, the family is not conceived as a symbolic pointer toward the divine and its claim. Rather, parents are joined to God in a value-continuum that endows the family with abiding worth, discloses the full stature of the human situation, and calls forth the response appropriate to that recognition. In medieval thought, however, filial responsibility becomes a more purposive vehicle of the encounter of God and man.

The assertion that parents are creators and share in God's creating acts reveals, too, the rabbis' wonder and astonishment, their enchantment and awe at the creative act. (Similarly, the *berakhot* before sensual experiences reveal their wonder at the world of nature.) In this sense, we ought not to hurry to the theological statement; in their focus on God, the rabbis carried enchantment and awe to their logical and experienced conclusion but did not eliminate them. God was seen in the world because the world revealed Him. The act of paternity, then, was perceived in all its staggering reality. As such, it demanded the divine.

The biblical text that preeminently demonstrated the participation of parents in the divine creative act was "Honor thy father and mother . . . " itself. Clearly, the Lawgiver considered the honoring of par-

ents a most significant and necessary component of the virtuous life.
But its presence in the Ten Commandments not only testified to the importance of filial responsibility but also provided a key to its meaning.
This was due to the structure of Exodus 20:1–14. The first four of the
ten statements (Exodus 20:1–11: the identity and claim of God; the ban
on the worship of other gods; the ban on swearing in God's name vain-
ly; the command to keep the Sabbath) all clearly establish and regulate
the relation of man and the divine. The last five (Exodus 20:13–14: the
bans on murder, adultery, theft, false witness, and covetousness) provide a basis for social morality.[14]

The fifth command, then, stands squarely between the command of
the Sabbath, in which God is honored as Creator, and the sixth command, in which the created man is declared inviolate. In the fifth commandment, man is significant, not because he is the created of God
(that is the burden of the sixth commandment: "You shall not murder"), but rather because he is the ever-present partner and imitator of
God, Whose single cosmic creation (the Sabbath) is celebrated in the
fourth commandment. The pivotal statement in the Ten Commandments, the one that moves man from contemplation of the divine to human society, is the fifth. But it is pivotal only because it dwells in both
these worlds, and celebrates the transient maker as a reflection of the
Creator. This characterization of the command to honor parents as being intimately related to the first four commands, in which the Divinity
is directly acknowledged and honored, is reinforced by the tradition
that the first five commandments were engraved on one tablet of stone
and the last five on the other.[15] Literary structure is a physical reality;
and the meaning of parenthood is ever more strongly seen as mediation
of the divine creation. Nahmanides (Ramban) articulates this analysis
most clearly:

> [With the fourth command] God has completed the description of
> our obligation to the Creator Himself. . . . He now continues by
> commanding us concerning the created things; and he begins with
> the father, because the father is like a creator to his progeny, a par-
> ticipant [as it were] in the making, for God is our first father, while
> our natural father is our last father. . . .
> . . . Of the ten statements, five deal with the honor due the Creator
> and five with the good of man. For "honor your father" is the honor
> of the Lord; it was for His honor that He commanded that one honor
> one's father, who participated in one's making. . . . And concern-
> ing the writing on the tablets itself, it would appear that the first
> five commandments were written on one tablet, for they relate to

the honor of God, and the last five on the other. . . .[16]

The exegeses of the 1st century Philo and the 13th century Nahmanides are remarkably similar, though Philo derived much from the Hellenic tradition. In his discussion of the Decalogue, Philo expounds the ideological underpinnings of filial piety:

This commandment [of filial piety] He placed on the border-line between the two groups of five. . . . The reason I consider is this: we see that parents by their nature stand on the border-line between the mortal and immortal sides of existence, the mortal because of their kinship with men and other animals through the perishableness of the body; the immortal because the act of generation assimilates them to God, the generator of the All. . . .

Some bolder spirits, glorifying the name of parenthood, say that a father and a mother are in fact gods revealed to sight who copy the Uncreated in His work as the Framer of life. He, they say, is the God or Maker of the world, they of those only whom they have begotten, and how can reverence be rendered to the invisible God by those who show irreverence to the gods who are near at hand and seen by the eye. Parents, in my opinion, are to their children what God is to the world, since just as He achieved existence for the non-existent, so they in imitation of His power, so far as they are capable, immortalize the race.[17]

The Greek origins of some of these sentiments are obvious. Plato had taught that "an ancestor . . . is . . . an image of God more marvellous than any lifeless statue";[18] Aristotle had written that "one should honor one's parents as one does the gods";[19] the idea that parents stood midway between the human and divine was a familiar Stoic idea.[20] Thus, the major motifs of Philo's presentation were part of his Greek heritage, and phrases like "a father and a mother are in fact gods" are totally alien to Jewish tradition. But the Philonic argument in its broader outline does dovetail neatly with the structure of the Ten Commandments, and it is consistent with the familiar talmudic teachings. The claim that "reverence [cannot] be rendered to the invisible God by those who show irreverence to the gods who are near at hand" is substantially identical with the talmudic report of God's reaction to the honoring or the dishonoring of parents: "I reckon it as though I abided with them and they honored me" or "I have done wisely not to abide with them, for if I did, they would pain me."[21]

Yet there still remain the marked differences in conception noted

above, and more subtle ones in stress and texture. For Philo, the attitude of a son toward his parent is a barometer of his attitude toward
God, and that—in this passage—is its significance. The rabbis, too,
speak of God's seeing His self-reflection in the filial encounter, but it is
done in such a way that the son-parent encounter gains depth and seriousness from the father-God analogy. God enters the family circle, rather than the reverse. The rabbis could say, "If Israel neglects God's commands, it is as though they cursed their father and mother,"[22] assuming
with the Bible the primal significance of the parental bond and inte-
grating God into that. And this subtle difference points to a more substantive one.

For Philo, God is the creator of "life," "the generator of the All"; parents are to children as "God is to the world." For the rabbis, on the other hand, the emphasis is personalistic throughout: parents are to a man
what God is to *him* in a deeper, more radical way. Though the rabbis
speak of God as creator, their thought is dominated by the image of God
as father; they are held by the biblical metaphor. Philo, however, uses
the Greek locution (parents are called "gods") and is true to the value
scheme it embodies, so that the parental stature is elevated by deper-
sonalization, beginning with God Whose grandeur lies in His having
"achieved existence for the non-existent."[23]

This discrimination is relevant in the inevitable discussion of the
possible Greek origins of the Hebraic concept. After all, the complex of
ideas we are considering makes its earliest recorded appearance in a
Jewish source (Ben-Sira) about 250 B.C.E., certainly late enough for Pla-
tonic influence. But both the pervasiveness of the primal biblical metaphor (God-father) and the thoroughly personalistic development of the
idea in the Jewish sources suggest that the two cultures pursued rough-
ly parallel courses, without the one necessarily influencing the other.

II.

The Ethos of Gratitude

Jewish tradition has long considered gratitude a basic human virtue.
One who bestows a kindness deserves thankfulness and loyalty: "Be
not stolidly unappreciative, like dumb cattle that offer no word of
gratitude."[24] While there is no biblical term for "gratitude," the concept itself undergirds the entire relationship of Israel and God. Israel is
covenanted to eternal service of the God Who took her out of Egypt, out
of the house of bondage: certainly, gratitude plays a major role in the
decision to accept the covenant.[25] The Jew repeats ceaselessly his
thanksgiving to the God Who redeemed him, and the Psalms never tire

of thankfully announcing God's mercies to His creation. Conversely, the *kofer* not only denies God and renounces Him but also declares and acts out his *ingratitude.*[26]

In their exposition of the bases of filial responsibility, Jewish thinkers teach that gratitude begins where life itself begins (assuming, of course, the unquestioned virtue of gratitude). Those who give life merit gratitude first; once this ethical impulse is successfully implanted, it will spill over into the total social situation—and will also be directed towards God. If the recognition of creatureliness moved man from awe of God to reverence of his parents, the theme of gratitude would move him contrarily, from the world of society to the divine. Or less schematically, the translation of the feeling of createdness into the language of ethics produces gratitude.

The primacy of gratitude in filial piety is a biblical concept. Deuteronomy 32, where God recounts His travails with His people and warns them of their disastrous end if they forsake Him, is textually and psychologically grounded on the parental role of God; the hurt suffered by God is understandable only when we see God as a father rejected by His sons.

Do you thus requite the Lord,
O dull and witless people?
Is not He the Father Who created you,
Fashioned you and made you endure!

(Deuteronomy 32:6)

Again, God is to be honored, as is one's father, because of the nexus of created and creator. But here this relationship is spoken of as a debt for which one ought to "requite" the Lord, and the heaping up of "created," "fashioned," "made you endure"[27] deepens the claim of gratitude.[28]

This, at any rate, is the reading we find in the *Sifre.* The midrashic comment exposes both the ethical motif implied in filial piety and the all-too-human motivations that often accompany it:

It is similar to one who stands and insults his father. He was told: "Fool! Whom do you insult? Your father?! How much did he labor with you! How much work did he put into you! If you have not honored him in the past, you certainly ought to honor him now, lest he make another his heir." So did Moses say to Israel: "Do you not remember the miracles and wonders God performed for you in Egypt? Imagine the good to be yours in the world to come."[29]

The point of the lesson is, of course, the filial devotion owed by the entire people Israel to God. But the model for this fealty is the gratitude owed the parent for his nurture of the child.[30] Here, God skillfully plays upon all the keys that produce the many strained theme of obedience: the love that surfaces through gratitude, but the hope and fear as well. By telling the people of his care and concern, He subtly reminds them of the similar benefits to be theirs in the future, and suggests the price to be paid for their ingratitude.[31]

It is quite clear, then, that the rabbis found gratitude a normal and compelling reason for filial piety. Thus, the Mishnah taught that a son owed his father service because "he brought him into this world."[32] Later the amoraim noted that:

> It is stated . . . ['Eduyyot 2:9] in the Mishnah: "A father endows his son with the blessings of beauty, strength, riches, wisdom, and length of years. . . ." . . . and just as the father endows the son with five things, so too is the son obliged in five things: "to feed him and give him drink, to clothe him, put on his shoes for him, and lead him."[33]

The two talmudic teachings are so juxtaposed as to suggest that the filial responsibilities represent compensation for the blessings given by the parent.[34] Naturally, this parallelism is in large part a characteristic pedagogic-literary device; but it does make an ethical claim nonetheless. Occasionally, a rabbinic source will be even more explicit and speak of filial piety as a "debt." Thus we find the following amoraic discussion of the rewards to be bestowed for the faithful implementation of divine commands.

> R. Abun said, *If an act which resembles the payment of a debt*[35] merits the promise, "that thy days may be long upon the land which the Lord thy God giveth thee" (Exodus 20:12–Honor thy father and thy mother that thy days may be long upon the land which the Lord thy God giveth thee), is it not clear that acts that demand financial sacrifice and the risking of one's life merit at least as much?[36] [My italics.]

The rabbinic sources do not, to my knowledge, speak of filial piety as a device for the inculcation of gratitude as an ethical norm. They do, however, expect that the gratitude shown parents will lead one to gratitude toward God. In this they are true to the biblical demand projected in Deuteronomy 32:6— "Do you thus requite the Lord? . . . Is he not the Father Who created you? . . ." —and elsewhere—"If I am a father, where is the honor that is mine" (Malachi 1:16). The Midrash also speaks of God's desire to be honored as a father:

> All . . . I have done for you [God says] was not done so that you should pay my price, but so that you should honor me as sons, and call me father.[37]

Yet here we note the rejection of the metaphor of debt and payment, and the deadly relationship it can create. God does not bestow His blessings upon the people so that they should "pay his price," and even the recognition of His Fatherhood is not to be seen as His "price." It is rather the sense that He Who cares so must be called "Father"; this is a human response, not a duty.

That parenthood compels gratitude is virtually a universal claim in ancient and medieval times, and its presence in Jewish sources need hardly be referred to as non-Jewish influence; certain ideas are the common property of humankind. But the stress placed upon this particular aspect of filial piety by Hellenistic-Jewish writers, the way they formulate the concept, may reflect both classical originals and the attempt to impress the non-Jewish reader.[38] Rarely, of course, is the parental claim to gratitude (or the virtue of gratitude itself, for that matter) rigorously analysed. It is a cultural assumption, similar to many others.

Ben-Sira, in an exposition of man's duties in society, wrote:

> Honor your father with all your heart,
> And do not forget the mother who created you.
> Remember that you came from them—
> And what can you give
>   like that which they have given you?[39]

And his Alexandrian near-contemporary "Aristaeas" placed the following dialogue in the mouths of Ptolemy Philadelphus and the Jewish sages:

> The king asked, "To whom ought we to exhibit gratitude?"
> And he replied, "To our parents continually, for even God has given us a most important commandment with regard the honor due to parents."[40]

Here again, we see the general significance attached to this *mitzvah:* it is a "most important command," and "even God" does not begrudge this honor of others but commands it. The specific ethical moment stressed by Aristaeas is, however, that of *gratitude.*

The dying Tobit instructs his son in a similar vein:

> . . . do not despise your mother, but honor her all the days of your life; do good to her and do not sadden her. Remember my son that she experienced many dangers on your behalf while you were in her womb.[41]

And Josephus defended the good sense and high ideals embodied in Judaism:

> Honor to parents ranks second only to honor to God, and if a son does not respond to the benefits received from them—for the slightest failure in his duty towards them—it [the Law] hands him over to be stoned.[42]

This summary of the law of the wilful and rebellious son (Deuteronomy 21:18–21) is more severe than the biblical original, which provides for the presentation of the son to the elders at the gate and their presumed scrutiny of the parental complaint.[43] The Josephan statement is quite characteristic, though, in its evaluation and understanding of filial piety as a duty second only to the honor of God, and one based upon the idea of gratitude.[44]

The most detailed exposition of the theme of gratitude is found in Philo. Men, it is acknowledged, owe a debt of gratitude to their benefactors, and

> . . . who could be more truly called benefactors than parents in relation to their children? First, they have brought them out of nonexistence; then, again, they have held them entitled to nurture and later to education of body and soul, so that they may have not only life, but a good life. They have benefitted the body by means of the gymnasium and the training there given . . . they have done the same for the soul by means of letters and arithmetic and geometry and music and philosophy. . . .[45]

The son who fails to show due respect to his parent is guilty of impiety to God because he insults "those who brought him forth from nonexistence to existence and in this were imitators of God." In the "human court," too, he is convicted of "inhumanity":

For to whom else will they show kindness if they despise the closest of their kinsfolk who have bestowed upon them the greatest boons? . . .

Philo continues with a long catalogue of filial gratitude in the natural world, and concludes:

With this example before them may not human beings who take no thought for their parents deservedly hide their faces for shame and revile themselves for their neglect of those whose welfare should necessarily have been their sole or their primary care, and that not so much as givers but as repayers of a due? For children have nothing of their own which does not come from their parents, either bestowed from their own resources or acquired by means which originate from them.

[He] . . . (who) does anything to dishonor his parents, let him die. He is the common and indeed the national enemy of all. For who could find kindness from him who is not kind even to the authors of his life. . . .[46]

Thus Philo presumes a filial debt for both existence and nurture, and stresses the cohesive function of gratitude and its expression in human society.

These same themes were repeated in the Middle Ages. In the medieval categorization of divine imperatives as either *sikhliyot* ("rational") or *shim'iyot* ("traditional"), filial piety is universally accounted "rational"; a key component of this "rationality" is the virtue of gratitude. Jewish philosophers and moralists identify filial piety as the root and first fruit of gratitude; gratitude itself is a basic social virtue that binds man to man and provides a rational basis for the worship of God.

Sa'adiah Gaon (10th century) mentions the ethical grounding of filial piety:

Furthermore, divine Wisdom forbade fornication in order that men might not become like the beasts with the result that no one would know his father so as to show him reverence in return for having raised him. . . .[47]

Curiously, Sa'adiah does not demand gratitude for the bestowal of being itself but for nurture. (Halakhically, as we shall see, the obligation to revere one's parents is not normally dependent upon their having been adequate to their parental duties.) Ibn Ezra considers both the be-

stowal of being itself and the continuous care given the child to be motives for gratitude: ". . . Reason, which God implanted in the heart of
man, demands that he repay with goodness all who have been good to
him; now, the child is brought into the world by his parents—and it is
they who diligently raised him, and clothed and fed him."[48]

But it is *Sefer ha-Hinnukh* which draws the portrait of this motif in
all its amplitude:

> Among the bases of this *mitzvah* is the fact that it is proper that a
> man recognize and bestow kindness upon one who has done him
> good, and that he not be base, a dissimulator, and one who denies
> the good done him by another. For that is an evil trait, held most
> obnoxious both by God and man.
>
> A man should realize that his mother and father are the cause of
> his being in the world, and therefore it is truly proper that he ren-
> der them all the honor and do them all the service he can. For they
> brought him into the world, and they labored greatly on his behalf
> during his childhood.
>
> Once a man has assimilated this trait, he will ascend by it to rec-
> ognize the good done him by the Lord, Who is the cause of his be-
> ing and the cause of the existence of all his forefathers, reaching
> back to Adam the first. It was He who brought him into the world
> and provided for his needs all his life; who structured him and per-
> fected his body; who gave him a soul and intelligence—for without
> the soul with which God graced us, man would be as the brute
> horse and mule. So a man ought to understand well how much ef-
> fort is owed the service of the Lord.[49]

Righteousness demands that a man feel gratitude to those who have
done him good and respond in kind. Gratitude, again, is considered rational as well as ethical; thus Sa'adiah Gaon states, ". . . logic demands that whoever does something good be compensated . . . by
means of thanks if he does not require any reward."[50] Inasmuch as parents bestow upon a man his very existence, they merit the utmost expression of gratefulness. As with Sa'adiah and Ibn Ezra, gratitude to
parents is not stimulated by their being the cause of one's existence
alone, but is evoked by all their efforts—their diligence and tender-
ness—during one's childhood. Both one's being and one's nurture and
upbringing demand the honor and service of parents. Finally, if parents
are seen as worthy of gratitude from their children, how obvious it becomes that God, Father of all men and author in truth of the life bestowed by parents, is worthy of honor and service.[51] Thus, the honor

done parents is a basic instance of a universally acknowledged ethical norm, and guides man (and Israel) to its broader application in social and religious existence.

Perhaps the most provocative exploration of this theme is found in the 11th century R. Bahya. In a discussion of the motives for the service of God, the author of *Hovot ha-Levavot* writes:

> . . . it is known[52] that we ought to acknowledge gratefully a kindness done us in proportion to the doer's intention of aiding us. . . . If some good happens to us through the act of someone who had no intention of benefitting us, we owe him no thanks. . . . It is known that the motives of a parent are purely egocentric, for the child is truly a limb of his parent. . . . Do you not see that the parent is more solicitous of the child's welfare—that he be fed and clothed—than of his own? That he tries to prevent any hurt to his child? That he will labor to exhaustion to guarantee the peace and security of his child? All this because of the instinctive feelings of parental love and mercy implanted in man. Nevertheless, both Torah and reason oblige man to serve, honor, and revere his parents . . . though the parent is forced to do his acts of kindness by nature itself; the kindness is truly God's, and the parent is His agent.[53]

R. Bahya is one with the other thinkers cited in this section; he too concludes that gratitude requires that a man honor and revere his parents, and that both revelation and reason so dictate. But he also subjects this obligation to rigorous scrutiny. If gratitude is properly felt in proportion to the absence of egocentric motivation on the part of the doer of the kind deed, R. Bahya asks: "What motivates parents to their many acts of dedication and self-sacrifice? Surely, natural drives and satisfactions. Does a clear understanding of this motivation affect—perhaps even completely sap—the traditional claim that gratitude requires the honor and service of parents?"[54]

The fundamental challenges that can be hurled at any theory of filial gratitude are fairly obvious. No man requests to be born, and life once given is a debatable good. The prospective parents join for mutual pleasure, not to do an act of kindness for their as-yet unconceived offspring; much of subsequent parental nurture and care is stimulated by instinct or compelled by societal expectations.

That man himself is no partner to his own creation was an old source of complaint. Thrust into a hostile life, Job contends (3:11–12; 10:18): "Why died I not from the womb? Why did I not perish at birth? Why did the knees receive me? And wherefore the breasts, that I should

suck? . . . Wherefore hast Thou brought me forth out of the womb?"
So too Jeremiah—though for different reasons—(20:14–18): "Cursed be
the day wherein I was born; . . . Wherefore came I out of the womb to
see labor and sorrow? . . ." Rabbi and visionary alike meditated on the
mighty fact that no man is consulted about his coming into being. R.
Elazar ha-Kappar used to say, " . . . not of thine own will were you
formed, and not of your will will you die. . . ."[55]   The same phrase is
found in the apocryphal IV Ezra.[56] Curiously, the rabbinic aggadah does
not (to my knowledge) conceive of man's complaining to God about the
injustice perpetrated upon him. Remember the brief filed by Milton on
Adam's behalf?

> Did I request thee, Maker, from my Clay
> To mould me Man, did I solicit thee
> From darkness to promote me, or here place
> In this delicious garden?

And Adam knows that his offspring, too, will ask,

> Wherefore didst thou beget me? I sought it not. . . .[57]

But Adam does not, in rabbinic aggadah, contend with his Maker on
that account. The agony of Job and the anger of Jeremiah were heard in
all their anguish, but they did not become part of a world-view, and the
rabbis do not labor to disarm man of claims against His maker. God is
both just and good. His creation is fair to behold and man is privileged
to participate. Life is good. Gratitude is in order.[58] The same is true of
the filial relation: rabbinic literature did not raise the question of the
filial "debt" having been unknowingly contracted and, in fact, constituting a claim against one's creators rather than a debt owed them!
     The Greeks, though, did raise our question, in the context of filial re-
sponsibility. Socrates, in urging filial gratitude upon his son Lampro-
cles, takes great pains to blunt the accusation of parental egocentricity:

> Whom, then, can we find receiving greater benefits from any per-
> son than children from their parents? Children whom their parents
> have brought from non-existence into existence, to so view so many
> beautiful objects, and to share in so many blessings, as the gods
> grant to men; . . . You do not, surely, suppose that men beget chil-
> dren merely to gratify their passions, since the streets are full, as
> well as the brothels, of means to allay desire. . . .[59]

Josephus is sufficiently sensitive to the point to imagine that the parents of a budding rebellious son (*ben sorer*) were instructed to tell their child "that they came together in matrimony not for pleasure's sake . . . but that they might have children who should tend their old age and who should receive from them everything that they needed."[60] Indeed, the Midrash is a good deal more realistic on this point: One midrashic explication of the famous verse in Psalms, "Behold, I was brought forth in iniquity; in sin did my mother conceive me" (51:7), reads, "Even the most pious are partly sinful here. David said—'Did father Jesse really intend to bring me into this world? Why, he had only his own pleasure in mind.' You know this is so, because as soon as they satisfy their desires, he turns away to one side and she turns away to the other side."[61]

R. Bahya admits the weakness of arguing from filial gratitude to filial piety. This is true even though the author of *Hovot ha-Levavot* does not base the major claim for filial gratitude upon the bestowal of existence itself, with the attendant skepticism as to the origins and worth of the gift, but upon parental nurture and concern. But this claim too is met by the more subtle rejoinder: human nature, for which no man can take credit, compels parental benevolence. A mother does not *choose* to love or to care. R. Bahya does not answer the filial question, nor is he compelled to; his purpose is to demonstrate the gratitude owed God, not parents. But he does assume that whatever the cause of parental care, even if it is largely a form of self-love, it merits gratitude.

Thus, despite the talmudic emphasis on parental "creatorhood" as a prime motive for filial piety, many medievals clearly are not impressed with the claim that the production of offspring *per se* merits gratitude. R. Israel ben Joseph Alnakawa (14th century) is explicit on this point:

> A man should honor his father and mother more for the moral instruction they gave him, than for their having brought him into this world. For in bringing him into this world, their own pleasure was their motive.

And *Orhot Zaddikim* (anonymous; 15th century) instructed his reader to love his parents by reflecting how "they raised him and took pains with him so as to teach him the ways of the Lord. . . ."[62] Gratitude, when employed by the medievals, is often an uncomfortable bedfellow with procreation, and rests more easily with the debt owed for nurture and education. This medieval insistence, which we have seen implied in Sa'adiah and R. Bahya and explicit in R. Joseph Alnakawa, that parental nurture and care compel filial gratitude and its expression in filial piety, would certainly displease the halakhic mind; the latter claimed that the fact of paternity alone established the nexus that compelled filial piety, and that this piety was an imperative that did not fluctuate with the merits of specific parents or the experiences encountered within specific relationships.[63]

But too much ought not to be made of this contrast. Though doubtless cognizant of the halakhic standard, the philosophers and moralists also knew that most parents not only bear children but also raise them with diligence, patience, and self-sacrifice. The appeal to filial gratitude was based upon the common experience of humanity, which confirms the devotion of most parents to their children. From this point of view, the ungrateful son is likely to reject not only his parents but the entire complex of sentiments and responsibilities that animate human fellowship and solidarity.

Despite a new vocabulary, the medieval philosophers have not radically reworked the motives for filial responsibility. There are new nuances, as a note of ambivalence toward physical creation *per se* can be heard; there is even a new stress. The ethical virtue of gratitude takes pride of place now and, with the crystallization of the religious and social significances of gratitude, filial responsibility is seen as instrumental in the formation of a healthy society. We shall soon have occasion to see how in their stress on the *political* implications of filial piety, medieval thinkers add a new dimension to the concept. Thus far, however, their emphasis on gratitude has fleshed out the biblical-talmudic tradition but has not radically altered it.

The relevance of gratitude to filial piety has remained a sore point. The late 18th century halakhist and moralist, R. Abraham Danzig, took up the argument again; despite the passion of his statement, he does not demonstrate the "rationality" of filial gratitude but rather its inevitability, its consistency with a world in which man owes gratitude to God, too. Behind it all, is the fear that man will one fine day declare that he owes God nothing, and that perhaps the Lord is the debtor:

> May the mouths speaking untruth be stopped. For they say that no gratitude is owed parents, for their immediate motive was self-gratification, and the child was merely created incidentally; that with the child born, the Lord made the nature of parents such that they would raise him, as indeed all animals raise their young, without the young being grateful for this. . . . For men who argue in this way show themselves to be, indeed, brutes, whom God denied reason and understanding. Concerning such opinions, our sages say, "Whoever is ungrateful toward his comrade will, in time, be

ungrateful to God." For according to their thinking, they need not fear or honor God either, since we are His creations, and it is only proper that one be good and merciful to one's creatures. Doubtless those who say these things deny God in their hearts.[64]

III.
Parents and Authority

Master Yu said: Those who in private life behave well toward their parents and elder brothers, in public life seldom show a disposition to resist the authority of their superiors. And as for such men starting a revolution, no instance of it has ever occurred.

(*Analects of Confucius*, I, 2; trans. A. Waley)

Can you deny . . . that you were our child and servant, both you and your ancestors? And if this is so, do you imagine that what is right for us is equally right for you? . . . . You did not have equality of rights with your father . . . to enable you to retaliate. . . . You were not allowed to answer back. . . . Do you expect to have such a license against your country and its laws? . . . . Do you not realize that you are even more bound to respect and placate the anger of your country than your father's anger? That if you cannot persuade your country, you must do whatever it orders. . . .?

(Plato, *Crito*, 50e–51c)

The family is the building-block of the state, and the habits of docility in the face of authority and veneration of the traditional order and values may be implanted at its hearth. It is true that authoritarian systems, whether politically or religiously totalitarian, educate their charges to reject parental authority in the interests of the higher authority represented by the state or the particular religious values in question. Nonetheless, the claim of the ancients may be profoundly true; the habits of docility in the face of authority, once inculcated at the parental hearth, can be transferred or redirected to their new object—the political or cultural system. Or as Leo Strauss put it, "The first man who uttered a word like 'father' . . . was the first political philosopher."[65a]

Some Jewish exegetes and moralists of the later Middle Ages are not too far from depicting a similar psychology, and applauding it. Maimonides, some centuries before, had spoken in more genial terms of social stability as based upon filial piety. But rabbinic literature does not note this result of filial piety at all. This, I believe, is due to its halakhic orientation. For despite the seemingly sweeping self-abnegation expected of the child, the claims of parental authority are judiciously winnowed and placed in relation to other aspects of the Jewish value structure. Indeed, filial *responsibility* replaces parental *authority.* Some of the medieval thinkers to be cited, then, do not extrapolate the authority function of filial piety from a close reading of the halakhic sources, rather they operate with a more general notion of filial submission.

The claim that social or familial or even personal well-being is advanced by a devotion to filial piety may be made by reference to the Decalogue itself:

> Honor your father and your mother, *that you may long endure on the land* which the Lord your God is giving you. [My italics]

"Long endure on the land" clearly suggests social vitality and durability,[65b] and filial piety functions pragmatically in the social context. Nor is it to the point to deny this functional effect by claiming that the verse describes the reward—and implies the punishment—to be bestowed by God; in the Bible, and certainly in a verse such as the one cited, the divine reward is often mediated through natural or historical processes. Morality and history do coincide in biblical theory, much as this may raise questions for both historian and philosopher.

The Mishnah—and Maimonides in his comment upon it—makes a similar claim (in its own idiom, of course):

> These are the deeds whose fruits are enjoyed in this world while the principle remains for their doer in the world to come: honoring one's father and mother. . . .[66]

To which Maimonides comments:

> . . . all the *mitzvot* fall, at the outset, into one of two categories; some *mitzvot* center on the individual and on his relation with God, such as the commands to wear *zizit* and *t'fillin,* to observe the Sabbath, and to avoid idolatry. Other *mitzvot* have as their aim the establishment of proper relations between men, such as the bans on robbery, fraud, hatred, vengeance, the command to love one another and . . . to honor one's parents and one's teachers, for they are the authors of all that is. . . . If a man has fulfilled those *mitzvot* that aid in the establishment of stable social relationships, he is re-

warded in the world to come for his fulfilling a *mitzvah,* and benefits in this world for his proper behavior with his fellow men, since
if he pursues this path and his neighbor behaves similarly, he too
will share in the (common) good.

Broadly speaking, then, Maimonides finds in the Mishnah the idea that
proper observance of the fifth commandment is essential to the stabili-
zation of society. He similarly designates as *mishpatim* those *"mitzvot
whose reason is apparent, and the wordly benefits of whose fulfillment
is known, such as the bans on robbery and murder, and the command
to honor one's father and mother."*[67]
Specifically, Maimonides considers the family unit the essential basis of social organization. If the fabric of the family is worn and weak
(and respect for parents is, for Maimonides, a key component in the
healthy family), the cloth of which society—and especially the state—
is woven, will disintegrate. Thus he writes, "He who strikes his father
or whose mother is killed on account of his great audacity, and because
he undermines the constitution of the family, which is the foundation
of the state."[68] The dependence of the state upon general acceptance of
its authority was uppermost in Maimonides' mind (he is, on the whole,
a realist about the importance of authority in human affairs), and authority is first respected or rejected within the family. Plato had written
long before that, " . . . when the right regulation of private
households within a society is neglected, it is idle to expect the foundations of public law to be secure."[69] And Aristotle understood the guidance of the family by the father to be a form of government,[70] just as
Maimonides himself does in his *Treatise on Logic,* where the "government of the household" is treated as a branch of political science.[71]
Later thinkers agree with Maimonides in finding pragmatic implications in the fifth commandment and also discover these implications in
the area of "authority." But they focus on the religious tradition as the
chief beneficiary rather than on the political structure. Both R. Levi ben
Gershom (14th century) and R. Isaac Abarbanel (15th century) stress
the significance of filial piety in the preservation of the tradition, a purpose more central to the Jewish experience (certainly the exilic experience) than the preservation of the state.
Thus, R. Levi ben Gershom (Ralbag) states:

> . . . this [respect for parents] will ensure that succeeding genera-
> tions will accept the teachings of their elders, generation after gen-
> eration, and they will all, therefore, be strong in their observance of
> the Torah of the Lord. . . . Also, this will bring the home to its pro-

per perfection, which is the first step toward the perfection of the state. And this perfection of the state encourages the agreement among men, so that the young accept the teachings of their masters; this will be a factor in the continued loyalty of Israel to the Torah of the Lord, generation after generation.[72]

So too, though perhaps more directly, with Abarbanel:

> The purpose of this *mitzvah* is to raise the importance of the traditions possessed by parents in men's eyes, so that they believe in them and rely upon them. And since the thrust of this command is to create belief in the tradition of earlier generations, . . . without which the Torah could not exist, therefore this command is found among the five divine commands on the first tablet, rather than among the five commands concerned with human relations that are on the second tablet.[73]

Both Ralbag and Abarbanel utilize motifs with which we are already familiar; Ralbag posits the dependence of social stability upon the stability of the home; Abarbanel works with the distinction between the first and last halves of the Decalogue. Their main point, though, is new. Respect for parents is likely to strengthen respect for, and then acceptance of, the tradition they represent; ultimately it will generate an atmosphere of commitment to the authority of the tradition generally. R. Joseph Albo (15th century) summed it up:

> The fifth commandment was given to urge respect for the tradition, that is to say, that a person should be drawn after the traditions of the fathers, for this is a main principle of all religions, the existence of which is inconceivable if men do not accept the traditions of the fathers and of the sages of that religion.[74]

And the parable Albo prefixed to this declaration emphasized the crucial nature of tradition for the religions of the West, based as they are on historical claims.

Kibbud av ve'aim, as seen by these thinkers, is a conservative force. As the effects of filial piety spill over into the political and ideological spheres, it becomes a force for the perpetuation of structures and traditions rather than their change; for stability rather than for ferment; for acquiescence rather than challenge. It is, of course, quite true that the biblical and rabbinic sources do not project the imperative of filial piety or its details with loyalty to the tradition as its goal. This is a medie-

val formulation. The more basic and less scholastic question is, however, whether filial piety as a phenomenon does not function in this
way, and whether *kibbud av* is not a necessary condition for the perpetuation and appropriation of a tradition by new generations. It seems
certain that it is. The son is expected to "ask your father—he will inform you" (Deuteronomy 32:7), and the father is expected to "impress
these words upon your children" (Deuteronomy 6:7). The filial loyalty
of the Rehabites insures the continuity of their heritage (Jeremiah 35);
Proverbs constantly uses filial regard and even affection as fulcra by
which the younger generation is turned toward the traditional culture,
its patterns and values. The rabbis urge faithfulness to custom as "the
minhag of your fathers," and Josephus speaks in countless places of the
entire Oral Law as the "laws of the fathers" (an expression often found
in Hellenistic documents). Indeed, it is a truism that for a culture to
endure it must be transmitted, and this can occur only between generations bonded by respect. If this is true of culture generally, it is certainly true of Judaism, which invested the tradition borne by the community with unusual potency, and relied, on the whole, on internal rather
than external sanctions to insure loyalty to that tradition.

The Midrash makes a related point in its own suggestive way. Joseph, it tells, was about to succumb to the blandishments of his master's wife when "he saw the image of his father and his blood cooled."[75]
The midrashic teaching is clear: Joseph rebuffs the first attempt at his
seduction by reliance upon the normative structure: "How then could I
do this most wicked thing and sin before God?" But conviction waned
while ardor waxed, so that the second attempt of Potiphar's wife (and
one tradition tells of Joseph's initiating this attempt) does not meet
with the normative rebuff. Rather, at the last minute, it is only "the image of his father" that rises before a speechless Joseph and impels him
to reject the woman. Centuries later, Nahmanides wrote to his son Solomon, a courtier at the royal court at Castile, urging him to be faithful to
Judaism and in particular to avoid sexual relations with non-Jewish
women. The father concluded his appeal thus: "My son, at all times remember me, and may my image be before your eyes—let it never depart
from you. Do not do anything that you know I hate. Be with me always;
observe the *mitzvot* and live."[76] In all this, the paradigmatic role of the
father and its ability both to inspire the son and evoke shame in him are
stressed.

Biblical and talmudic reality contain a sphere of filial regard whose
outer periphery is both wide and blurred. Biblical verses counsel allegiance to paternal commands; rabbinic masters transmit paternal teachings with special loyalty; communities remain bound by "customs of

the fathers," and so on. All these, in varying measure, draw upon echoes of the father-son relationship and its normative timbre. But filial responsibility itself is not mobilized in these instances in any specific and definable way. We do not read that loyalty to custom (*minhag*) or to tradition is an aspect of the fifth commandment. By and large, the community transcends the family; it may draw upon filial metaphors, but these remain peripheral to its claim. Indeed, the identical filial metaphor can sometimes point to the stultification of tradition; the religious performances of some men, we read, are mere "loyalty to the traditions of their fathers"—and are not to be taken with full seriousness![77]

Thus despite the classic recognitions of the centrality of the filial connection in the survival of a tradition, the medieval stress is new. For the first time we find an explicit focus on the pedagogic role of the parent and a purposive instrumental role assigned filial responsibility. The talmudic rabbis did not discuss *kibbud av* as a factor in the preservation of the tradition, though they were obviously aware, as is the Bible, of the pedagogic and paradigmatic role of parents. Rather, *kibbud av* isolated and stressed the responsibilities inhering in the personal relationship. The articulation of a purposive orientation toward filial piety is a distinctly medieval phenomenon. Maimonides, Albo, Ralbag, and Abarbanel all formulate in a distinctly new way this value of filial piety for a society buffeted by internal stresses and external challenges, all of which press upon the traditionalist the knowledge of the tenuousness of historical survival. Filial reverence is not only reverence for the *parent*; it is now become reverence for and faith in his *values*. Filial piety is now the vehicle through which one generation affirms the heritage of its predecessor. Noble as this may sound, it is actually a sign of weakness and insecurity. It is unnecessary in an age of classic faith, and insufficient when that faith declines.

The medieval focus betrays the inner atomization and insecurity—both political and religious—of the Jewish Middle Ages. But it also expresses suggestive insights. Reverence of young for old can exist only when the values of one generation are respected by the other, however subtly and even selectively. Filial reverence and responsibility reflect, in broad social dimensions, a sharing of meaning, though they cannot of themselves create that sharing of meaning. Moreover, if we take these medieval comments in balanced perspective as merely pointing to one of the many factors that are necessary for a tradition to be perpetuated, it is clear that they are accurate: a society in which parents are held in genuine regard is apt to create a similar aura around the tradition to which they testify.

IV.
Filial Responsibility and Human Nature

The term "natural" is notoriously difficult to define or even to use intelligently. Biblical and rabbinic Hebrew, for example, do not possess such a word at all.[78] Nonetheless, I think it is fair to state that for both the Bible and the rabbis some form of filial piety, respect, and honor were part of the normal, natural make-up of man. Corresponding to this assertion would be the acknowledgment that filial piety is not a distinctively Jewish trait, or one that without its source in the Sinaitic revelation would be alien to humanity.

The Bible assumes throughout that men naturally revere and honor their fathers. God demands, over and over again, that He be granted the honor of a father, that His will be decisive as a father's ought to be. Biblical imagery draws upon the human situation and demands from man and Israel the wealth of feeling he naturally bestows upon his father:

> Children unworthy of Him,
> That crooked and twisted generation—
> Their baseness has played Him false.
> Do you thus requite the Lord,
> O dull and witless people?
> Is not He the father who created you,
> Fashioned you and made you endure?

> *   *   *   *

> You neglected the Rock that begot you,
> Forgot the God who brought you forth.
> The Lord saw and was vexed
> And spurned His sons and His daughters.
>   (Deuteronomy 32:5–6, 18–19)

> A son honors his father, and a servant his master;
> If then I be a father, where is my honor?
> And if I be a master, where is my fear?
>   (Malachi 1:6)

The integration of filial piety into the biblical *humanitas* is seen from another, different perspective as well. In the following descriptions of man's betrayal of God and himself, filial impiety and dishonor not only violate the will of God as objective Lawgiver and author of "Honor your father and your mother"; filial impiety is denounced as a betrayal of natural decency and a violation of the *humanitas* with which God endowed man.

> The godly man is perished out of the earth,
> And the upright man is no more;
> They all lie in wait for blood;
> They hunt every man his brother with a net. . . .
>
> Trust ye not in a friend,
> Put yet not confidence in a familiar friend. . . .
> For the son dishonors the father,
> The daughter rises up against her mother,
> The daughter-in-law against her mother-in-law;
> A man's enemies are the men of his own house.
>
> (Micah 7:2, 5–6)
>
> There is a generation that curse their father,
> And do not bless their mother.
> There is a generation that are pure in their own eyes,
> And yet are not washed from their filthiness. . . .
> There is a generation whose teeth are as swords,
>   and their great teeth as knives,
> To devour the poor from off the earth, and the needy
>   from among men. . . .
>
> The eye that mocks at his father,
> And despises to obey his mother,
> The ravens of the valley shall pick it out,
> And the young vultures shall eat it.
>
> (Proverbs 30:11–14, 17)

*   *   *   *   *   *

The concept of "natural law" is one of the most elusive bequeathed modern man by the ancients. Most scholars claim that "natural" in this phrase is identical with "rational," and it is questionable whether the rabbis ever developed an equivalent concept.[79] Certain biblical commands are designated by the rabbis, however, as *mishpatim* and defined as "commands which, had they not been written in the Torah, would have been worthy [or, would have had] to be written." The element compelling adoption of these *mishpatim* is nowhere spelled out, but some have loosely applied the term "natural law" to this rabbinic structure.[80] Do the rabbis include filial piety as a component of man's "natural" equipment? The material here is much more varied than was the case with the biblical sources, but by and large we must answer our question with a cautious affirmative.

The rabbis do not overpopulate nature with moral instincts. In a rare excursion into animal morality, R. Hiyya and R. Yohanan do state:

> " . . . God . . . who teaches us by the beasts of the earth, and through the fowl of heaven makes us wise" (Job 35:10–11). R. Hiyya said: " 'by the beasts of the earth'—this is the mule, which kneels [modestly] to urinate; 'through the fowl of heaven makes us wise'— this is the cock, which woos before it mates."
>
> R. Yohanan said, "Had the Torah not been given, we could learn decorousness from the cat [which does not defecate before men, and covers her excrement with earth—Rashi]; respect for the property of others from the ants [ants do not steal from each other— Rashi]; faithfulness from the dove [which is faithful to its mate— Rashi]; and sexual decency from the cock [which woos before it mates].[81]

"Go to the ant, thou sluggard; Consider her ways and be wise" (Proverbs 6:6) is traditional folk wisdom; R. Yohanan is more cautious: the Torah, he carefully writes, is man's proper pedagogue, not the ant—but the ant, too, possesses exemplary moral traits, as do cocks and cats and doves. Let us praise famous animals. R. Hiyya is more enthusiastic: Man can, and ought indeed to, learn from the animals.

The rabbis do not say, here or elsewhere (an argument from silence, of course), that animals display filial piety; there is no claim for a pattern of filial honor or concern binding all of nature's progeny. The rabbis will say—for hortatory purposes, at least—that both man and animal possess in common the trait of *paternal* concern and care:

> When parents who refused to support their children were brought before R. Hisda, he would say: "Make a public announcement, and say, 'The raven cares for its young, but this man does not care for his young.' "[82]

But the Talmud knows that parents display more concern for their children than children do for their parents, and it expresses this fact in both anecdote and law:

> R. Hunna once found a juicy date which he took and wrapped in his mantle. His son, Rabbah, came and said to him, "I smell the fragrance of a juicy date." He said to him, "My son, there is purity in thee," and gave him the date.
> Meanwhile, Rabbah's son, Abbah, came ; Rabbah took it and gave it to him. R. Hunna said to Rabbah: "My son, you have gladdened my heart [with your purity] and blunted my teeth [by loving your son more than you love me]." That is what the popular proverb says: "A father's love is for his children; the children's love is for their own children."[83]

In a legal context, the Talmud assumes[84] that a father burglarizing his son would not kill him, while in the reverse situation the son is not expected to behave any differently toward his father than toward a stranger.[85] Whatever human drive toward filial piety does exist, then, is not predicated on a "moral" instinct held in common with other animal life.

The talmudic statement which comes closest to utilizing or drawing upon these natural sentiments is the following tannaitic sermon:

> R. Simeon ben Yohai said: "Just as the reward of the honoring of parents and the dispatch of the mother from a nest before the fledglings are taken (Deuteronomy 22:6–7) are equal [both are rewarded with length of days], so is the punishment for their violation similar. As it is written, 'The eye that mocks his father, and despises to heed his mother/ The ravens of the valley shall pick it out, and the young vultures shall eat it' (Proverbs 30:17). The eye which mocks at the honor due parents, and despises the command to dispatch the mother from the nest, should be picked out by the ravens. Let the raven which is cruel pick it out and be denied its enjoyment, for the eagle which is merciful will eat it and enjoy it."[86]

The cruel or merciful son finds his counterpart, it would seem, in the cruel raven or the merciful eagle; these should then serve as models. But the raven and eagle are chosen, not because of their behavior toward their parents, but because of the merciful (or cruel) way *they treat their children.*[87] Once again, the rabbis found no natural model for filial piety. Indeed, a measure of caution is in order even with regard to those rabbinic expressions of an animal-human continuum that we have noted, expressions which are often taken as evidence of rabbinic "natural law." These statements are uncommon and isolated, more aptly described as occasional sermons than aspects of a philosophy of law. Sermons can disclose much that is serious and basic, of course, but they can also utilize any and every argument likely to improve the listener.

We turn from an examination of rabbinic comment on the animal world and its "morality" to survey the attitude of the rabbis toward "natural" or "universal" human morality and to learn whether filial piety is ever seen as an expression of this "natural" morality.

The rabbis never lose sight of the fact that it is only the reality of a Lawgiver and His Law that constitutes an imperative. But they are free both to affirm the ultimate authority of the Lawgiver and yet speculate about the pragmatic roots of law in human conscience and society. Thus we find the following reflection, one that would later serve the medieval philosophers well:

> "My judgments shall ye do, and my statutes shall ye keep to walk therein: I am the Lord your God" (Leviticus 18:4). "My judgments' —these are things which, if they had not been written, would have had to be written, such as idolatry, unchastity, bloodshed, robbery, blasphemy.
>
> "My statutes"—these are things to which Satan and the Gentiles raise objections, such as not eating pig, not wearing linen and woolen together, the law of *halizah* (Deuteronomy 25:5–10), the scapegoat. Should you say, "These are empty things," the Scripture adds, "I am the Lord, I have made decrees; you are not at liberty to criticize them."
>
> (*Yoma* 67b)

Two categories are set up here, *mishpatim* ("judgments") and *hukkim* ("statutes"); the latter are particularist, they defy reason, or at least utility, and merit obedience by virtue of their divine origin, while the former are "rationally" acceptable and recognizably purposeful. This catalogue resembles the "Seven Commandments of the Sons of Noah," the universal code of morals and religion found in rabbinic literature (which adds to the five *mishpatim* listed above a command to establish law and a ban on eating a limb torn from a living creature), and is also related to the three cardinal sins of talmudic law: idolatry, unchastity, and bloodshed.

The rabbis knew full well that the *mishpatim* were not yet universally observed, nor even universally acknowledged; Roman idolatry alone testified to that. But in stating that "the Gentiles" could raise no objection to these imperatives and, even more, by affirming that had these imperatives not been written in the Torah they "would have had to be written," they were declaring the reasonableness and necessity of these imperatives and the ability of humanity guided by innate conscience to discover them.[88] It is interesting, then (again, the argument from silence), that filial piety is not listed among these *mishpatim.*[89] Nor is it considered one of the Seven Noahide Commands[90] nor included among those imperatives that some tannaim would add to that list.[91]

But while filial piety is absent from the list of *mishpatim* of which our source says that "were they not written they would have had to be written," one tannaitic comment does declare this imperative to be a command of *mishpat,* as contrasted with *hok:*[92]

> "There He made for them a statute and a judgment"—'A statute' [hok], this is the Sabbath; 'a judgment' [mishpat], this is filial piety": so said R. Joshua.[93]

It is quite fair to read the *mishpat* of this rabbinic comment as informed by the same "rational" character as the *mishpatim* of the *baraita* cited above; here too there is a contrast with *hok.* For R. Joshua, then, filial piety is a universal, "natural" aspect of human society.

Furthermore, there is at least one tannaitic source that directly treats the Sinaitic pattern of filial piety as an extension of a natural human phenomenon. Rabbi Judah the Prince explains why "father" precedes "mother" in Exodus 20:12 ("Honor your father and your mother . . ."), while the reverse is true in Leviticus 19:3 ("You shall each revere his mother and his father . . ."):

> The Creator knew that a son honors his mother more than his father, because she sways him by persuasive words—therefore, the Torah gave precedence to the honor of one's father. . . . The Creator knew that a son fears his father more than his mother, because he teaches him Torah—therefore, the Torah gave precedence to the reverence due one's mother. . . . Where a deficiency exists—He filled it.[94]

Where a deficiency exists, He filled it. The Torah relies on the natural inclination of a son to honor (or serve) his mother and to stand in reverence of his father. This reliance is not total—after all, the honoring of mothers and the reverencing of fathers is commanded! But the existence of the natural inclination in these areas allows the Torah to stress the honor of fathers and the reverence of mothers, or to draw these out more fully. Certainly, the legislated norm to, say, honor one's mother now possesses a new and different sanction, but there is no indication that the natural posture is rejected or even transcended— quite the contrary. "Where a deficiency exists, He filled it": this is the language of continuum, not of a break. Filial piety is rabbinic *humanitas,* though the rabbis did feel that Judaism deepened and strengthened the normal human ethos.

Are All Parents Equal?

This passage merits consideration from other points of view as well. The biblical family ethos is generally described as "patriarchal," and this description may have much truth to it.[95] It is crucial, however, that the Bible never commands honor or reverence of the father alone, but always commands filial respect and service of both parents.[96] Indeed, it will sometimes give precedence to the duty owed the mother, as it does in Leviticus 19:3. The Septuagint, however, departs from the Masoretic text at this point, translating, "You shall each revere his father and his mother . . ." (adding extra urgency to the tannaitic exegesis cited above), and Philo, who follows this version, stresses the patriarchal role in instances where the Bible clearly involves both parents.[97] The rabbis, though, did not neglect to stress parental equality.

Other rabbinic teachings reinforce this posture, even where a superficial reading seems to disclose a contradiction:

> Everywhere Scripture speaks of the father before the mother. Does the honor due to the father exceed that honor due to his mother? Scripture says, "You shall each revere his mother and his father," to teach that both are equal. But the sages have said: "Everywhere Scripture speaks of the father before the mother because both a man and his mother are bound to honor his father."[98]

The Sages are saying that, practically speaking, the honor and reverence of the father take precedence, and they justify this assertion by the fact that the wife is bidden to honor and revere her husband. (It is revealing that later students of the Talmud found this judgment difficult to maintain; does the Talmud itself not declare that a husband must "honor his wife more than himself"?[99]) But the essential affirmation is the same as that made by R. Judah the Prince: inherently, both father and mother "are equal"; the honor due the father from the son "does not exceed that due the mother." Thus, R. Joshua implies that if the parents were divorced, freeing the wife of all obligations toward her former husband, the son in fact would be left in a quandary as to which of his parents he ought to give preference.[100]

If it would be overly speculative to elicit from the sources cited conflicting tannaitic postures on the issue of the quality of parents, it does seem that different exegeses of the two contrasting verses were given, and that the varying stresses may have had practical correlates. The fact that one verse speaks first of father and the other speaks first of mother means for R. Judah the Prince that each verse speaks of specific aspects of the relationship, and that there is a deliberate correlation between this specificity and the literary structure. The second view (perhaps that of R. Simeon b. Yohai, against which Rabbi Judah the Prince would then be reacting)[101] is that the variation is deliberately arbitrary, and indicates that "both are equal."[102] A third view notes that Scripture generally mentions the father before the mother, and reads this consistent precedence as testimony to the priority of the father—but this is predicated not on the inherent superiority of his claim as a parent but on the dynamics of the marital ethos.

This rejection of partriarchal priority in filial piety, a posture that is in fact biblical, may have had significant impact upon Western mores and civilization generally. It has long been noted that the later Roman Empire significantly humanized its concept of filial piety; in addition to the weakening of the law of *patria potestas* (which gave the father great powers over the person of his son), Roman law elevated the status of the mother and expected the son to give her much the same loyalty proffered his father. This has generally been explained to have been a result of the influence of Christian ethics on Roman law.[103] Inasmuch as the rabbinic discussions represent no revision of the biblical perspective but rather its faithful exposition, it is quite likely that the "newer" laws reflect a much older Jewish ethos. This ethos could well have influenced Roman mores through both the extensive Jewish settlements in the Roman Empire and the Jewish presence in Rome itself, and indirectly through the absorption of Jewish ideals into Christianity. Needless to say, the influence of other cultural spheres, such as the Hellenistic and the Greco-Egyptian, and the possibility of concurrent internal development ought not to be ignored. But if historians do point to the impact of the Christian ethic, it is not unreasonable to pursue the matter on native ground.

Returning to our passage once again, we also note with interest the reason for the son's partiality in the reverence of his father, "because he teaches him Torah." It is not the physical presence of the father that transmits filial awe, nor his familial role in punishment, nor his social role; rather, it is as the source of normative teaching and value that he is the object of filial reverence. The father evokes this attitude in his son to the degree that he is identified with the transcendent source of values.

We have seen that rabbinic sources sometimes do identify *kibbud av* with the natural patterns of filial piety, and that sometimes they ignore this identification. There is certainly no overwhelming thrust in the former direction; neither is there any overt, positive rejection of it. On balance, though, the idea of "natural patterns" seems to be cautiously and indirectly affirmed.

One may speculate that the reserve of the rabbis in this regard is due to their awareness that feelings toward parents, far from being homogeneous or placid, are indeed complex, ranging from love to hostility and usually embracing some measure of both. Furthermore, the halakhic crystallization of filial piety stressed a pattern of behavior governing the relations of one generation of adults to another generation of adults, and not the duties of minors to their adult parents. This complicates the matter of "feelings" considerably. On both accounts, then, the rabbis preferred to keep their silence—with some exceptions—on the natural roots of *kibbud av*.

Philo

The Hellenistic-Jewish writers, Philo preeminent among them, do not display the reserve characteristic of the rabbis. We have already seen the Hellenists' general agreement that gratitude requires that children honor their parents, and their general assumption that gratitude is a natural and rational act. The participation of filial piety in the "law of nature" and, at times, its identification with love of parents are also found in this outlook.

The Fourth Book of Maccabees was written in Alexandria, most probably in the century preceding the destruction of the Temple in 70 C.E.[104] In demonstrating the rule of reason (Torah) over nature, the author argues that " . . . we see that wisdom rules over the instincts. Does not the Torah rule over the love of parents, forbidding us to abandon virtue for their sake?"[105] I believe that this refers not to "love of parents" in general but to the fifth commandment, which, the tannaim state, is overridden if the parent commands his child to violate a law of the Torah.[106] If our author does indeed refer to this tannaitic teaching, we can conclude that he considers *kibbud av* a natural (indeed, instinctive!) pattern. Furthermore, the instinct is called "love." Love of parents is also stressed by the author of IV Maccabees in his telling of the epic martyrdom of Hannah and her seven sons. The sons, we are told, "loved their mother so that they obeyed her till their death, and observed the *mitzvot.* " So significant is this element that the author hymns it: "O sublime quality, love of parents and fondness of parents. . . . "[107] Love of parents here seems to replace the biblical honor of parents, and explicitly functions to stimulate an abiding loyalty to the tradition.

Philo himself touches on our problem in two places; the first bears on the integration of filial piety into the "morality" found in nature, while the second discusses the role of filial love in filial piety.

We have already cited part of Philo's discussion of filial gratitude. A fuller citation is now in place:

> . . . let us turn for a lesson in right conduct to the winged tribe that ranges the air. Among the storks, the old birds stay in the nests when they are unable to fly while the children fly, I might almost say, over sea and land, gathering from every quarter provision for the needs of their parents . . . [so the children,] moved by piety and the expectation that the same treatment will be meted to them by their offspring, repay the debt which they may not refuse. . . . And thus, without any teacher but their natural instinct, they gladly give to age the nurture which fostered their youth.
>
> With this example before them, may not human beings, who take no thought for their parents, deservedly hide their faces for shame? . . .[108]

This selection contains many themes we have noted before: gratitude, the repayment of a debt, and the expectation of children that they, in turn, will be honored. What is new is the assertion that filial piety is so natural as even to be found in the community of beasts. Philo does not say that men possess the same "natural instinct" as do storks; indeed, men are asked to learn—a decidedly "unnatural" activity—from the bird. Yet the overriding fact for Philo is that the conduct of the stork reflects upon human conduct in this area and, if he takes his analogy seriously, must mean that there is a moral community of bird and man.

In a second passage, Philo directly confronts the role of instinct and nature in filial piety. Commenting on the fact that Scripture nowhere commands filial affection, he writes:

> . . . it would not be suitable to include in the enactments of a lawgiver an instruction on the duty of filial affection, for nature has

implanted this as an imperative instinct from the very cradle in the souls of those who are thus united by kinship. And therefore he omitted any mention of love for parents because it is learned and taught by instinct and requires no injunction, but did enjoin fear for the sake of those who are in the habit of neglecting their duty. . . .

Filial *affection* is instinctive, and there is no need to command it. Filial *reverence,* on the other hand, is indeed part of the divine instruction to man. This does not mean that filial reverence has no basis in human nature. On the contrary, Philo generally affirms the total agreement of the Torah and nature, maintaining that it is only Torah, whose author is the Creator of nature, that contains a Law consonant with the Law of Nature (reason).[109] Furthermore, we have just seen that filial gratitude is found even in the animal world, and Philo argues that it would be most unnatural of man not to learn this lesson from the beasts. Filial reverence, our passage even implies, is found in all men who are not "in the habit of neglecting their duty," the divine command being addressed to those who are forgetful of this standard of *humanitas.*

Thus Philo distinguishes two levels of filial piety: the one is instinctive, and need not be commanded; the second must be learned, either by observation of nature and attention to the dictates of reason or by fealty to the divine imperative. The filial piety commanded by the Torah does not in fact include the love of parents, Philo notes accurately, but this ought not to imply that there is no expectation of such love. On the other hand, the Torah's command of filial reverence and honor does not signify that these imperatives derive from a standard otherwise closed to the human conscience. For Philo, then (as for many classical thinkers), filial piety is an integral part of a natural, universal *humanitas.*

Sons and Gentiles

One final aspect of rabbinic thought seems relevant to our discussion of filial piety and *humanitas.* The rabbis teach that the exemplars of *kibbud av* are to be found in the gentile rather than the Jewish world. (They do, of course, cite numerous instances of exemplary filial piety among Jews also.) The point is not whether we can establish that a universal pattern of filial piety exists in human cultures; it is, rather, that the rabbis thought gentiles, specifically representatives of Roman culture, who were "not commanded" the norms of filial piety,[110] to be the paragons of this virtue.[111] The purposes of this teaching may have been varied: to chastise Jews for their neglect of this command, to explain the otherwise inexplicable dominion of "wicked" Rome in a world ruled by a just God; perhaps other motivations were at work as well. What is of significance for our inquiry, though, is the fact that filial piety is almost *the* gentile virtue. This certainly testifies to its roots in the soil of human culture as the rabbis understood it.

The great talmudic examples of filial piety are drawn from the life of Dama ben Netinah, "a non-Jew from Ashkelon."[112] In this he followed in the footsteps of Esau, of whom R. Simeon ben Gamliel said, "I served my father all my life, but I never served him a hundredth as well as Esau served his father."[113] So highly valued was this filial devotion that God granted Rome (Esau) all "this glory" (or, dominion) as reward.[114]

What induced the rabbis to find in Esau and his descendants models whom Jews might well emulate? The biblical suggestion that Esau was ever ready to fulfill his father's command (Genesis 27:3–4) hardly warrants, in itself, such fulsome exposition; furthermore, the Bible has already presented Esau as paining his father greatly through his marriage (Genesis 26:34–5) and will show him cynically expectant of his father's death (Genesis 27:41).[115] A reasonable suggestion is that the rabbis were, in fact, impressed with the gravity and importance of filial piety among the Romans. They were certainly aware of both *patria potestas* and the concern for filial piety evinced by moralists and thinkers. *Patria potestas* and, in fact, the entire "legal" conception of the family were in an irreversible decline during the rabbinic period, it is true, but as part of the history of Rome, they provided a good justification for the origins of Rome's greatness. Furthermore, the ethic expressed in *patria potestas* was imbued, in more humane fashion, throughout the Roman world in this period. In Hellenistic Alexandria, "the honor of parents was a popular theme of pedagogic moralizing,"[116] and it was a staple of Stoic thought. *Patria potestas* was doubtless considered savage and inhumane in allowing parents to expose an unwanted child and to deny all property rights to the son. But the rabbis found the Romans exemplary even when measured by the Jewish standard of filial ethics. The behavior singled out for rabbinic praise—Esau's eagerness to satisfy his father's wish and the royal clothes he wore while serving him; Dama's refusal to disturb his father even at the price of financial loss and his patient and passive endurance of his mother's rage and blows—is not that described by *patria potestas* but rather by *pietas* and *reverentia,* the kind of filial respect and honor deemed exemplary in Jewish ethics. Clearly, then, this ethic was considered part of the heritage of all mankind.

II
The Scope of Responsibility

Filial Responsibility

How does one honor his parents? How does one fear them? These questions, directed as they are to the individual, require intimate and individual answers that emerge from the singularity of persons and their relationship in the creative play of the unique situation. Judaism, though, does not reject the answers to be found in patterns of behavior objectively imposed upon persons and situations rather than spontaneously and subjectively growing from them. Man's response draws upon both his individual resources and a universal heritage; it moves in a context that is both unique and common.

A number of pentateuchal verses define the relationship we call "filial responsibility." Some are specific and punitive:

> He who strikes his father or his mother shall be put to death.
> (Exodus 21:15)

> He who curses his father or his mother shall be put to death.
> (Exodus 21:17)

> Cursed be he that dishonors his father or his mother.
> (Deuteronomy 27:16)[1]

The law of the "wayward and defiant" son, who "does not heed his father or mother and does not obey them" (Deuteronomy 21:18–21) may also belong to this pattern.[2] But the overriding foci of Jewish filial piety are stated in the two general and positive imperatives of the Torah, taken in rabbinic thought as typological categories:

(1) Honor your father and your mother. . . . (Exodus 20:12)
(2) You shall each revere his mother and his father . . . . (Leviticus 19:3

"Honor" would seem to demand behavioral concretization, while

37

"reverence" might primarily describe an inner feeling. For the Halakha[3] both have normative manifestations:

> Our rabbis taught: What is reverence and what is honor? Reverence means that he (the son) must neither stand nor sit in his [father's] place, nor contradict his words, nor tip the scale against him.
> Honor means that he must give him food and drink, clothe and cover him, and lead him in and out.
>
> (*Kiddushin* 31b)[4]

All this expresses what the Mishnah calls "the obligations (*mitzvot*) of a son toward a father," which are incumbent on both men and women.[5] The mishnaic[6] vocabulary shows that the filial relationship was to be concretized in an expected pattern of behavior; this is revealed, too, in the Aramaic documents from Elephantine (see note 3). The *baraita,* because of its greater specificity, has been most seminal in the Jewish ethos. Let us examine it from both morphological and substantive points of view.

The terminological compartmentalization of *kibbud* ("honor") and *morah* ("reverence") introduced by the *baraita* is hardly absolute. *Kibbud,* which here denotes acts of service, is often used by the rabbis for the entire area of filial piety, including those characteristics listed here under the rubric of *morah.*[7] The terminological distinction between *kibbud* and *morah* does, however, reflect an attentive and pedagogic reading of the biblical verses and functions broadly in halakhic writing. The *baraita* also reverses the pentateuchal sequence ("honor" in Exodus, and "fear" in Leviticus) in favor of a conceptual one: fear, or reverence, demands the avoidance of certain acts, while honor goes beyond it to claim positive deeds.

Furthermore, the specifics listed hardly exhaust the meaning of "honor" or "reverence"; rather they serve as types, as examples. We shall see both Talmud and later authorities articulating other ways in which honor and reverence are displayed, and in doing this they are true to the inner dynamic of the *baraita* cited. "Honor" and "reverence" are both goals to be attained through faithfulness to many specifics; they are guides to conduct in situations where no specific response had been plotted. So comments Maimonides on the mishnaic "*mitzvot* concerning the parent incumbent upon the son": "These are too numerous to list, and discussion of them would be overly long. They are included, however, in two basic principles—fear and honor; and we find examples given of these. . . . "[8] The specifics given are, of course, meaningful in themselves and are also significant as pedagogic types, illustrations of a norm capable of both momentary, partial achievement and of infinite demand and suggestiveness. Other *rishonim* say much the same thing when they write that *kibbud av ve'aim* knows no limits.[9] R. Samson of Sens considers the honor of parents an act of *gemilut hesed* ("acts of lovingkindness") capable of infinite development.[10]

These concretizations of reverence are not unique to the filial relationship. A *baraita* explains the command to "honor [*vehadarta*] the face of the old man" (Leviticus 19:32) thus: "What is the honor [*hiddur*] demanded by the Torah? That you not stand in his place, nor speak in his place, nor contradict his words, but behave toward him with reverence and fear. . . . "[11] (We do note, though, that the *hiddur* of the aged man does not include the positive patterns of filial "honor.") These standards are not restricted to filial piety but are in place wherever reverence is to be expressed.[12]

II.

Filial Reverence

The Talmud illustrates "reverence" tersely: "Reverence means that *the son must neither stand nor sit in his [father's] place, nor contradict his words, nor tip the scale against him.*"[13] The principle behind this pattern is clear: nothing is to be done that might diminish the dignity, and hence the feeling of worth, of one's parent—either father or mother.[14] Reverence (*morah*) is expressed by this unegalitarian reserve, which demonstrates behaviorally the qualitative gulf in status separating parent and child. Indeed, parental dignity is here virtually identical with inviolability and superiority, just as respect shown others generally expresses itself in self-abnegation of some sort.

These rules reflect the general norms of behavior in traditional biblical society for both parents and elders alike. If one is to rise before the hoary head (Leviticus 19:32), one will certainly not stand or sit in his place; indeed, we have just seen that the *baraita* considers this very pattern of "filial" reverence equally applicable to elders. Similarly with regard to speech: "Elihu," we read, "had waited to speak with Job, because they [the other friends of Job] were older than he" (Job 32:4). The son will doubtless not speak before the father, and will certainly not argue with him publically, although he will be a ready defender of his father's opinion (see Psalms 127:4–5). Indeed, the version of the *Sifra* states, "He may not speak in his place."[15] This ethos, too, is not restricted to the filial relationship: it is one of the "seven traits of the fool" to speak in the presence of those wiser than he.[16]

The medieval commentators, however, are not satisfied with elucidations of a general type. The classic Jewish thrust from the Bible onward, after all, is toward specificity, and this process is evident in the interpretation of our *baraita*. Actually, it deceives by its terseness and seeming simplicity; in reality it is ambiguous and even obscure, making interpretation a necessity, not a luxury.

The *baraita's* insistence upon a formal etiquette of filial reverence is limited by Rashi to public situations outside the home. There, parental worth or disgrace may ride on externals, and these must be scrupulously safeguarded. In the home, he implies, a more informal, fluid, standard prevails. Thus, he interprets the first of these phrases ("do not stand . . . in his place") to mean: "Do not stand in the place reserved for your father at the council of the elders, at deliberations with his friends."[17] The context for Rashi is spatial in the narrow sense but also symbolic of the role of the father, which is not to be usurped. Rashi sees the *baraita* as concerned with the audience of peers rather than with the family hearth.

Others, however, rejected such relaxation. R. Me'ir ha-Levi Abulafia added that the phrase does not lose its literal significance: if your father habitually occupies a certain place, say, for prayer or at meals, do not displace him. The *Shulhan Arukh* accepted this latter view, and it is safe to say that Jewish homes were ordered accordingly.[18] Finally, R. Menahem ha-Me'iri—influenced no doubt by a similar Maimonidean ruling with regard to one's teacher—writes that the son may not even leave the presence of his father without first getting permission.[19]

" . . . *Nor contradict his words, nor tip the scale against him.*" Rashi takes the latter phrase to mean, "If his father and another scholar disagree on a matter of Halakha, he should not say, 'The opinion of X seems to me correct.'" Rashi focuses on the halakhic arena, but his thrust is to require that the son be sensitive to the father's dignity and importance in weighty areas, rather than in matters of halakhic debate alone. Once again, the home and private discussion are excluded from the regimen of the *baraita*. More subtly, R. Me'ir Abulafia understands by "tipping the scale" an expression of *support* for one's father: the fundamental arrogance is to suppose that one can lend support to one's father, while supporting his adversary is no better than contradicting him.[20]

Is silent agreement, then, the public price of discourse with one's father? It would be all too facile to reject the apparent Talmudic norm out of hand, to claim that it does not mean what it seems to say. What we can point to, though, are the many father-son debates scattered throughout the Talmud and, beyond that, to the idealization of the father and son who do battle on the field of Torah.[21] Clearly, vigorous assertion and honest disagreement were valued. We might do well, now, to return to R. Me'ir Abulafia. Noting that Rashi ruled out personal identification with the adversary, rather than substantive contribution to the debate in his behalf, R. Me'ir (having made the adjustments demanded by his own interpretation) explicates: "Even if he agreed with his father's point of view, he may not say, 'My father's words appear to me correct,' for he seems to be implying that he needs to support his father [for his father requires support]; rather, if he has an answer to the claims of his father's opponent, let him offer it." The words of Rashi do, indeed, carry this implication. It is the unsupported assertiveness of the son that is banned, not his genuine contribution.

But in spelling out the difficulties felt by the medieval scholars in their grappling with the question, "What is reverence?" we ought to point out explicitly that for some the paramount difficulty in the demand that the son not "contradict" the father did not lie in the kind of ethical or social relationship this would presuppose, but in its application to the universe of Torah study. A son *could* be bidden to silence in all secular, mundane matters; but how could he be expected to maintain his silence in the "war of Torah"? Thus R. Israel ben Joseph Alnakawa, the 14th-century moralist, wrote:[22]

" . . . he may not contradict him"—in wordly things, but not in matters of Torah.[22]

Thus, many medieval scholars took the passage at its word and understood the Talmud to forbid the son to disagree publically with his father, except perhaps in discussions of Torah.[23] Public disagreement ("to his face"—*Shulhan Arukh*[24]) was an embarrassment, an affront.

All the interpretations cited thus far take "nor tip the scale against him" as restraining the assertion of opinion or ideas because such assertion may imply a devaluation of the status of the parent. R. Aha, the 8th-century author of *Sefer She'iltot,* focuses on a different and much broader area. He interpreted: "Nor tip the scale *to judge him harshly.*"[25] One is, of course, obliged "to interpret the actions of each man in the most generous light"(Avot 1:6) and "not to tip the scale harshly against any man" (*Derekh Eretz Zuttah,* 3)." One is required—on the basis of *kibbud av*—to extend toward one's parents the generosity of spirit that one ought to extend to all. The refusal to do so would carry special weight where one's parents are concerned, and would imply not only niggardliness but irreverence. Perhaps, too, it was felt that filial dynamics often lead to a cynical suspicion of parental actions, thus necessitating a special sensitivity not to judge one's parents harshly.

"Do not judge your parents ungenerously" is, thus, both a broader reflection of reverence than the other specifics listed, and a narrower one. Narrower, because it demands for parents that which one ought to extend to all as an expression of social morality. Broader, because in distinction to the seemingly localized behavioral concretizations, we have here an attitudinal requirement, a demand of the internalization of generosity. Filial reverence includes both these dimensions: special expressions and concretizations, and the bestowal of added weight to normal and expected patterns of social behavior. Thus we find: "And he that smites his father or his mother, shall surely be put to death" (Exodus 21:15); "And he that curses his father or his mother shall surely be put to death" (Exodus 21:17); "Cursed be he that dishonors his father or his mother" (Deuteronomy 27:16). One should not strike, curse, or dishonor any human being; yet these actions reflect a deeper meaning when directed against parents.[26]

Through these bans and punishments, the Bible reinforces the universal moral code as it applies to parents. Yet the term translated "insults," *makleh,* really means "to make light of, to show contempt towards," and denotes the opposite of "honor," which in its root *k-b-d* means, "to consider weighty, important." *Makleh* straddles social and filial standards: it includes both the universally improper insult and the disapproval—unique to the filial relationship—of acts that reflect disrespect in the specific context of the father-son relationship.[27] The medievals picked up both strands of biblical thought; Maimonides is both realistic and specific, yet necessarily vague as to the minimum threshold of "contempt":

> The Torah is rigorous not only with him who strikes or curses his parents, but also with him who treats them with contempt. For he who treats them with contempt, even by using harsh words against them, aye, even by a discourteous gesture, is cursed out of the mouth of God. . . .[28]

Indeed, the talmudic rabbis had already focussed on speech as an instrument of reverence and its opposite:

"A man should not refer to his father by name, neither during his lifetime nor after his death, but should say, 'My father, my master.' "[29] Even passive acquiescence to irreverence is condemned: "R. Ishmael said, 'Ten times did the sons of Jacob call their father 'thy servant' before Joseph. Joseph heard this, yet was silent—therefore, his life was shortened by ten years.' "[30] This last midrash is, of course, a suggestive

insight into the anguished and tangled relationship of Joseph to his father after the lad was snatched away to Egypt; but it taught most effectively that the Jew was to be a zealous guardian of his father's name,
and that he could not allow its devaluation in even the most detached
way. A son, we read, must restore to their owner goods taken in usury
or stolen by his late father—"for the honor of his father."[31]

The Talmud does not, by and large, undertake any conceptual explorations of filial reverence, but its anecdotes of heroic filial concern
have had a telling impact upon Jewish ethics.

> They asked R. Eliezer how far must one go in *kibbud av ve'aim?* He
> replied: "Go and learn from the behavior of an Ashkelonite gentile,
> Dama ben Netinah, to his father. The sages wished to buy jewels for
> the [priestly] *ephod* at sixty thousand, . . . but the key [to the jew-
> el-box] was under his sleeping father's head, and he did not disturb
> him. In the next year, God caused a red heifer to be born in his flock
> as a reward. When the sages of Israel came to him [to buy the heifer]
> he said: 'I know that I can ask of you all the money in the world,
> and you will pay it—but I ask only for the amount I lost in honoring
> my father.' "
>
> (*Kiddushin* 31a)

In another version of this story, Dama, seeing his father asleep and not
wishing to rouse him, simply told the sages he could not provide them
with the stone. Thinking he was trying to raise the price, they offered
him more and more money—but he was adamant. Upon his father's
wakening, he was able to deliver the stone; to the offer of the sages to
pay the highest sum they had previously mentioned, he replied, "Do
you think I will sell my father's honor for money? I refuse to derive any
benefit from the honor of my parents!"[32]

Here is a man who refuses to disturb his parent in any way, even
when the magnitude of annoyance to the father is so inconsequential,
so unproportionate to the loss taken by the son. The guideline is obvious: when such a conflict arises, the effect on the parent becomes an absolute, evaluated without respect to the effect on the son. However
obvious the guideline, though, such conduct is heroic. Perhaps more
heroic—though in another sense more easily understandable—is the
behavior of the same man in the following narrative:

> Once he [Dama ben Netinah] was seated among the great men of
> Rome,[33] dressed in a silken gold garment, when his mother came
> and tore the garment from him, slapped him on the head, and spat

in his face—but he did not shame her.

(*Kiddushin* 31a)

Another version adds: "When the slipper [with which she was hitting him][34] fell from her hand, he reached forward and returned it to her; he only said: 'Enough, mother.'"[35] A final detail is provided by another midrash: "His mother was mentally disturbed."[36]

Here again, halakhic analysis of the problem of the wicked parent, or of the mentally incompetent parent, must defer to the lesson of the episode: however trying the provocation, the honor of the parent remains an absolute in relation to the difficulties of the son. The obvious psychological and even physical suffering of the son are never to be relieved at the expense of the parent, even when the parent is their cause. As we shall see, the parent is condemned for his behavior most strongly; but this condemnation remains a matter between God and the parent and is irrelevant to the plight of the son.

A final instance of filial self-control is presented by R. Eliezer: "They asked R. Eliezer, 'How far must one go in *kibbud av ve'aim?'* He said, Till the father throws the wallet of the son into the sea, and his son does not shame him.'"[37]

Other incidents recorded in the Talmud served as ideals of concern and solicitousness:

> The mother of R. Tarfon went walking in the courtyard one Sabbath day, and her shoe tore and came off. R. Tarfon came and placed his hands under her feet, and she walked in this manner until she reached her couch. Once when he fell ill and the sages came to visit him, his mother said to them: "Pray for my son R. Tarfon, for he serves me with excessive honor." They said to her, "What did he do for you?" She told them what had happened. They responded, "Were he to do that a thousand times, he has not yet bestowed even half the honor demanded by the Torah."
>
> (P. *Pe'ah* 1:1)

This incident is often cited in the subsequent literature, both scholarly and popular. Picturesque and clear, it presented a model that Jewish children ought to imitate and by which they ought to measure themselves. However much the sages might proclaim that R. Tarfon had not exhausted the infinite possibilities of filial piety, the people found in his patient palms a full measure of filial care. It is illuminating, parenthetically, to learn that there were other facets to this relationship, too:

Once, as R. Tarfon sat teaching the disciples, a bride passed by in his presence. He ordered that she be brought into his house, and said to his mother and wife: "Wash her, anoint her, have her outfitted, and dance before her, until she goes on to her husband's house."[38]

Here R. Tarfon is seen instructing his mother and directing her in the fulfillment of an act of *gemilut hesed* towards others. But let us return to filial service:

R. Abahu said: "My son Abimi has fulfilled the commandment of filial respect." Abimi was the father of five sons who were all ordained during the lifetime of his father. When R. Abahu would arrive at his son's door, Abimi would [himself] race to open the door, saying, "Yes, yes," until he reached it. Once R. Abahu asked his son for a drink of water. Until Abimi brought the water to his father, the older man fell asleep. Abimi sat down and waited until his father waked.

(*Kiddushin* 31b)

Through such incidents related in the Talmud does the heroic, the exemplary, become the expected. The wondrous is codified. Indeed, heroic incidents are always pedagogic; their inner thrust is, paradoxically, to elevate all men to their standard. A measure of uniqueness is lost in the process, it is true, but this is the price paid for the advancement of the community of man. (It is crucial, moreover, that originality should not be identified with spontaneity, the personal zest and meaning with which the deed is done. Spontaneity retains a high priority in the normative system, irrespective of the originality of an act.) This phenomenon is well-known to students of ethics and law. Edmond Cahn writes:

. . . . many duties are now assigned to the law which used to be fulfilled by other methods of social ordering. . . . what is more significant . . . is . . . the considerable rise that has occurred in the moral level of legal standards. . . . Yesterday's moral-but-not-legal right frequently becomes today's moral-and-legal right. . . . The real purpose of moral ideals is to teach; they are . . . tools for educating ourselves. Once we recognize this, the old static diagram of commands and precepts changes before our gaze into a fluid, moving process. . . . Thus, what was heroic may become commonplace. . . . This moving process in the life of morals does not-

. . . fail to engender similar movement in the life of the law. What was legally optional in one generation may, in this manner, become a strict obligation in the next. . . .[39]

In codifying the heroic, exemplary act, the halakhist must reckon with another, most delicate question. A heroic standard of behavior should sometimes compel only the hero; to turn it into a norm for all men demands of them something beyond their powers, and transforms a pedagogic and inspiring model into an oppressive goad. Any experiential evaluation or description of the ethos of filial piety must recognize this transformation of exemplary model into norm and explore its human implications.

This transformation was, in large measure, implied in the very question of R. Eliezer's disciples: "How far does *kibbud av* go?" For they posed the question in the generalized terms of the normative structure. In the more formal statement of Maimonides we find the completed process:

> How far must one go to honor one's father and mother? Even if they took his wallet full of gold pieces and threw it into the sea before his very eyes, he must not shame them, show pain before them, or display anger to them: but he must accept the decree of Scripture and keep his silence.
>
> And how far must one go in their reverence? Even if he is dressed in precious clothes and is sitting in an honored place before many people, and his parents come and tear his clothes, hitting him in the head and spitting in his face, he may not shame them, but he must keep silent, and be in awe and fear of the King of Kings Who commanded him thus. For if a king of flesh and blood had decreed that he do something more painful than this, he could not hesitate in its performance. How much more so, then, when he is commanded by Him Who created the world at His will![40]

Interestingly, Maimonides does more than codify. Deeply aware of the nature of the demand that is here made upon a man's normal self-respect, he supplies a motive force for restraint: "be in awe and fear of the King of Kings" Who has commanded reverence of parents. In order to transform the heroic into the required, Maimonides must mobilize the fear and reverence of God, for he believes that reverence for parents alone could not universally produce the desired response. Perhaps Maimonides also thought that ethical considerations alone would not require considerate treatment of parents who are so malicious. In either case, the Maimonidean formulation offers a fascinating insight into his theory of the psychology of filial responsibility. As we shall see, other thinkers found this approach remote and bleak.

III.

Honor and Service

The second term to be clarified is *kabbed* ("honor"). *Kabbed* is the verb found in the fifth commandment, and it has also provided the phrase around which all aspects of filial piety and responsibility have clustered: *kibbud av ve'aim*. Its definition is central.

The basic meaning of the root (according to Brown, Driver, Briggs, *Lexicon of the Old Testament*) is "be heavy, weighty"; "be honored" is given fourth in the list of definitions. "Honor" is a response to, a recognition of, the weightiness of the person honored, his worth. All societies—democratic or not—and all individuals designate certain persons as men of greater worth than others, though they may differ on the persons and qualities singled out. This designation carries with it both internalized and behavioral responses: the man of worth is treated differently, and one relates to him differently from other men.

Father and mother are to be perceived and treated as persons of import, worth, significance. We have already seen the expression of this attitude in the reverence with which parents are treated. What more positive expression is cultivated by the Jewish ethic?

> Honor means that he must give food and drink, dress and cover him, and lead him in and out.[41]

The fundamental motif of *kibbud* is personal service.[42] Though the passage cited above does indeed serve as a springboard for the talmudic and medieval discussions of filial support of parents, its primary meaning is to require personal service in the parent's behalf quite similar to that performed by the servant for his master. To feed and clothe requires, primarily, not the financial expenditure for food and clothing, though it may imply that as well, but the physical deed itself. Thus, the personal responsibilities of the son to his father are analogous to those of a servant to his master. These include the symbolic gestures of attentiveness as well as the satisfaction of real needs, for both dimensions of service underscore the worth of the person so served and honored.

Son and servant were linked by the prophet Malachi:

A son honors his father,
And a servant his master;
If then I be a father,
Where is my honor?
And if I be a master,
Where is my fear?   (1:6)

The juxtaposition of roles does not in itself prove very much; it can suggest contrast as well as comparison. The same prophet is more explicit, though. On the "Day of the Lord," he predicts, God will spare the righteous "as a man spares his own son who serves him" [3:17]. The apocryphal Ben-Sira is concretely prescriptive:

The fearer of God honors his father,
He honors his parents as masters.   (3:6)

The talmudic ethic agrees fully with this formulation.

The Tosefta's version of our *baraita* adds to its list of personal services those of "washing his face, hands, and feet."[43] A later midrash[44] contains this same *baraita* with the added provisos that he "sprinkle (the floor) before him, wash and anoint him, and put his shoes on."[45] The similarity of the services of both a son and a servant is clear if we compare the following:

What are the services through which a servant is acquired? If he looses his master's shoe, carries his clothes after him to the bathhouse, undresses him, washes him, anoints and scrapes him [with the *strigil*], dresses him, and puts his shoes on.[46]

The performance by the servant of the personal duties normally expected by a master from a servant constitutes the act of acquisition. Despite some variation between the service to be rendered a master and that to be rendered a parent, it is clear that the two can be called upon to perform virtually identical personal tasks.

Even more direct evidence for this assertion is found in a *baraita* that first distinguishes between the Canaanite servant—from whom these services may be demanded—and the Hebrew servant—from whom they may not—and then identifies the tasks of the son with those of the Canaanite servant:

> "When you acquire a Hebrew slave, he shall serve six years . . . " (Exodus 21:2). I might think that he must do all sorts of service for you, therefore Scripture teaches: "If your brother . . . must give himself over to you, do not make him serve as a slave" (Leviticus 25:39).
>
> Hence they taught: The Hebrew servant should not wash his master's feet or put his shoes on, carry his clothes to the bathhouse, support him when he climbs, or carry him on a bed, chair, or *lectica*, as slaves usually do.
>
> Scripture teaches: " . . . over your brethren the children of Israel you shall not rule, one over another, with rigor" (Leviticus 25:46). *But you may do so to your son or your disciple.*[47]

The passage, besides demonstrating that the previous lists of filial and servile services are hardly complete, clearly shows that the personal tasks of the son (and a disciple) are in fact identical with those of the slave. And a later midrash describes the contrast between the gentile service of God (even in Messianic times) and that of the Jews as the difference between "a son who ministers to his father happily, for he says, 'Even if I spoil something somewhat, my father will not become angry with me, for he loves me,' " and a slave "who ministers to his master in fear" lest his master grow angry with him.[48] Both son and servant are, however, set the same task.

As this midrash itself hints, the analogy was only an analogy. Sons, even when they served their parents, were not slaves. A talmudic *baraita*, in fact, distinguishes between a man who serves another "as a slave," and he who serves him "as a son."[49] And a Palestinian amora claims that only Nabataeans exact the service of slaves from their sons.[50] But these distinctions grew out of life; they were not imposed by the law.

The force with which a similar requirement was taught (again, the degree to which it was practiced is another matter) centuries later in amoraic Babylon is apparent in the following record:

> R. Joshua b. Levi [fl. in Palestine, early 3rd century] said: "A disciple must serve his master in all the ways that a slave serves his mas-

ter, except that he does not loose his shoe" ('lest an observer think he is a Canaanite slave'—Rashi).

Rava [Bayblon, d. 352] said: "This is said only for places where the disciple is not known, but where he is known (and will not be mistaken for a slave) it is not so (and he must loose his master's shoe)."

R. Ashi [Bablylon, 352–427] said: "Even where he is not known, the teaching is true only if he is not wearing phylacteries, but if he is, he must loose his master's shoe" ('because a slave is not accustomed to wear phylacteries'—Rashi).[51]

It is clear, then, that a major component of "honor" (*kibbud*) is personal service, and that this service includes even menial and servile tasks. Maimonides justly generalizes from the talmudic evidence when he writes, " . . . and the son must serve the parent in all the ways that one serves a master."[52]

It is crucial that, if one wishes to understand the Jewish filial ethic, the fundamental role of personal service be appreciated. The very person, nay body, of the son is claimed. Furthermore, the son is always to recognize his parent as in some way his master, the filial posture never becoming one of egalitarian comradeship. It is wise, at the same time, to anticipate our later discussion and point out that the rabbinic tradition also cautioned the father to exercise his prerogatives wisely and creatively, lest he gain a servant and lose a son. But it places this initiative—and responsibility—in parental hands. The father, from the halakhic point of view, may—and, indeed, should—refuse to be master; but the son cannot refuse to serve. The knowledge of this disparity is itself a significant element of filial consciousness.

Finally, to be true to the ethos of Hebraic law, we must note that it is inaccurate and indeed somewhat insensitive to speak of "parental rights" or the "claim of the father." For Hebraic law, as has been pointed out, is fundamentally a system of duties owed, not of rights possessed. The son serves his father but not because he "is in his power," as the Roman code has it, or because of "parental authority"; it is the son's responsibility. The *baraita* does not ask, "What power does a father have over his son?" or "What are the rights of a parent with relation to his son?" but rather, "What must a son do to fulfill the command of 'Honor'?" Though the answer is one of personal service, the actual performance of such service has its origin in filial purpose. By the same token, service is valued not for its utility alone but as a response to an imperative that a son *honor* his father. It is characteristic of Halakha that a statement of worth and dignity is hammered out of actual mundane need and functional gesture.

The talmudic realia of filial "honor" focus on acts of service.[53] The typical parental request in the discussion of the legists is, "Get me a drink of water."[54] Again, the ethos of service (as that of reverence) was impressed upon Jewish society by heroic and extreme exemplars of attentiveness and zeal, as we recall from the filial behavior of Dama ben Netinah, R. Tarfon, and Abimi the son of R. Abahu. Biblical characters, too, were extolled as models of filial service, and the lesson was not lost on the students of the tradition:

> Naftali honored his father to an extreme. His father would send him
> wherever he wished, and Naftali eagerly fulfilled his father's task.
> Jacob took pleasure in him, and found his words pleasing. . . .
>   (*Numbers Rabbah* 14:11)

> " . . . Reuben came upon some mandrakes . . . and brought
> them to his mother Leah" (Genesis 30:14): This teaches how fully
> he honored his mother, for he did not taste them but brought them
> to her first.[55]
>   (*Genesis Rabbah* 72:2)

R. Simeon ben Gamliel said: "I served my father all my life, but I did not extend to him even one-hundredth of the honor given Jacob by Esau. For I would serve my father dressed in dirty clothes, and when I would go to my affairs would change into clean clothes, but Esau always dressed as royalty to serve his father. . . ."
                                                                  (*Genesis Rabbah* 65:16)

Here, Bible lesson (Esau) and biographical incident (R. Simeon b. Gamliel) reinforce each other, both teaching filial service in all its specificity. Furthermore, the point made by R. Simeon b. Gamliel is not to be taken lightly; he is concerned, not with the externals of the service *per se,* but with their precision in mirroring the centrality and significance of this service (and hence, of the person served) in the eyes of its performer. Is filial service dashed off ungracefully, resentfully—or is it performed nobly, winningly? Here, indeed, is the subtle yet substantial measure of true honor and regard.

The rabbis found, in their attentively read Bible, the same lesson. The sale of Joseph is precipitated by the following incident:

> One time, when his brothers had gone to pasture their father's flock

at Shekhem, Israel said to Joseph, "Your brothers are pasturing at
Shekhem. Come, I will send you to them." He answered, "I am
ready." . . . So he sent him from the valley of Hebron. When he
reached Shekhem, a man came upon him wandering in the fields.
The man asked him, "What are you looking for?" He answered, "I
am looking for my brothers. Could you tell me where they are pasturing?" The man said, "They have gone from here. . . . " So Joseph followed his brothers and found them at Dothan.

(Genesis 37:12–17)

The midrashic comments follow:[56]

a. "Israel said to Joseph"—R. Tanhum in the name of R. Berekhia
said, "He behaved toward him with the proper honor, as befits the
reverential obligations of a son toward a father."

b. "He answered, 'I am ready' "—R. Hama b. Hanina said, "Our father Jacob would later remember these words, and feel his bowels
cut up. 'I know that your brothers hate you, and yet you answer, "I
am ready.' "

The medievals understood the one midrashic comment to reinforce
and interpret the other, and so Rashi writes: "Joseph answered, 'I am
ready,' eager to fulfill his father's wish, though he knew that his brothers hated him." And Nahmanides finds additional evidence of this motif in the episode: " '. . . A man came upon him wandering in the
fields. . . .' Scripture tells this entire tale to show that though Joseph
had good cause to turn back, he suffered it all for the honor of his
father."[57] The same lesson was taught in the many midrashic treat-
ments of biblical material which we have cited elsewhere in our discussion. Rabbinic reflection on the Joseph-story could elicit even the more
extreme demand that "a man's father is like his king."[58] Indeed, one
wonders whether this preoccupation with Joseph's filial conduct did
not grow, in part at least, out of the uncomfortable question posed by
Joseph's allowing his father to mourn him as dead all the years he was
living as vice-regent in Egypt. In any case, the virtue of filial honor
through personal service was exemplified by unimpeachable biblical
and talmudic models.

And the medieval moralist R. Israel Alnakawa systematically spelled out the full (and realistic) dimensions of the services listed by the *baraita:*

> "Clothe them"—How is this to be done? He must clothe them as is befitting, covering them from winter's cold in a wrap befitting them, and giving them proper beds.
>
> "Lead them out"—How is this to be done? The son is obliged to accompany his father and mother, and not to turn back until they are out of sight.
>
> "Take them in"—How is this to be done? He is obliged to give them a fitting dwelling, or rent one for them. And when the father or mother enters the son's home, he must rejoice in their coming and receive them happily.[59]

IV.
The Internalization of Reverence

Alnakawa explicitly includes in his list of "services" the cultivation of an emotional attitude: "When the father or mother enters the son's home, he must rejoice in their coming. . . ." A resentful and hostile attitude makes the filial hearth an uncomfortable and uninviting place, and effectively checks the "honor" that the physical fact of domicile supposedly implies. Externals alone become a torturesome burlesque. Our medieval moralist, moreover, had a good ear for dialogue:

> A son must not dishonor his father in his speech. How so? For example, when the father is old and wants to eat early in the morning, as old men do because they are weak, . . . and the son says, "The sun is not yet up, and you're already up and eating!"
>
> Or when the father says, "My son, how much did you pay for this coat (which you have given to me)?" And the son says, "What do you bother yourself for? I bought it and I have paid for it, it is no business of yours to ask about it!"
>
> Or when he thinks to himself, saying, "When will this old man die and I shall be free of what he costs me?"

Nor is speech itself but another external pattern, to be controlled perhaps but not reflecting the inner life of the son. "The son," he writes, "must rejoice always in his expenditures on his father's behalf." And R.

Eleazar Azkari (16th century) claimed that "the plain sense" of *kabbed*
("honor") refers to the respect and concern evinced in speech as the
most crucial determinant of worth; all else—even service—is derivative. Indeed, "the essence of *kabbed*" lies in "the heart," and only from
the heart can come the proper deeds of speech and action. Even compliance with the divine command is a poor motive for respectful speech![60]

The masters of the Halakha knew well that the behavioral concretization often deceives. Compliance with the rule can be bought at the
price of utter disregard for the purpose of the law and thus betray, not
the spirit of the law alone, but even the ostensibly fulfilled rule itself:

> Abimi the son of R. Abahu taught the *baraita:* A man may feed his
> parent pheasant, and (yet) be driven from the world (to come); he
> may chain him to the millstone, and merit the world to come
> thereby.[61]

Rashi comments: " 'Be driven from the world'—he is punished . . .
for he displays a mean spirit as he feeds him. 'Merit the world to
come'—for he honors him by speaking good and comforting words, imposing the labor gently by showing him . . . that they could not sustain themselves without his labor." The rich man who feeds his father
well but meanly perverts the expression of reverence, for his "good
deed" telegraphs only contempt and scorn. Conversely, the son who
imposes toil upon his father nonetheless honors him well, for the generous and respectful relationship is not undermined by the imposition;
the father retains the dignity and degree he is denied by his resentful
though dutiful son. The Palestinian Talmud illustrates pungently:
"There was a man who always fed his father fattened hens. Once the father asked, 'Son, where do you get these hens?' The son answered, 'Old
man, eat and be quiet; just as dogs eat and are quiet.' "[62]

Both the Palestinian Talmud and Rashi (in part) do explicate the *baraita,* it is true, as referring to the display of emotion revealed in
speech.[63] This is largely an exegetical necessity: the Halakha is after all
concerned with the feelings of the father and these can be affected only
by some filial demonstration. The root of the matter is internal, but its
focus is concrete. The talmudic stress is relational (as is the biblical in
this area) and not therapeutic; it is laid upon the "other," not upon the
self. Despite this general reserve, rabbinic literature does, on occasion,
speak to the inner experience of filial piety, as when it contrasts the
man who "fulfills the wishes of his father, but in his heart is disrespectful of the will of his father" with the man whose heart and hand are at

peace.[64]

Contempt or resentment are not really the major offenses; they are merely the most easily dramatized and the most justly condemned. The poverty of internal emptiness is possibly the most common want; the simple absence of all feeling may be more devastating than actual hostility, for it testifies to a complete lack of relation. Acts of reverence and honor in this context ("a man often honors his parents for fear, or for shame")[65] ring hauntingly hollow.

To conclude: The internalized emotional correlates of behavior are just that—correlates. They do not minimize the list of concrete obligations; rather, the acted specifics are the necessary ground of the felt attitudes. The *baraita* of Abimi does not oppose the *baraita* of "service" and "reverence"—they complement each other. One is obliged to honor one's parents in very concrete ways, extending even to personal service. But the more overt aspects of the law do not negate the more subtle ones; externals do not substitute for the internal (nor, of course, is the reverse true). The absence of real reverence is never compensated for by an overabundance of the substance, but not the spirit, of honor.

Love of Parents

The Torah commands man to "love thy neighbor" as himself, and it commands man to honor his parents. It does not instruct man to love his parents either more or differently than he ought to love his fellowman. Nor is such an imperative found in the Talmud. The implications of this silence were articulated by Maimonides, who also noted that love for parents is not a prerequisite for either reverence or honor. The relevant passage occurs in a responsum discussing the obligation to embrace the convert (*ger*) in love; Maimonides writes:

> Know that the Torah has placed us under a heavy obligation in regard to the proselyte. For we were commanded to honor and revere our parents, and to obey the prophets—*now it is possible for a man to honor and revere and obey those whom he does not love.* But with the proselyte there is a command to love him with a great, heartfelt love . . . much as we are commanded to love God Himself.[66]

Maimonides believes, then, that reverence and honor possess emotional correlatives of their own, which can sustain a generous and respectful relationship.[67] But filial responsibility is not derived from, or connected to, unique filial love. We recall Maimonides' assertion that filial patience must sometimes fall back upon the "awe and fear of the King of Kings who commanded him thus."

The Midrash similarly dissociates honor and love when discussing a problem to which we shall return in detail: the relationship of a man to his wife and his relationship to his parents:

> Until a man takes a wife, he directs his love toward his parents. Once he marries, he directs his love toward his wife, as we read, "Therefore shall a man leave his father and his mother, and shall cleave unto his wife, and they shall be one flesh" (Genesis 2:24). Does a man leave his parents in the sense that he is free of the obligation to honor them? Rather, his soul's love cleaves to his wife. . . . [68]

The imperatives of honor and reverence do not depend upon love, but are ordered and sustained by other sources.[69]

No demand for a unique filial love is found in the traditional material, by and large. This should not be overemphasized, as though the ethos of filial piety presumed a unique filial hostility. Nonetheless, it is true that neither law nor lore find filial love a significant category; the basic categories are those of reverence, honor, service—and these do embrace feelings as well as behavior. It would seem that the tradition is, in fact, concerned with guaranteeing the reverence and honor due parents; these are necessary whether the son loves his parent or not. It is almost obvious, in fact, that instruction in reverence is necessary precisely where affection is absent. (And reverence and honor are, of course, not superfluous even where affection is present—they are different, and therefore the affectionate son must undertake to revere his parent as well as to love him.) Obviously this perspective embodies both an opportunity and a challenge: the son is given the emotional and behavioral tools with which he may fashion a filial relationship, in which his father is loved as his fellow and honored as his father, without forcing the flow of the relationship into the channel of filial love.[70] On the other hand, it is an imperative that the absence of reverence and honor cannot be excused by the absence of love. Finally, the focus on expressions of honor and reverence is true to the reluctance of the tradition to speak even of love of one's fellow, and its preference to let that love function in the concrete, loving deed.[71] Filial love, then, is best expressed in filial service, reverence, and honor.

As might be expected, the Maimonidean posture is not shared by all. Rashi, for example, assumed that filial love is the reason why a son supports his parents.[72] *Sefer Haredim,* one of the most popular moral-halakhic tracts of the Middle Ages, argued passionately that the essence of honor is internal and that it must include "a powerful love." This discussion of filial responsibility was taken almost verbatim into R. Abraham Danzig's halakhic digest, *Hayye Adam:*

> . . . obviously, a man ought to love his parents as himself, for they are included in "You shall love your neighbor as yourself." But the love of parents is compared to the love of God, as we read in *Zohar:* "a man ought to do all for his mother and father and love them more than himself, and his soul and all he possesses ought to be held as nought in his zeal to do their will."
>
> Our sages have said that the obligations of a son toward his father are repayment of the debt owed the parents for their good nurture. . . . Part of this repayment must be that he love them strongly, as they loved him, and that he not consider them an unwelcome burden. . . .
>
> "Honor" is a matter of thought, deed, and speech. In thought, . . . he must honor them in his heart, that they be in his eyes great and distinguished, though they are unimportant in the eyes of other men. And this is the essence of "honor," for if one does not do so, he fits the description of Scripture: "Forasmuch as this people draw near, and with their mouth and with their lips do honor Me, but have removed their heart far from Me . . . " (Isaiah 29:13).[73]

Both love and reverence for parents take as their model love and reverence for God. Now, heartfelt reverence in the presence of God, the internalizing of honor, must fuel the behavioral commitment. The ritual gestures remain shells if they are not the expressions of an inner state seeking concrete release. This is all the more blatant where, as in the situation described by Isaiah, the ritual gesture is one of prayer, or speech, for speech ought above all else to communicate and express the inner man. The Torah does not shrink from commanding the emotions: "And thou shalt love the Lord thy God with all thy heart, and with all thy soul, and with all thy might."[74]

Thus, continues *Sefer Haredim,* honor—modeled on the honor of God—implies both an inner valuation and the concrete objectivization of that valuation. The external proceeds from, reflects, the internal. The common man is not only to be *treated* by his son as though he were uncommon; he is to be so treated because in his son's eyes he *is* extraordinary. (Needless to say, this preciousness "in his eyes" does not conflict with the ability to see one's parent as he really is.) One must feel reverence in one's soul before one can be reverent in deed. The centrality of the parent is crucial here, a centrality born of concern and expressed in acts of service and care. To return to the situation discussed by Maimonides, the man provoked by his parent will restrain his anger ideally, not because of his commitment to the command of God, but because he possesses an inner reverence for his parent, and anger that would conflict with that reverence is checked by it.[75]

The demand that the expressions of service and reverence be impelled by an inner concern is prefaced by the imperative of filial love.[76] One stands before parents as one stands before God: one discovers an imperative to love one's parents matching the imperative to love God. Furthermore, gratitude compels that one respond to parents with their own most precious gift—the love they lavished on the child. Basic to these arguments is the deep conviction that behavior cultivated as an external response to an external divine demand, service without inner concern, etiquette without inner reverence, performance without love—all these are grotesque, bankrupt, and ultimately impossible.

Can love be commanded? That is the obvious and just question, but in a sense it is improper to focus the question this way. Can the reverence and honor of parents be commanded? These, too, are internalizations as well as behavioral patterns. Can the love of God be commanded? The Bible does command the Jew to "love the Lord your God with all your heart and with all your soul and with all your might." The imperatives are clearly there; yet, at the same time, they cannot be expounded simplistically. The *mitzvah* ("command") is a subtle concept and merits delicate understanding. The commanding God, first of all, is as much teacher of the right way as its legislator; He is the ultimate source of the right and good, not their arbitrary promulgator. Hence *mitzvot* are given in love and lived in joy.

Many *mitzvot,* moreover, are not given to swift and exhaustive execution. On the contrary, a terse imperative can imply a lifelong program and a beckoning goal. Love of both God and man can often be attained, as the rabbis declared, through a pattern of loving deeds. It is characteristic, then, that the *Zohar* (cited by *Hayye Adam*) brackets the love for parents with its concrete expression, and that R. Abraham Danzig, too, moves from "he loves them strongly" to "and not consider them a burden." At the same time, the love of which he speaks is clearly not exhausted by its expressions; sometimes nurtured by them, it must finally sustain them.

* * * * * *

It should be clear that this discussion concerned the roots and bases of
filial responsibility (*kibbud av ve'aim*) as an imperative, and it was
from that point of view that we considered the role of filial love. But
Judaism always knew the nobility, power, and meaning of the love that
could bind father and son, a love that served most often to express the
love of God for Israel and the love of Israel for God. Such love best described the achievement of Elijah, who would come "before the coming
of the great and terrible day of the Lord" to

> . . . turn the heart of the fathers to the children,
> And the heart of the children to the fathers. . . .
>
> (Malachi 3:24)

And if in one perspective Maimonides and *Sefer Haredim* represent
two distinct postures, may it not also be possible to see them as occupy-
ing two positions along one continuum? In such a perspective, Maimonides safeguards the possibility of service and reverence even where a
unique filial love is absent, while *Sefer Haredim* speaks of the fullest
flower of the filial experience.

III
The Support of Parents

The single problem of filial responsibility that is discussed at any length in the Talmud concerns the support of parents. In context, the problem is not precisely the support of indigent parents, but is somewhat broader: The Talmud asks whether or not the son is expected to supply the goods underlying the personal services for his parent—Is the son merely to help his parent physically to dress, or is he also to supply him with clothes?[1] Nor does the Talmud pause to inquire into the financial status of the parent under discussion. But it is quite easy to recognize in that discussion—as the post-talmudic scholars immediately did—the components of a legal and/or moral posture on the question of filial responsibility for poor parents.

I.

Tannaitic Teaching

There had been substantial tannaitic teaching on the subject before the talmudic (i.e., amoraic) problem had been put. These teachings all obliged the son to expend his own resources on his parents' behalf,[2] certainly implying his responsibility to support them, if not more.[3] One can detect in these teachings varying degrees of stress, but the basic attitude is the same: the honor of parents requires their support.[4]

Thus we find the following:

> Simeon b. Yohai taught: "Great is the honor one must accord one's parents—for God elevates it even beyond the honor one must accord Him. Here it says, 'Honor your father and your mother'; there it says, 'Honor the Lord with thy substance, and with the first-fruits of thy increase' (Proverbs 3:9). How do you honor Him? With the wealth in your possession—you give the gleanings to the poor and tithes and *terumah* and *halah*, you build a *sukkah*, make a *lulav*, a *shofar*, *zizit*, and *tefillin*, you feed the hungry, and give drink to the

thirsty. If you have the means, you are obliged to do all this—if you do not have the means, you are not. But with 'Honor your father and your mother' it is not so: whether you have the means or you do not, 'Honor your father and mother,' even if you must become a beggar at the door."[5]

"Honor your father and your mother": Perhaps this means with words alone? We are taught: "Honor the Lord with thy substance"—in food and drink, and with clean garments.[6]

It is stated: "Honor your father and your mother." And it is also stated: "Honor the Lord with thy substance." Just as one demands economic sacrifice, so does the other demand economic sacrifice.[7]

The general declaration that "Scripture equates the honor of parents with the honor of God" here finds characteristic concrete expression. The latter two teachings equate the son's responsibility toward his parents with his responsibility for the honor of God through His commands, while R. Simeon b. Yohai goes further and declares that the filial duties are even more extensive.[8] But all agree that the son is responsible for his parents' support.

The Mishnah also implies that a son honors his parents by sharing his possessions with them, and suggests that he is required to do so:

R. Eliezer said: "One may suggest to a man as an opening [for absolution from a vow] the honor of his father and mother,[9]" . . . The sages admit that in a matter concerning himself and his father and mother their honor is suggested as an opening.[10]

The latter section of the Mishnah means that where the son has banned the use of his property by his parents, an "opening" for absolution of the vow may be that he has thereby made it impossible for himself properly to honor his parents.[11] It is clear that the enjoyment of the property of the son is an aspect of the honor due parents. But it is difficult to gauge its nature or extent. Does the Mishnah presume a *duty* to so honor parents, or merely an opportunity and an everyday occurrence of such honor? (We speak of the discrimination between *hiyyuv* and *kiyyum,* or distinguish with Melden between "obligatory actions" and "actions that meet obligations.") The Mishnah might also refer to the needs of normal social intercourse rather than to actual support.[12] Whatever vagueness exists, though, it is clear that parents can expect to enjoy and use the property of their children. Anecdote and midrash also assume that the sharing of property with one's parents is a normal mode of *kibbud.* Joseph fulfilled the fifth commandment, we are told, because he sustained his father in Goshen. And the *baraita* told of the son "who fed his father pheasants. . . . "

More light is seemingly shed on the tannaitic situation by the report that:

> It was enacted at Usha that if a man assigned his entire estate in writing to his sons, he and his wife are nevertheless to be maintained out of it. . . . [13]

This apparently speaks of children who abandon their parents, and of an enactment that guarantees the parents maintenance from the property that was originally theirs.

The situation here described is a classic one, and we find Ben-Sira cautioning his reader, some three hundred years earlier, lest he allow "son, woman, comrade, or friend rule over your life. . . . Do not give your substance to another, lest you have to entreat him. For it is better that your sons beg of you, than you look to them for succor."[14] But the legislation of a specific enactment indicates an upsurge in such behavior. Why were parents assigning their entire estates to their children? The synod at Usha of which our source speaks is probably to be dated around 140 C.E., that is, in the generation following the Bar-Kokhba revolt.[15] One aspect of the declining economic situation at that time, according to A. H. M. Jones, was the employment of "ingenious legal devices" by men otherwise subject to certain Roman levies, "to divest themselves formally of their property while retaining its use."[16] Our enactment probably reflects this usage, and mobilizes the resources of Jewish law to protect—up to a point—the man who wished to evade the Roman duty.

Thus, the Usha *takkanah* is no indication that sons were otherwise not obliged to support their parents. Rather, it formalized parental rights in their erstwhile property, and made the parental claim enforceable and binding in civil law; the obligations stemming from filial responsibility were probably not enforceable.[17] But the criterion of enforceability does not distinguish "law" from "piety" in rabbinic thought; the unenforceable obligation may be a halakhically compelling obligation for all that. Certainly, children could not always be counted upon properly to support their parents. This fact emerges from some of the anecdotal talmudic material of a later period (see note 24) as well as from the oft-repeated tannaitic admonitions and teachings on the subject. The rabbis' enactment, interestingly, guaranteed parental rights only in what had originally been their own property—no enactment compelling general filial support was made.

Something more of the relevant social history and ethic of the time is revealed in the following discussion, later cited by the Talmud for its juridic implications:

> Two brothers, two partners, a father and son, may each redeem the Second Tithe for each other [and not add the normal "fifth"], and may give each other Poor Tithe. Said R. Judah: "Cursed is he who gives Poor Tithe to his father." They said to him: "But what if they are both poor?"
>
> (*Tosefta Ma'aser Sheni* 4:7)

R. Judah (a contemporary of R. Simeon) clearly expects a son to support his poor parent, and reviles the son who demeans his father by feeding him from the Poor Tithe (another instance, incidentally, of attention to spirit as well as substance). His companions respond that his sensitivity is indeed proper in respect to the prosperous son, but is misplaced when both father and son are needy, and it is all the son can do to maintain the Poor Tithe. Both R. Judah and the other sages expect the son to provide in some fashion for his father.

II.

Talmudic Problematics

Both Babylonian and Palestinian Talmuds ask the identical question: "At whose expense" is the son (in the language of the *baraita*) to "give his father food and drink, and clothe him? . . . " Some rabbis claimed that the son owed his father personal services alone, while others argued that to so restrict filial piety by excluding the concrete responsibility for parental needs made it ineffective and perhaps meaningless. The first opinion stressed the old analogy of son-servant and read the *baraita*, with its list of personal services, as characteristic (though not exhaustive) of the range of filial responsibility; the second opinion doubtless regarded both the son-servant analogy and the *baraita* as valid guides, so far as they went, but certainly not complete or thorough-going accounts of all types of filial responsibility—a responsibility they claimed to be both personal and financial. The discussion in the Palestinian Talmud concluded that filial piety includes financial responsibility, while that in the Babylonian Talmud concluded it does not.

The historical question is, of course, very much in place here: Why did the amoraic period, at least in Babylon, and to a certain degree in Palestine as well, see a rejection of the clearly articulated tannaitic emphasis on filial responsibility for parental well-being,[18] and a return to a singular stress on filial service as the total definition of filial honor? I am unable to isolate the economic or social data that would answer this question in historical terms; perhaps, indeed, the historical perspective can shed little light on our problem. My analysis, then, must be in the main a conceptual and juridical one.

In the Palestinian Talmud, we read:

> What is reverence? He must not sit in his place, nor speak in his place, nor contradict his words. What is honor? He must give him food and drink, clothe and shoe him, lead him in and lead him out.
>
> At whose expense? Hunna b. Hiyya said, "At the expense of the older man (the parent)." Others wished to say, "At his own expense." Did not R. Abahu say in the name of R. Jose b. Hanina, "Even if one is told by his father, 'Throw this wallet into the sea,' he must obey him?" That refers to a case where he has another wallet, and is giving his father pleasure. . . .
>
> The statement of Hunna b. Hiyya conflicts with the teaching of R. Simeon b. Yohai [cited above]. . . .
>
> R. Yannai and R. Jonathan were sitting. A man came up and kissed the feet of R. Jonathan. R. Yannai asked, "What did you do for this man that he repays you so?" R. Jonathan answered, "Once this man came to me and complained about his son, that he does not support him. I told him, 'Go gather the congregation in the synagogue[19] and publicly shame him.'" R. Yannai asked, "And why did you not compel the son to support his father?" R. Jonathan responded, "Can one compel that?" R. Yannai answered, "You don't know that?" R. Jonathan then began to teach as a fixed rule, "One may compel a son to support his father." . . . R. Jose said, "Would that I were as certain of all my traditions as I am of that one that 'one may compel a son to support his father.' "[20]

Though many points in this passage are not fully clear, the discussion concludes that a son must support his parent. The care implicit in *kibbud* is total; it demands the gift of substance as well as the gift of self. This opinion is clearly that of R. Simeon b. Yohai, it is implied by the statement of R. Abahu (though the Talmud cannot accept it as unambiguous and hence sufficient support for that position), and assumed by R. Yannai and R. Jonathan. Furthermore, the son is not only *obliged* to support his parent, he can be *compelled* to do so. So, at least, taught R. Yannai, and R. Jonathan accepted this teaching.

In the Babylonian Talmud we read:

What is reverence and what is honor? . . .

At whose expense [is the son to feed and clothe his father]? R. Judah said, "At the son's expense." R. Nathan b. 'Oshaya said, "At the father's expense." The sages taught R. Jeremiah . . . that the decision was as he who said, "At the father's expense."

It was asked: "(We have learnt:) It is stated, 'Honor your father and your mother,' and it is stated, 'Honor the Lord with your substance'; just as the latter demands economic sacrifice, so does the former demand economic sacrifice. And if the father is honored at his own expense, what economic sacrifice is asked of the son?" That he must lose working time. . . .

Come and learn: They asked R. Eliezer, "How far must one go in honoring one's father and mother?" He answered, "So that he throws a wallet into the sea before your very eyes and you do not shame him. And if you say that the father is honored at his own expense [and the wallet, perforce, is the father's own], what difference does it make to the son? Because the son will inherit the father [and so feels the loss as his own]." It is as the case of Rabbah bar R. Huna; R. Hunna tore clothes before the eyes of his son Rabbah, saying, "Let me see if he becomes incensed [and says something disrespectful to his father], or not." But perhaps he would be incensed, and his father will have thus transgressed the Scriptural command, "You shall not place a stumbling-block before the blind" [Leviticus 19:14]? R. Hunna waived the honor due him. But did he not transgress the Scriptural " . . . you must not destroy? . . . " (Deut. 20:19)? He tore the clothes at the seams. Then perhaps that is the reason that Rabbah did not become incensed? He did it when he was already in a temper.[21]

(b. Kiddushin 32a)

The position of the Babylonian Talmud on the questions of support and the obligation of the son to incur financial loss in the service of his parent is clear:

It presents two opinions on the question of support, but reports a decision according to which the son is not obliged to contribute to the support of his parent.[22] *Kibbud av* entails personal care and service (as in the primary *baraita*), but not the shouldering of the financial burden. All inferences to the contrary are parried, though as we shall see some limitation to filial non-responsibility is thereby introduced.

While the son is not obliged to make a direct financial contribution to the welfare of his parents, he is obliged to render them service even when the performance of that service restricts his economic activity and hence forces the loss of gain and opportunity. This exception to the general rule articulated above is well integrated, despite its origins in textual harmonization, into the conceptual dynamic of that rule: even though financial loss results, the direct demand made upon the son remains one of personal service.[23]

It would seem, then, that the Talmuds differ on the obligation of filial support and financial contribution. The Palestinian (TP) obligates the son, and holds that both personal service and economic care fuse in the organic category of concern and centrality called *kibbud av*. The Babylonian (TB), on the contrary, discriminates between the two; personal service is a valid demand, but financial responsibility lies outside *kibbud av*. TP, moreover, concludes that the son can be compelled to provide for his parents; TB does not consider this issue, inasmuch as it frees the son from such responsibility altogether. But other sources indicate that some Babylonian rabbis did compel sons to live up to their responsibility, though we are not told its specific nature. At the court of R. Hisda, in late 3rd-century Sura, "they brought in a man who did not honor his father and mother, and bound him. Rami b. Tamri said to them, 'Leave him alone, for so it has been taught, "The earthly court is not forewarned concerning an affirmative commandment that carries its reward by its side." ' "[24] While current practice did sanction compulsion, TB, consistently, presented Rami b. Tamri's stricture as the last word on the subject. Finally, the Babylonian version of the R. Yannai–R. Jonathan incident harmonizes with these conclusions: the story is understood to revolve around the obligations in civil law (legislated at the Usha Synod) of children who had been assigned parental estates, not around the general rubric of filial piety.[25]

Despite the relatively extended treatment given this problem in both Talmuds, it is clear that certain basic questions have not been clarified, or even asked. What, for instance, is the economic status of the parent we are discussing? Doubtless, the talmudic discussion is most immediately relevant—socially and morally—if the poor parent is its subject. It would only be natural, in fact, to assume that the question presupposes this pragmatic need. Yet the question is not framed in these functional terms; the Talmud asks, "Who is to pay for the food the son feeds his father, and the clothes in which he dresses him?" This vagueness, whatever the true concern of the Talmuds, was the literary catalyst for the next stage of the rabbinic discussion. The pragmatic and moral catalyst was the filial laissez-faire apparently endorsed by the Babylonian Talmud. Could the normative Jewish filial ethos consent to the economic abandonment of the parent? It would seem perverse for the Halakhah scrupulously to legislate in the area of personal service, yet to remain blind to the crucial need of financial support.[26]

III.
Reconsiderations and Conclusions

The earliest post-talmudic authorities grappled with this problem within the context of an assumption, implicit if not explicit, that the primary responsibility for a man in need is his son's. Two major juridic approaches translated this assumption into pragmatic legal categories: (a) the imperative of charity (zedakah) obligated the son, even if the norms of filial responsibility did not; (b) despite the conclusion of the Babylonian Talmud, the rubrics of filial responsibility do in fact obligate the son to support his father.

R. Ahai, author of the She'iltot (8th century), formulated the decision that was accepted (though with significant variation) by the majority of legists, including the authors of the Shulhan Arukh:

> . . . where the son is prosperous, and the father has naught, there is no question but that since he must give him charity, he is obligated [to do so]. The talmudic question is raised concerning a case where the son has nothing, or where the father is not in need. . . .[27]

The specific command to "honor your father and mother" may indeed be directed toward the service of parents, but one is not thereby released from their support when they are poor, for they are the most deserving recipients of zedakah. As R. Me'ir of Rothenberg was to note centuries later, the Talmud declares (though in its own idiom) that charity begins at home. It is, of course, most demeaning to support one's parent as an object of charity, and the baraita (which is repeated by the medievals) rages, "May he who supports his parents from his

alms-box be cursed."[28] But from a purely practical point of view, since
the Jewish community often considered itself empowered to force a res-
ident to give charity, the ruling of R. Ahai gave the community the in-
strumentality with which it could direct most children to contribute to
the support of their parents.[29] This is clearly a fact of the first order in
Jewish social ethics.

R. Ahai's decision merits analysis from a number of perspectives.
The major obstacle in the path of filial responsibility in this area is, of
course, the conclusion of the Babylonian Talmud that the substance in
which the father is served is to be "of the father." R. Ahai neutralizes
this discussion by reducing its scope to those situations where *zedakah*
cannot apply and only filial responsibility can: the situation of a prosperous father,[30] or that of a son who is himself possessed of very little
and cannot be expected to make substantial contributions to charity.
Where, however, the rubric of *zedakah* does apply—and this would
probably include most cases of parental need—the son is to conform to
it. This is a bold exposition of the talmudic *sugyah,* and one that does
not fully dovetail with the talmudic give-and-take at all points.[31] Its
moral logic, on the other hand, is most compelling.

This textual exposition has broad conceptual implications. As Prof. I.
Twersky notes, "With regard to one's parents, the material assistance,
when required, is probably also to be viewed from the vantage point of
charity. Indeed, the Halakhah states that honoring one's parents means
providing them with food and drink, clothing and covering, but the expense is to be borne by the parents. What counts, on the part of the son,
is the zeal and quality of service. In other words, the fulfillment of 'honoring thy father and mother' and 'ye shall fear, every man, his mother
and father' is not contingent upon finance. Indeed, since it was em-
phatically maintained that the honoring of parents was on a level with
the honoring of God, this could not be, in essence, a materially conditioned act. In socially ideal situations, where the parents have independent resources, the duty of honor and reverence is unimpaired and
their scope unrestricted."[32]

The conceptual distinction between *zedakah* and specifically filial
responsibility has important juridical as well as functional conse-
quences. The question of legal compulsion aside, the scope of *zedakah*
is limited compared with the range of filial piety; historically, quantitative criteria—often fixed at a tithe—limited the expected contribution
and, needless to say, the financial situation of the donor was also taken
into account. These factors were much less potent, as R. Ahai himself
noted, in obligations born of filial responsibility. "Even if you have
nothing," R. Simeon b. Yohai had said, " 'Honor your father and moth-

er' even if you must become a beggar at the door."

Despite this flaw, R. Ahai's solution was a useful instrument, and was accepted by R. Hai,[33] R. Hanan'el,[34] R. Alfas,[35] and many others; later, it was adopted by R. Moses Isserles in his *Mappah*.[36] The following responsum of R. Solomon ben Aderet (13th century Spain) illustrates both the workings of this instrument and its limitations, as well as the social situation it endeavored to correct:

> You have asked: Rebuen demanded before the court that his son Hanokh grant him support. The son claims that he must support his own children, and furthermore that his father has a quantity of debts outstanding that would afford support if collected. The father argues that it is doubtful if these debts could be collected, and that he would die of starvation before he could collect them. The father remonstrated with his son, who paid no attention; finally, enraged, he placed his son under a ban *(niddui)*, forbidding his participation in public prayers and in communal grace, and compelling him to adopt the habit of a mourner, until he grants the support. Please advise me if the court ought to compel him to support his father, or not.

> Response: According to the conclusion of the Talmud in the first chapter of *Kiddushin*, the law declares that the son is not obliged to support his father. . . . However, the son ought to be shamed, and the services ought to be halted on his account,[37] so that he will support his father, for we read in the Jerusalem Talmud: "R. Yannai and R. Jonathan were sitting. . . . " Here we see that even he who argues that the son may not be compelled to support his father agrees that the synagogue may be closed to him, and that he is to be publically shamed. But he may not be placed under the ban, for there is no compulsion greater than that. . . . It would seem correct, finally, that if the son is prosperous, we may compel him to support his father according to the laws of charity, much as a father is compelled to support his minor children. . . . [38]

Rashba rules here that the decision of the Babylonian Talmud precludes legal compulsion except in cases where the son's economic situation is such as to allow compulsion for *zedakah;* and where this is the situation, the power of the court is to be used to force the son to support his father, at least to the amount that the levy for charity will allow.[39] (We note, incidentally, that Rashba takes the discussion in the Palestinian Talmud at face value, claiming that its conclusion is opposed to that of the Babylonian Talmud and would sanction compulsion of the son on the actionable grounds of filial piety. Other medievals similarly understood PT.[40] But there were some who sought to harmonize the two Talmuds; they argued that PT describes a situation of parental impoverishment, and that the legal compulsion applied derived from the rubric of zedakah.)[41]

A second group of medieval scholars—R. Tam,[42] Rabiah,[43] and Maimonides[44] (and if we list Maimonides, we must also include R. Joseph Karo, who reproduces the Maimonidean formulation verbatim in his Shulhan Arukh), among others—utilized the exposition of R. Ahai but derived a more potent social and moral instrument from it. If it be granted that the talmudic sugyah can be so treated that it concerns only the prosperous father or the impoverished son, the more normal situation of the comfortable son and the needy parent has not been touched at all. R. Ahai decides, at this point, that the talmudic discussion has exhausted the range of filial responsibility and that the Halakhah must perforce operate within the structures of zedakah. The other approach asserts that it is ethically grotesque to thus reduce filial responsibility. The son who is relatively well off must support his needy parent, and this support is an expression of filial responsibility. It is true that the talmudic conclusion is that the substance is to be "of the father," but R. Ahai had already limited that conclusion to a narrow set of ideal circumstances. Other circumstances demand a different response—not, as for R. Ahai, of zedakah, but of filial piety itself.

This approach presents, perhaps, even greater problems in the analysis of the talmudic text itself. On the other hand, it directly resolves that most disturbing ethical problem: Can filial piety remain blind to the plight of the needy parent? It is quite true that the discussion of this latter group of scholars often utilizes the zedakah motif. But a close reading indicates that this motif is not a legal source, rather it is utilized as part of a moral rhetorical question: If a man can be compelled to make his contribution to charity, certainly he ought to be compelled to support his parents![45] Finally, this approach was, in fact, closer to the conclusion of the Palestinian Talmud, and while loyalty to the Babylonian Talmud was asserted, the precedent of the Palestinian conclusion could be utilized directly; one merely had to add, if one wished to harmonize the two, that PT described a case of parental need, but that the compulsion then applied was certainly on the grounds of filial responsibility.[46] But the norms of filial responsibility, while broader in scope than those of zedakah, were also less enforceable: the payment of zedakah assessments could be compelled by the full utilization of the power of the court, while the requirements of filial piety were not supported by that same armory—though the power of social pressure and ostracism that could be called into play should not be underestimated. Rashba was most reluctant to "compel" filial support; on the other hand, social and personal pressures often proved their potency in Jewish law and life as effective substitutes for the more clear-cut corporal compulsion. In any case, the exponents of parental support as an expression of filial piety would doubtless utilize the resources of enforcement available through the *zedakah* framework to compel the support.[47]

The thrust of the Halakha, then, is to focus responsibility upon the son. This is, of course, true of the juridic approach outlined just above; it is also true of R. Ahai and the approach associated with his name. Making due allowances for a characteristic hyperbole, we find in *Seder Eliyyahu* the view doubtless held by the halakhists: "If a man has much food in his house and is not a benefactor of his parents in their old age, it is as though he were a murderer before God."[48] Moralists such as the author of *Menorat ha-Ma'or* integrated the demand that the son provide his parents with food and clothes into the very *baraita* of *Kiddushin* 31b! Two responsa—one of the 16th century, the other of the 19th; both ostensibly committed to the talmudic conclusion that the son is not to spend his own money on his father's needs—typify the drive of halakhists to expand the filial responsibility.

R. David ben Zimra (Ridbaz) concludes a lengthy discussion of the talmudic texts with the following directive:

> And know that though the *poskim* have written that one compels the child to support his parent as though it were charity, the parent is not treated as the other poor, but according to the prosperity of the son, in the sense of one who is behaving charitably toward his own father, for it is customary for a father to be supported in a manner reflecting the prosperity of the son. This opinion is . . . midway between that of our Babylonian Talmud and the Jerusalem Talmud.[49]

Another, more radical attempt to integrate the demands made of the son in the name of "charity" and those made in the name of *kibbud av* is found in a responsum of the 19th-century jurist, R. Moses Sofer *(Hatam Sofer)*. R. Moses was asked about a son "of honored, well-born parents, who cannot sustain themselves from public charity. The son cannot afford to give them all they need, for his own personal and familial expenses are extensive. May he support them from the tithe he would normally give to charity, refusing money to all the other poor . . . until his parents live honorably and comfortably?"[50]

In his response, *Hatam Sofer* makes two basic points. First, the son is duty-bound to devote the complete tithe to the welfare of his parents, for it is precisely this priority within the charity structure that constitutes *kibbud av*.[51] Secondly, while the rabbis did ordain that no man give more than one-fifth of his income to charity, the original standard of the Torah was doubtless that "he who had sustenance for the day, must give the superfluity to the poor, . . . and with regard to one's parents, the rabbis made no ordinance but let the law of the Torah stand . . . that as long as he (the son) possessed enough for his own sustenance, he must give the rest to his parents." Here we see how bold and far-reaching even the "charity"-rooted approach to parental support could be. *Zedakah* remains the juridical category as it must, given R. Moses Sofer's submission to the authority of R. Moses Isserles. But most significantly, this category is emptied of its limiting disabilities and is made into a new juridic mode that reflects the old tannaitic demand: everything a son possesses must be placed at the disposal of his needy parent. It is quite true that the responsum is not addressed to a recalcitrant, niggardly son; quite the contrary—the son wishes to stretch his resources to provide for his parents. Yet whatever its social origins and effects, the opinion of *Hatam Sofer* is a legal and ethical landmark.

Nor can one omit the famous anecdote (adumbrated, in fact, in the responsa literature) told of R. Hayyim of Brisk:

> A man once came to R. Hayyim with the following question: He had heard that his father was ill, and hence felt obliged to journey to visit him. But since the law states that a child need not spend money in the honoring of his parent, he thinks that he may not be obliged to take the trip, for he would, of course, be forced to buy a train ticket. R. Hayyim answered tersely: "Correct—you are not obliged to spend the money—walk. . . . "[52]

We witness here an ongoing halakhic and ethical dialectic. One pole of this dialectic is composed of a steady stream of authoritative rulings limiting filial piety to acts of personal service and concern and suggesting that the plight of the needy parent is similar to the plight of all society's needy, to be meliorated by the same general structures. The Babylonian Talmud rules that expenses are not to be borne by the son, and some thousand years later this ruling is codified in the last code, the *Shulhan Arukh;* Ramah notes that filial contributions to parental welfare need not exceed the normal charity levy. Doubtless, this position bodies forth not only a functional economic conclusion, but a theory of filial piety as well: "what counts . . . is the zeal and quality of service."

This pole is in constant tension with its opposite, which insisted that filial responsibility must—in one way or another—protect the needy parent.[53] The very demand that the structures of *zedakah* be mobilized and focussed upon the recalcitrant son, a demand later integrated into the more conservative of the two postures, was at its origin an attempt by R. Ahai to fix filial responsibility. A more vigorous stance was expressed by those who would enforce filial responsibility as part of a filial piety unlimited by the various restrictions built into the structures of *zedakah.* Despite the fact that this wing, too, has textual authority behind it—the Palestinian Talmud and the antecedent tannaitic opinions—its basic weapons could not be texts but had to be a logic generated by an overarching grasp of the halakhic ethos and a skilled utilization of halakhic dialectics.

Of more immediate significance than the methodological observations above is the concrete social ethic that was hammered out. Children were made responsible for the economic security of their parents. This was preeminently true for those who saw this responsibility in terms of the extensive demands contained in the rubric of filial responsibility. It was true as well—though to a significantly lesser degree—for those who utilized the structures of *zedakah* alone; despite the theoretical fact that by using these structures parental need is identified with that of society's poor, this generalized instrument is also differentiated so as to focus responsibility upon the son, bringing in its train whatever techniques of enforcement were available. And though *zedakah* operates within quantitative limits, we have seen the tendency to expand this category where parental support is concerned (which, of course, is no more than a tendency: R. Moses Isserles stated explicitly, for example, that "[the son] is obliged to give him no more than he is required to contribute to charity," adding immediately though that "if he is prosperous he is cursed for supporting his father from the alms-box").[54]

*   *   *   *   *   *   *

A late midrash tells that God commanded Israel to build a Sanctuary for Him only after the people had petitioned for the right to so honor the Lord. God then said to the people:

> If you now insist upon carrying out your wish, do so, but do it in the way that I command you. It is customary in the world that whosoever has a little son cares for him, annoints him, washes him,

feeds him, and carries him; but as soon as the son is come of age, he provides for his father a beautiful dwelling, a table, and a candlestick. So long as you were young, I provided for you: washed you, fed you with bread and meat, gave you water to drink, and bore you on eagles' wings; but now that you are come of age, I wish you to build a house for me, set therein a table and a candlestick, and make an altar of incense within it.[55]

IV
Responsibility and Conflict

The Extent of Filial Piety

We live, notoriously, in a complex world in which responsibilities and rights, desires and needs never remain simple, and unconflicted. The noblest of wishes are often at cross-purposes, and we must choose between them. The human situation itself is certain to create a variety of needs from the most mundane to the most sublime, all demanding instant fulfillment or the next best thing (though actually a sorry second!)—right and fair adjudication.

So too with filial piety: How and where are its legitimate limits to be drawn? The *baraita* that specifies the content of reverence and honor does not make infinite demands; especially within certain cultural milieus, these expectations can be reasonably well integrated into the daily routine. The talmudic anecdotes and exegeses, on the other hand, project a service and a reverence infinite as the service and reverence of God Himself—that, indeed, is the very comparison drawn. Historically, this anecdotal, exegetical material became a normative ethos, and its authors themselves trembled at its magnitude:

> R. Simeon b. Yohai said " . . . the most difficult of all *mitzvot* is 'Honor your father and your mother. . . . '"
>
> (*Tanhuma, 'Ekev*, 2) [1]

> Mishnah: He who performs a single *mitzvah* receives much good, his life is lengthened, and he inherits the land. . . . R. Jose b. Bon said: "This refers to one who selected one *mitzvah* and never violated it all his life." Which *mitzvah* is this? Mar Ukban said: "Such as the honoring of parents."
>
> (p. *Kiddushin* 1:9) [2]

> R. Johanan said: "Blessed is he who never set eyes on his parents." (Because it is impossible to honor them adequately, and one is punished for failures—Rashi.) When R. Yohanan was conceived, his father died; when he was born, his mother died. So too Abbaye.
>
> (b. *Kiddushin* 31b)

R. Ze'era was wont to say, regretfully: "Would that I had a mother
and father (alive) so that I might honor them and inherit Paradise."
After he heard these two lessons [that of R. Tarfon, cited above,
Chap. 2; and that of R. Ishmael, who was forced to allow his mother
to wash his feet, for "her desire is her honor"] he said: "Thank God
that I have neither mother nor father—I could not do as R. Tarfon
did, nor could I accept what R. Ishmael accepted."

(p. *Kiddushin* 1:7)

These sources do not present the monochromatic picture that is suggested by my lumping them together this way. R. Simeon b. Yohai and
R. Jose b. Bon speak as much of the profound achievement promised by
filial piety as of its difficulties, which are vividly stressed by R. Yohanan and R. Ze'era. And even the words of these two—"Thank God" for
neither father nor mother—are momentary exclamations. Yet with all
these disclaimers, it cannot be denied that these citations betray an awe
at the magnitude and extent—both quantitative and qualitative—of the
ethos of filial piety.

As I have noted, the extent of filial piety is indeterminate. Its basic
floor is set down in the *baraita* of reverence and honor, but its ceiling
(as indeed that of any noble pursuit) eludes quantification. It is this
quality that inspires the feelings expressed above, this consciousness of
an ultimate challenge. But the more pragmatic and essential question
is, How does one integrate this demand into the totality of values and
quests that comprise a human life? To put the problem less vacuously,
How does the Jewish ethic adjudicate the claims of filial piety, on the
one hand, and the conflicting demands for the legitimate fulfillment of
different goals, on the other? The goal of a meaningful and happy family life might be one example, and that example is indeed the classic
arena in which the problem moves.

The passage of time itself seems to have complicated our dilemma.
The anecdotes surrounding filial piety, the exhortations urging the seriousness of this ethos, were taken with increasing resoluteness as
unexceptional norms. This was true in the halakhic sphere, and it was
perhaps truer in the sphere of popular (though not unlearned!) moralizing. The 14th-century martyr and moralist R. Israel Alnakawa wrote:

A person should always try to honor his father, and should not
do even a single thing that his father tells him not to do . . . for
the father always guides the son in the straight and good way, because he loves him. . . . Sometimes a father and mother advise the
son well and wisely, but it appears to him that their advice is poor

and he despises it, because the nature of youth is different from the nature of the older man, and therefore it appears to the young man as foolish counsel. But when he tries their suggestion, he discovers it to be good and correct.[3]

The claims of parental love and of the wisdom that comes with years are traditional devices—the one psychological, the other intellectual—in the conflict of generations. Our source prefaces them with what is for him primary: filial piety, which of itself compels adherence to parental wishes with the authority of Sinai. Another example is found in the 14th-century ethical will of Kalonymus b. Kalonymus. The writing of an "ethical will"—a last testament to one's family containing ethical, religious, and personal instruction—itself testifies to a faith in filial loyalty to parental guidance, and the prevalence of such wills is a revealing aspect of Jewish culture. R. Judah the Prince, who, a millennium earlier, had urged his sons to "be careful of the honor of your mother,"[4] perhaps served as a model for those who exhorted their children to filial piety toward their surviving parent. But the specifics noted by Kalonymus are a valuable testimony to the expectations of filial piety then prevalent:

> My son, I give you one command, which I declare you must fulfill with great and powerful zeal. Honor your honored mother with the greatest honor, submit to her with the greatest submission, and revere her greatly. Do not reject her commands or do something of which she disapproves, in either important or unimportant matters. For truly no one loves you more faithfully than she does. All the more should you behave this way, since the Torah commands you in the honor of your mother and her reverence.[5]

In a sense, this is the ethic glorified by the biblical Rehabites:

> . . . and I set before the sons of the house of the Rehabites goblets full of wine . . . and I said unto them, "Drink ye wine." But they said, "We will drink no wine; for Jonadab the son of Rehab our father commanded us, saying, 'Ye shall drink no wine, neither ye nor your sons for ever; neither shall ye build house, nor sow seed, nor plant vineyard, nor have any; but all your days ye shall dwell in tents. . . .' And we have hearkened to the voice of Jonadab the son of Rehab our father in all that he has charged us . . . and done according to all that Jonadab our father commanded us."

> Will ye not receive instruction to hearken to My words? saith the
> Lord. The words of Jonadab the son of Rehab, that he commanded
> his sons . . . are performed . . . for they hearken to their father's
> commandment. . . .
>
> (Jeremiah 35:5–14)

Biblical historians generally focus on the nomadic ethos to which the
Rehabites remained faithful. But of greater significance for biblical
thought—for it made the Rehabites a model for the people of Israel—
was their loyalty to the command of their father. Thus, Judah ben Tib-
bon (12th century, Provence) concluded his ethical will by commanding his son to read the Rehabite episode "every Sabbath," as a spur to
obedience.

Rabbinic declarations that "A man's father is like his king,"[6] and
"You are obliged to obey your father in all he tells you,"[7] doubtless
contributed to the crystallization of this ethic; the "servant" metaphor
and status (which we have described in Chapter II) contributed as well,
but in a less powerful and direct way. The midrashic apogee of these
sentiments is perhaps found in the observation that Isaac, by allowing
his father to bring him as a sacrifice to God, fulfilled the fifth
commandment.[8]

Indeed, the midrashic treatment of certain aspects of the *akedah* itself demonstrates the development. In the earliest midrash, the filial
role of Isaac in the *akedah* is not explored.[9] The compiler of *Tanhuma*,
which does focus on the willingness of Isaac to be sacrificed, includes
the detail that Isaac asked Abraham to bind him, lest he jerk away from
the descending knife and render the sacrifice unfit. Finally, a later midrash portrays Isaac as asking that he be bound for two reasons: the one
just given, and second, lest he kick out at his father and thus violate the
command of filial piety. This dual motive is found in many medieval
midrashim, as well as in medieval liturgical poetry. What we see here
is, fundamentally, an instance of literary but not cultural development.
It is not that the earliest midrash would not speak of Isaac's filial obedience; rather, it hardly explored the role of Isaac at all.[10] Once *Tanhuma*
and its contemporaries do focus on Isaac, it is only a matter of time until all the nuances of his behavior are exposed. But this natural development does nonetheless add new stress and weight to the older values
and responsibilities.

Great importance is attached to parental pain and distress, and the
obedient son is expected never to be their source. The Torah had spok-
en of the curse laid upon any who treated their parents lightly, and required the honor and reverence of parents. Other sources are more spe-

cific on this point. Proverbs taught that "A wise son makes a glad father; but a foolish son is the grief of his mother,"[11] and while wisdom and foolishness are the virtue and vice that are stressed, it is clear that a son should not grieve his mother. So too, " . . . he that is a companion of gluttonous men shames his father."[12] Ben-Sira tells the son to conjure up the memory of his parents and their certain shame before he would use foul language.[13]

The power of such apprehension is dramatized in Tobit: Reguel's daughter, Sarah, all of whose seven betrothals ended with the deaths of the young men, is dissuaded from hanging herself by the thought that her suicide would shame her father to death.[14] The Mishnah spoke of the shame suffered by parents of a son free with vows as a possible device by which the vow could be annulled.[15] And the Talmud spoke of the son who "pained his parent" as one who pained God. A representative medieval voice is the 13th-century Spanish talmudist and moralist, R. Jonah Gerondi, who found in filial piety the most apt and impressive topic with which to conclude his *Iggeret ha-Teshuva*:

> Know that the entire world was created for the glory of God. . . . Now if one wishes to honor God . . . let him honor his father and mother. As our Sages of blessed memory said: "When a man honors his father and mother, I count it as though I lived among them and they honored Me." Now the essence of the honor of parents is to give them pleasure, whether in words or in deeds. And he who pains them by his speech bears an insupportable sin. . . .

All this fed into the pentateuchal ethos of filial honor, expanding and enriching it. An ethos that expected honor would disapprove of the dishonor implicit in parental anguish; the willingness to act as the source of this pain would run directly counter to the concern presumably at the core of *kibbud av ve'aim*. Thus, the biblical curse and the rabbinic categories of reverence combine to develop into the generalized norm—obviously present in some talmudic narratives and in one or two halakhic discussions, and formulated in the abstract in early medieval times—that "one not cause one's parents any pain."[16] This norm, freighted with the burdens of human sensitivity and vulnerability (one is reminded here of Proust's meticulous explorations), becomes a major theme of both the literature and the living, transmitted, ethos.

The Zoharic analysis of the untimely death of Rachel (Genesis 35:16–19) is characteristic. With the standard midrashic interpretations, it, too, sees this event as bound up with Rachel's theft of her father's idols. But while these latter sources focus—as the Bible itself implies—on Jacob's curse ("With whomsoever you find your gods, he shall not live" [Genesis 31:32]), the *Zohar* understands her death as a punishment for the distress she caused her father by depriving him of his idols, "though her intentions were for the best."[17] Despite this gesture in the direction of the more usual antipathy towards idolatry (one thinks immediately, for contrast, of Gideon smashing his father's Ba'al altar [Judges 6:25] and of the robust delight the Midrash takes in Abraham's childhood demolition of his father's idol shop!), the value scale of the *Zohar* is clear: the pain caused Laban by his daughter is the single most significant component of the episode. R. Isaiah Horowitz, the 16th-century mystic, offers another instance: commenting on Joseph's willingness to abide by Jacob's wish that he search out his brothers though he knew that they hated him to the death, the *Shelah* remarks, ". . . a man must sacrifice his life to do the will of his father."[18]

The halakhic literature, too, I believe, displays this tendency. But Halakha is not hortatory, and does not grow in the deliberately simple and monochromatic, sermonic atmosphere. It is ever aware of a myriad of competitive possibilities, and strives to establish hierarchies of value and act. The halakhic literature must come to grips, then—as the hortatory or moralistic writer need not—with the concrete situation in which filial piety is a value among others, to be preferred or rejected after thoughtful reflection.

II.
Parental Commands and Divine Imperatives

What is the profile of filial submissiveness to parental authority? The first limitation placed upon filial submissiveness is born of the primary responsibility of both parent and child to God and His law. (It is, characteristically, a limitation born of responsibility, not of right.)

> "You shall each revere his father and his mother, and keep My sabbaths: I the Lord am your God" (Leviticus 19:3)—"You shall each revere . . .": perhaps I might think that one is obliged to obey even if one's father or mother desired that one violate a commandment— therefore the Torah says, ". . . and keep My sabbaths . . . : you are all required to honor Me."[19]

The Talmud understands this to mean that one is obliged to disobey a parent not only if he demands the gratuitous performance of an antinomian act, but even if he requires an act of service that would willy-nilly force the son to violate the law (e.g., that the son cook food for him on the Sabbath)[20] Loyalty to God and right take precedence for both parent and son over filial reverence and honor.

An elementary example of the workings of this doctrine is afforded by a responsum of R. Asher:

> You have asked about a father who forbade his son to speak to a certain Jew, or to pardon him . . . until a specified date. The son wishes to become reconciled with the individual, but hesitates because of his father's command. . . .
>
> (Response) Know that it is forbidden to hate any Jew, unless he is seen violating the law. The father who commanded his son to hate a man does not have the right to command him to violate the words of the Torah, which says, " 'I am the Lord' "—reverence of Me precedes reverence of yourself." Furthermore, the father is thus violating the law himself and not behaving in this matter as a member of the Jewish people ought to, and he need not be honored.[21]

Both the argument and decision of R. Asher flow quite naturally from the talmudic sources themselves.[22] It is interesting, nonetheless, to recall a complementary responsum of R. Me'ir of Rothenberg, the master of R. Asher. The case concerned an informer who was judged liable for the damages he caused another through his informing. The defense of the informer (a defense acceptable, apparently, to some, as the responsum indicates!) was that his act was motivated by a desire to strike a blow for his father's honor, inasmuch as his father had been physically assaulted by the plaintiff. R. Me'ir briskly ruled that the argument of the defendant holds no water, "for even if his father had commanded him to turn informer, he ought not to have done it . . . certainly, now, that his father never did so command him; furthermore, it was his father who struck the first blow. . . ."[23]

It is relatively simple to declare that a parental desire that would violate an ethical or ritual norm is itself to be rejected. What, though, if one is faced with the choice between fulfillment of a parental wish and fulfillment of some other divine command, the opportunity to rejoice with the bride, engage in an act of social welfare, or hear the *shofar* blown, for example? Tannaitic authorities disagreed:

> El'azar ben Matya said, "If my father says, 'Give me a drink of water,' and I am simultaneously presented with an opportunity to perform another divinely commanded act, I must waive the honoring

of my parent and perform the other *mitzvah*, for both I and my father are obliged to perform the *mitzvah*."

'Issi ben Judah said, "If the commandment can be performed by others, let it be done by others, and he must attend to his father's honor."

R. Matnah said, "The law follows the opinion of Issi ben Judah."[24]

Operating under a general rule that prefers the fulfillment of any *mitzvah* to the command of filial piety, the tannaim differ in approach and result. For El'azar ben Matya, this rubric is rooted in the claim of any *mitzvah* upon one's person—a claim that overrides filial piety—as both father and son are "required to honor Me." For many practical purposes, then, filial responsibility comes last. 'Issi ben Judah disagrees: the achievement of the divine imperative, it is true, takes precedence over filial responsibility, but the son may not neglect his filial responsibilities to ensure that *he*—rather than someone else—bring the *mitzvah* to fruition. Theoretically, then, filial responsibilities cannot be fulfilled at the expense of another *mitzvah*, but practically speaking the son must prefer these responsibilities to involvement with other *mitzvot*. El'azar ben Matya would sacrifice the parental desire; 'Issi ben Judah rejects this posture, so often maintained by children overwhelmed by divine imperatives,[25] and declares that the service of parents must take priority over one's fulfillment of other, more obviously God-oriented *mitzvot*.[26] The talmudic decision was rendered in favor of 'Issi. Where, however, the *mitzvah* is a personal one (e.g., the hearing of *shofar*) or would otherwise not be achieved, it is preferred to filial responsibility.

Pragmatically, yet another perspective emerges. 'Issi ben Judah distinguishes between commands that "can be performed by others" and those that cannot be fulfilled through others. Normally, those that can are imperatives directed toward meeting social needs; commands that cannot be so fulfilled but can be met only by oneself are usually (though not necessarily) acts of individual religious expression (e.g., hearing *shofar*, etc.). 'Issi ben Judah says, therefore, that religio-ritual achievement does take precedence over filial responsibility. This is not usually true of the sphere of social responsibility: father and mother come before other men. Finally, despite 'Issi's declaration that parental service takes precedence over other kinds of social involvement, both he and El'azar ben Matya agree that observance of ritual *mitzvot* is more compelling than *kibbud av*. In this they contrast strongly with R. Simeon b. Yohai who taught, we recall, that God ranks the honor due parents higher than the honor due Him, and commands men to behave accordingly.

Our analysis notwithstanding, this passage is tantalizing in its generality. *All* parental needs are apparently included in, "Get me a drink of water," which, though doubtless a stock formula, does refer to the least of parental wants. Evaluation—by the son—of the parental request is discounted. But are all *mitzvot* of equal weight? And when does the parental wish carry with it the active violation of a divine imperative? What are the bounds of a divine command—cannot virtually any human activity be part of a *mitzvah* structure? And when does one's participation become crucial to the success of the enterprise, when is one superfluous or replaceable? These are the obvious questions that illustrate how much remains unanswered by the *baraita,* seemingly so objective yet in reality open and in need of definition.

The Nature of Parental Authority

The second limitation on filial submissiveness cuts more directly to the heart of the matter. In essence, it is not a limitation at all; rather, it is an attempt to define the nature and judge the uses of parental authority and filial submission to it.

Some talmudic sources—the more anecdotal among them—speak of the filial obligation to avoid causing parents pain or anxiety at virtually any cost. Other, more normatively structured sources speak of substantive service and concern as the basic category of filial piety. Obviously, expansion or development originating from the former sources place a high premium on parental authority whatever its context; discussion rooted in the latter sources evaluate parental authority in terms of substantive need and right.

Discussion of this question, both theoretical and practical, emerged in the Middle Ages during the period of the *rishonim,* and has continued to recent times. The clear talmudic imperative of filial service included filial obedience to a parental wish when what is expected is a purposeful act, an act from which the parent derives concrete benefit, if only indirectly. It is a matter of disagreement, though, whether the parent is to be obeyed when he simply desires that his will be done for its own sake, when filial submission is itself his goal. Some medievals and moderns argue that the child is obliged to honor his parents' every wish within the limits of religious propriety and financial responsibility discussed above; they grant him little or no right to evaluate the motives or purposes embodied in the requests. The tosafists, on the other hand, distinguish sharply between opportunities for purposeful service—which are to be seized—and purposeless impositions upon the child—which may be ignored.[27]

The logic and implications of this latter position—which I believe reflects the stance of most authorities—are most suggestive. On the one hand, there is no limit to filial obedience—whether selfishness of motive on the part of the parent or difficulty of accomplishment for the son—when the parent desires to derive some concrete benefit from the child; "service," again, is the crux of "honor." If, however, the parent's goal is self-assertion, and he chooses for that purpose the most casual and minor of arbitrary requests, the son need not comply. (One is, indeed, tempted to speculate about the right of the son to adjudge even an objectively beneficial request as proceeding from an objectionable motive.) This halakhic dialectic is controlled, obviously, not by considerations of stress—whether physical or psychological—but by an indigenous dynamic flowing from an understanding of *kabbed,* a dynamic best described as ethical in the broadest sense of that term. The limits of "parental authority" are determined by its source and essence, the responsibility of the child to serve and revere his parents. Service, especially, requires selflessness in constructive pursuits. Thus, the assertion of authority *per se* is rejected.[28]

Revealing as this theoretical discussion has been, it is only through an examination of some concrete problems treated in the responsa literature that one can gain an appreciation of the ethos of the Halakha and see its contextual crystallization.

Various problems were discussed in light of the first rubric summarized above: when the son wished to perform a divinely commanded act and the parent objected, the respondent generally supported the son.

Thus we find the following question asked of R. Meir of Rothenberg:

> You have asked: "Can a father prevent his son from going to the land of Israel, since we rule that it is a *mitzvah* to go up to the land, and it is stated, 'I am the Lord,' that wherever a parental request conflicts with a *mitzvah* the parent is not to be obeyed, for the honor of God takes precedence over the honoring of parents. . . . "[29]

The response of R. Meir is, apparently, not preserved. A similar question was asked of R. Moses of Trani, who responded that "the son need not heed the command of his father and mother," since he would be fulfilling a divine command by settling in the land of Israel, "and he is not punished for neglecting the honor of his parents, since they can go the land of Israel with him, and thus both divine commands—the settling of the land and the honor of parents—could be fulfilled."[30]

R. Israel Isserlein wrote a responsum discussing a "student who wished to leave his home to study Torah with a certain teacher under whose guidance he was sure he would make great progress; and his father objects strongly, saying, 'I know, my son, that if you go you shall cause me great distress, for I shall constantly worry about you, lest you have been imprisoned or become the subject of accusations, as is common in that place. . . .' "[31]

R. Isserlein rules that the son need not heed his father's declaration, for he goes to perform a *mitzvah;* furthermore, he explains, "it would not appear correct to distinguish between failing to render service to parents and disobeying them when they object, even causing his father pain when he disobeys his command, for both honor and reverence are equally positive commands"; just as one may neglect the service of a parent if one is engaged in the performance of a *mitzvah,* so may one cause them pain. This last, crucial point was to be disputed by later respondents, as we shall see. It is quite clear, though, that without a ruling allowing the child to pain a parent if he wishes to fulfill a *mitzvah,* the scope of the priority given to the child's performance of a *mitzvah* as against the honoring of his parents would be severely restricted. The principle employed by R. Israel Isserlein settled more homely disagreements as well: "If one wishes to worship in a synagogue where the congregants pray with greater *kavvanah* (devotion), and his mother objects, he need not obey her," we read in an early 19th-century responsum.[32] Respondents were also sensitive, though, to the pleading of "divine imperative" as a cloak for less admirable motives. A son who vowed to study in the Land of Israel was told to cancel both vow and voyage when it was discovered that his real purpose was to abandon his widowed mother.[32a]

The Mitzvah of Marriage

Over and above the many parent-child conflicts that the Halakha and its interpreters were called upon to adjudicate, one issue has seemed to elicit the most persistent appeals to filial piety. Here, moreover, the Halakha was forced to articulate clear guidelines in an area where the conflict of the primary categories outlined above—the duty of filial compliance with parental wishes, the desire for individual happiness, the primacy of *mitzvah* over parental command, the impropriety of arbitrary, nonconstructive parental demands—could be clearly discerned and evaluated. Challenges to the filial relationship were often precipitated by the marriage of the child, first by the choice of the mate and then by the variety of stresses that the filial and marital states impose upon each other.

The patriarchs provided clear models here. Of Esau it was written, "When Esau was forty years old, he took to wife Judith daughter of Bee-ri the Hittite, and Basemath daughter of Elon the Hittite; and they were a source of bitterness to Isaac and Rebekah" (Genesis 26:34–35). But of Jacob it was told that he "obeyed his father and mother" and went to Paddan-aram to take a wife of his mother's family (Genesis 28:7). The Midrash is more explicit:

> "The way of a fool is straight in his own eyes; But he that is wise hearkens to counsel" (Proverbs 12:15). "The way of a fool"—this is Samson, who said, "Get her for me, for she is good in my eyes" (Judges 14:3). "But he that is wise"—this is Jacob, as it is said, "He listened to his father and mother."[33]

It is to be noted, though, that in all the incidents cited above, the parental preference or antipathy is not arbitrary but is substantively grounded: a wife of Israelite or related stock is preferable to a Hittite or Philistine woman. What is stressed, therefore, is not parental prerogative but parental wisdom—and, of course, the propriety of parental involvement.

Biblical practice was not monochromatic. On the one hand, ". . . the parents took all the decisions when a marriage was being arranged." Yet this was most true with regard to the marriage of children; the mature man is more likely to be guided, directed (see Genesis 28:1–2), or advised (see Tobit 4:12–13) by his parent but left free to come to his own decision. And so de Vaux concludes, ". . . parental authority was not such as to leave no room for the feelings of the young couple. There were love marriages in Israel . . . young people had ample opportunity for falling in love . . . for they were very free."

But the young daughter was especially subject to paternal control—he could sell her into slavery, and received monetary compensation (*mohar*) when she married and the penalty money if she were raped or maligned. Clearly, he had the right to give her in marriage, though her consent might be asked later (see Genesis 24:57–58).[34]

In rabbinic times, too, the father had the right to give his daughter in marriage until puberty (*boggeret*).[35] It was taught, though, that "it is forbidden for a man to marry off his daughter while she is a minor (*ketanah*); let him wait until she matures and says, 'I desire so-and-so,'"[36] at which time the father ought to help her fulfill her desire—

although medieval times saw a large-scale erosion of this rule. But though the father never had any legal rights in his son's marriage or in that of his mature daughter, the rabbinic leaders of talmudic Babylon prohibited sudden or private marriages; this increased the possibility of parental supervision, although it did not guarantee parental control.[37] Furthermore, the Jewish ethos involved the father in his child's matrimonial plans by requiring him to see to it that his child found a proper mate.[38] Indeed, the aggadah claimed that Joshua the high-priest was punished because he did not object to his sons' improper marriages.[39]

The normative requirement that the father marry his son off, though suggestive of parental control, neither sanctioned nor guaranteed it. Moreover, we ought not to assume that traditional societies consistently succeed in damping ardor; the story of R. Akiba and his wife Rachel is adequate demonstration of that.[40] Yet, certain traditional societies succeed quite well in controlling marriage; witness the statement of R. Solomon ben Aderet about 13th-century Spain:

> Praise be to the Almighty that in these areas the generation is moral and the daughters of Israel are chaste, so as not to take for husbands those whom they might fancy without the assent of their father during his lifetime; that is not the manner of the daughters of the land. Whoever heard of such a thing?[41]

In 15th-century Germany, too, "it is not the way of the land for a son to marry a woman without his father's agreement."[42]

The widespread attempt of medieval Jewish communities to guarantee restraint through legislation (*takkanot*) reveals, though, that parents and children would often disagree on the choice of a mate, and that the son or daughter was apt to settle the matter as they liked. Thus, R. Solomon ben Aderet also notes "that in all the communities between Narbonne, Arles, Avingnon, and Alez, the regulations required the assent of the father or (if fatherless) the mother and brother of the maiden . . . for a betrothal to take place."[43] The Synod of Ferrara, Italy (1554), declared that any man who married a woman without the presence of ten witnesses and the consent of her parents was to be excommunicated; a similar *takkanah* had been decreed by Castilian Jewry in Valladolid in 1432.[44] The community of Salonika (Greece) agreed, sometime before 1529, not to allow the marriage of any girl without parental consent;[45] the Council of Lithuania declared in 1523 that no man younger than eighteen years old might enter into an agreement to marry without first receiving parental consent; a similar edict was de-

creed by the Council of the Four Lands in 1534.[46] But the legal effectiveness of some of these *takkanot* was either limited or arguable, and
even when communities did legislate in this vein, their overriding concern was generally not with youthful ardor or rebellion (which might
best be handled in other ways) but with scoundrels capable of manipu-
lating both daughter and law.[47]

The more direct and halakhically impressive appeal was to the fifth
commandment. Could a child, of whatever age, go counter to the expressed desire of his parent, and marry though his parent had banned
the match? There is no talmudic comment on the problem, nor any direct gaonic discussion.[48] Yet from a codificatory point of view, the law
is clear. R. Moses Isserles ruled in his gloss (*Yore De'ah* 240:25) that,
". . . if the father objects to his son's marriage to the woman of his
choice, the son is not obliged to listen to his father." The responsa both
antedating and postdating this gloss offer a fascinating insight into the
halakhic dynamic at work in both the conceptual and moral spheres,
and display the fusion of law and value.

The two basic documents are the responsa of R. Solomon ben Aderet
(Rashba) and R. Joseph Kolon.[49] The opinion of Rashba was offered in a
responsum devoted primarily to another, though related, question. A
son is allowed to override parental objections in order to marry, he
ruled, for to marry is to fulfill a divine command before which the
claims of parents must be silent. Furthermore, this "command cannot
be fulfilled by others," for one must marry one's proper mate, and cannot be put off by a parental "others are as good as she." In the words of
the Talmud, "Forty days before the child is formed a heavenly voice declares, 'The daughter of X to the son of Y. . . .' "[50] No other wife will
do and, presumably, the man searching for his mate is best able to hear
the heavenly verdict. The value judgment that clearly provides the base
for this entire discussion is that while the individual cannot set aside
his obligation toward his parent on the ground that it interferes with
his own personal growth, he can, however, reject the parental claim
when this personal growth coincides with the fulfillment of a divine
norm. In a similar vein, R. Asher disallowed parental interference in
the formation of social relationships because the normative "love of
one's fellow" is at stake.[51] A crucial pragmatic question for this axiology is, obviously, whether to place a narrow or a broad constuction upon
the "normative"; almost every form of human activity can, after all, become an opportunity for divine service—at least for argument's sake.
Yet keeping faith with this value scheme demands that the individual
be prepared to sacrifice his own fulfillment to parental honor.

The discussion of R. Joseph Kolon is more complex and exposes the full problem. Addressing himself directly to the question of marriage in violation of parental wishes, Maharik firmly rejects any appeal to filial obligations.

Citing R. Asher, Maharik argues that in fulfilling a *mitzvah* one may ignore parental wishes; the tradition, he continues (in a different treatment than that of Rashba, *supra*), strives to make the partners in marriage beloved to each other—a possibility made infinitely more difficult by the introduction of compulsion into the very seed of the relationship. Marriage is thus an instance of the love of fellowman, and is immune to parental interference.

Furthermore, he continues, the Talmud has already ruled that the son need not sacrifice his own substance in the honoring of parents—certainly, then, he need not suffer physical "discomfort."[52] The entire talmudic discussion concerns, in fact, the obligation laid upon the child to render service to the parent—that is to say, to provide him with his needs, and to prevent his falling prey to those displeasures and pains to which he would otherwise be heir. What is essential, then, is that the claims of filial piety exist only in those areas in which the parent is inexorably involved— his own pleasure or pain. They do not exist in areas that are not of immediate personal concern to the parent, such as the behavior of his child, even if the parent chooses to involve himself and thereby make the issue one of parental pain or pleasure.[52]

Much the same point is implied by another responsum of Rashba. A father, he ruled, cannot bind his son to the employ of a third person without the agreement of the former; and barring other complicating factors, the son need not comply with such a contract: "The father possesses," to use the language of the questioner that is tacitly accepted by Rashba, "no right other than that of honor."[53] Clearly, the fulfillment of the parental will is not considered, of itself, an aspect of honor.

We first encountered this limitation of the sphere of filial responsibility to those areas that are properly the concern of parents—their own physical comfort and the demands of their own beings—in the theoretical discussion of the tosafists.[54] Now we see this concept as a potent legal and ethical instrument. For though the overarching axiological pattern just formulated still holds, and the son is indeed asked to surrender personal growth to parental needs, the sphere of these needs is limited both pragmatically and ethically. Parental pain or pleasure *per se* are no longer the criteria; rather, these become legitimate demands upon the child only insofar as they are not inappropriate intrusions. The two principles articulated by Maharik—the integrity of acts in which a *mitzvah* is crystallized, and the illegitimacy of parental coercion in areas not directly of concern to them—complement each other,

serving as opposing arms of an integrated halakhic instrument. The former allows the evaluation of the act contemplated by the son, while the
latter demands the independent evaluation of the parental wish.

Sixteenth-century Greece provided the fullest exposition of the landmark responsum of Maharik. A father in the Greek town of Patras forbade his son to marry the woman whom "his soul desired." Does the
son's filial responsibility demand compliance? R. Elijah Capsali of
Crete ruled that it did not, in a responsum that richly embroiders that of
Maharik; special stress is here laid upon the bonds of marital affection:

> . . . Though the command of filial honor and reverence is inex-
> pressibly great . . . nonetheless it appears in my humble opinion
> that if the girl about whom you ask is a proper wife for the afore-
> mentioned Reuben—that is, there is in her or in her family no
> blemish[55]—then the commmand of filial honor and reverence is ir-
> relevant, and the son is not to abandon her so as to fulfill his fa-
> ther's command.
>
> For it is nearly certain that this father virtually commands his son
> to violate the Torah. . . . For we see (in the Talmud) that a man
> ought not to marry a woman who does not please him. So that
> when the father commands his son not to marry this woman, it is as
> though he commands him to violate the Torah; and it is well
> known that the son is not to obey his father in such cases. . . .
>
> Now, if we were to decide that a son is obliged to obey his par-
> ents and marry though his heart is not in the match, we should
> cause the growth of hatred and strife in the home, which is not the
> way of our holy Torah. Most certainly in this case, where he loves
> her. Indeed, we can cite in this situation: "Many waters cannot
> quench love, neither can the floods drown it . . . (Song of Songs
> 8:7)." Were he to marry another whom he does not desire, his entire
> life would be painful and bitter.
>
> . . . Moreover, we may also argue that the Torah obliges the son
> to filial honor and reverence only in matters that affect the parent's
> physical well-being and support . . . but in matters that do not
> affect the parent in these areas, we may say that the Torah does not
> oblige the son to be obedient. Therefore, the son is not obliged by
> the rubrics of reverence and honor to accept his father's command
> in the matter of marriage.
>
> . . . All this is according to the letter of the law (shurat ha-din).
> However, so far as behavior beyond the line of the law (lifnim
> mishurat ha-din) is concerned, the son should not do any-
> thing—whether important or not—without the agreement of his

parents.

And it is proper for the son to subdue his own desires as much as possible so as to fulfill the desires of his parents. . . . But if he sees that it is impossible for him to do so, let him do as seems good and proper to him in the matter of his own marriage; for God considers marriage to depend upon the will of the son, as I have explained.[56]

Here we see the arguments of Maharik marshaled and expanded: marriage is a *mitzvah* and love is a necessary component of marriage; parental authority, moreover, extends only to the areas of parental well-being for which the son is responsible, not beyond.

R. Elijah Capsali is hardly intent upon undermining the institution of filial reverence. His last paragraph above, in which the son is asked to render general submission to a parent's wish, is typical of his available writings on the subject; the argument that filial responsibility is limited to areas of parental well-being is offered quite grudgingly. He was moreover, the only author to write an entire volume on the topic of filial responsibility (the volume, *Me'ah She'arim,* is still in manuscript), and we may safely assume that it encouraged dutifulness. Indeed, he tells us elsewhere[57] of his admiration for a custom he saw in Padua, where "every Sabbath and festival, after the evening prayer, the sons come to their fathers to prostrate themselves, bow down on their knees, and kiss their palms. . . . From the time I observed this custom I said, 'This must be an old tradition of the pious.' . . . I also said . . . I shall follow this practice myself. And so I did. . . . And if God should grant me sons, I would instruct them in this same custom. . . ." This responsum on marriage, therefore, results from the weighing of right and responsibility so as to provide guidance in an area where both sides have just claims.

The ruling of Maharik was codified by R. Moses Isserles, and both it and its analytical underpinnings are considered normative by most discussants of this problem.[58]

Nonetheless, some opinions required, with varying degrees of vigor, filial obedience even in this most personal of decisions. An anonymous—and in its context, irregular—Gaonic responsum had assumed that a proper daughter of Israel would never refuse to marry him whom her father had chosen, and had constructed a legally effective presumption of this observation; this opinion remained an eccentricity, however (see note 48). Some centuries later, the pietistic *Sefer Hassidim* cautioned: "If the mother or father sees that the daughters of the land are evil, and the son wishes to marry one of them, and the father commands him to desist, the son sins if he proceeds to marry, for Jacob

obeyed Isaac and Rebekah."[59] Certainly, an ethos different from that of
Maharik is taught here, though no general mandate was read into these
words until fairly recent times: For one thing, there is the objective requirement that "the daughters of the land [be] evil"; for another, the
standards of *Sefer Hassidim* were not necessarily given normative cre-
dence.

A number of 16th- and 17th- century Italian and Greek respondents
declare, in strictly halakhic contexts, that filial piety extends to the
choice of one's mate. In the course of his lengthy deliberations, the elder R. Joseph of Trani (Maharit) allows a young man to rescind a vow by
which he barred a particular woman as his wife, arguing that the claim
that the vow was made in respect of the father's instructions (the father
having since changed his mind) is fully reasonable, for filial compliance in these matters is an aspect of *kibbud*.[60] And R. Samuel Abohab
wrote that a son who abided by his father's wish and married a poor orphan girl was a man of virtue on many scores, among them *kibbud av*.[61]

Yet, when seen in context, these data are less impressive than it
might appear. In neither responsum is filial responsibility the decisive
factor; rather, the questions were, in effect, decided on quite other
grounds with which the component of filial piety is then integrated.
Equally pertinent is the fact that while both respondents claim that obedience is a form of filial piety, neither argues (or has to, for that matter)
that rejection of paternal advice is banned as a violation of filial piety.[62]
It is this latter determination that would be truly crucial. In short, neither responsum really discusses our question with any amplitude or as
more than a tangential aspect of other more central problems. Despite
this disclaimer, it is clear that we find here an approach that would include matrimony as a proper arena for parental involvement (R. Joseph
of Trani cites, in fact, the talmudic statement that a father is responsible
for marrying off his son) and hence, for filial piety.

In more recent times, however, a fully articulated posture requiring
filial submission in marriage and other matters has been articulated.
Thus, it has been argued that the tosafists' exclusion of parental will as
an aspect of parental honor is in fact a minority position (see note 27),
though some medieval sources must be pushed rather hard to justify
this conclusion; furthermore, a rigorously systematic reading of talmudic sources disclosed to one 20th-century discussant that Maharik
had exceeded all talmudic precedent: "In conclusion," wrote Rabbi Y.
Perlow, "I know of no source for the opinion of Maharik, nor any citation that implies it."[63] More concretely, it has been held that in certain
circumstances—and these are, as we shall see, rather elastic—filial submission to parental wishes in matters matrimonial is the rule.

The two major sources cited by proponents of this position are *Sefer Hassidim,* and Maharik: *Sefer Hassidim* does counsel filial acquiescence when the "daughters of the land are evil."[64] And Maharik began his reply by stating (and this detail is omitted in the gloss of R. Moses Isserles): ". . . it appears that *if she is a proper wife* for him, the father cannot object to his son's behavior. . . ." If, however, she is not a proper wife, the argument continues, the father is within his rights in objecting to the match, and the son must respect his objection.

But neither of these sources provides the unambiguous mandate for parental authority that has been claimed. Maharik, in point of fact, is saying no more than that a father—and perhaps any relation—ought to object to an improper match.[65] He does not suggest that filial piety ought to compel filial compliance, but that the son, as any man, ought to heed wise and proper counsel. Furthermore, where child and parent disagree over the match, the parent always says, "She is not a proper wife"; the wisdom of the match is precisely the issue about which there is no objective testimony. Thus, *Sefer Hassidim* also advises a son to disobey his parents and not marry the "evil girl" they prefer: Here the son is expected to decide.[66] Halakhists, moreover, have been wary of utilizing the pietistic *Sefer Hassidim* as a source of normative law, though exceptions abound. We may say, then, that though both Maharik and *Sefer Hassidim* do suggest, with varying degrees of emphasis, that the parental negative ought sometimes be a weighty consideration, the expansion of this suggestion into a normative rule, and the claim of juridical clarity for what is originally marked by ambiguity, betrays a *tendenz.*

One noted rabbinic authority of the last century argued that, in general, a son can, at the utmost, refuse to honor his parents in order to fulfill a *mitzvah*—he cannot disgrace them and pain them, and should not marry the woman if this will ensue.[67] If taken at face value, this last opinion would give the parent a veto over the son's choice of mate, for which parent who disapproves strongly of a match does not feel himself disgraced and pained by it? Nor would matrimony be the only area in which filial initiative would be inhibited. The distinction between honor and irreverence functions in a manner rejected some six centuries earlier by R. Israel Isserlein and betrays the shift noted above. One does sense, intuitively, that a greater premium ought to be placed on parental disgrace than on parental honor; a man who should embarrass his parents so that he might perform a *mitzvah* is perverse.[68] But this judgment is accompanied by the conviction—articulated in halakhhic terminology by Maharik—that it is ethically not legitimate for the parent to preempt areas of filial growth and fulfillment by his own personal involvement. And to the degree that R. Moses Isserles remains a crucially authoritative voice, his opinion, together with its theoretical base in Rashba and Maharik, remains normative.

It is possible, of course, to see this entire debate from a different perspective. This would pit a revisionist trend, represented first by the tosafists and later by R. Joseph Kolon, against the traditional mores of both Bible and Talmud. In the Bible, sons are expected to obey parental advice; the Talmud, too, tells of the inviolability of parental authority— the parent, in short, is "not to be contradicted." By codifying the response of Maharik, R. Moses Isserles legitimates a new departure in the Jewish teaching on filial piety. His opponents, on the other hand, simply defend the standard implicit in the Bible and Talmud, in which parental authority is central to filial piety.

Despite the attractiveness of this reconstruction, it oversimplifies. It is true that biblical and talmudic cultures do project a picture of inviolable parental authority. But as we have pointed out, talmudic teaching is given in two strains: the anecdotes of total filial submissiveness, and the more pointedly definitive *baraita*. The latter, certainly, stresses filial responsibility—not parental authority. (Nor is it unlikely that the elements of *morah* would be evaluated by the halakhist *in situ.*) It is by this ethos of substantive responsibility that the tosafists and Maharik evaluate and define the place of parental authority.[69]

III.
Parents, Mates, and In-laws

Our concern with filial submission and parental authority has led us to focus on conflicts arising out of the choice of mate. But the basic challenge to the filial relationship is not delivered by this single aspect of marriage, but rather by the marital situation and process as a whole, by the emotional as well as physical development and displacement that are its cause and corollary. This tension and its resolution must be integrated into Jewish thought, not only because marriage is the common human experience, but especially because it is, in Judaism, a *mitzvah* . Indeed, it was this very quality that insured recognition of the problem and structured the axiology of its solution.

The first statement made by the Torah on the subject remained the guide for subsequent Jewish thinking. After telling of Eve's creation by God from Adam's rib ("bone of my bones and flesh of my flesh," says man), the Torah says:

Hence a man leaves his father and mother and clings to his wife, so that they become one flesh.

(Genesis 2:24)

The terse sentence is richly suggestive, yet lucidly pedagogic. The join-
ing of man to woman, an event inherent in their very origins, requires
for its achievement that a man "leave his father and mother. " The
movement toward one's new partner attains its fullness only when the
individual has moved away from the parental hearth and its ties. Both
physical and psychic movement are implied here. The building of a
new family necessitates the destruction, in part, of the old.

These few biblical words inform subsequent Jewish thought, and
predict its posture. This does not mean to say that all or even a majority
of the subsequent discussants cite this verse, or deal explicitly with its
contents. They do not and need not: The attitude expressed in this sentence impregnated the very process in which the problem was thrashed
out, it was a fundamental and presupposed assumption. More concretely, the normative character of marriage, which is of course a basic component of all discussion, is the translation of the biblical verse into halakhic structures. Yet, one reservation must be set down: Jewish tradition—both in its analytic and in its lived expressions—did not cultivate
the potentially harsh and extreme possibilities of the biblical verse.
With some exception, of course, the verse did not become the subject of
aggadic exploration, and its implications for the human experience
were not articulated. The halakhic tradition, needless to say, mobilized
the normative character of marriage only when a concrete conflict between the marital situation and the filial one was exposed, with the
hope that such conflicts could be minimized rather than expanded.
Whatever the existential truth of Genesis 2:24, then, it was often tem-
pered by filial responsibility and the attitudes that accompany the command to "Honor your father and your mother." Yet, all in all, aggadah
and Halakha confront both the emotional development and the displacement which occur with marriage—though this need not affect filial piety—and the concrete displacement of responsibility and energy—
which do affect filial piety in its concrete expression of service.

The rabbis focus on both the elementary fact of the shift in physical
domicile that occurs with marriage, and the more meaningful psycho-
logical-experiential development.

The Aramaic translation of Onkelos (followed closely by Pseudo-
Jonathan and Targum Jerusalem) renders Genesis 2:24 in the following,
somewhat puzzling, manner: " . . . a man will leave the sleeping
place of his father and mother and cleave to his wife. . . . "[70] The sim-

plest meaning of this translation is that with marriage the new husband leaves the house of his parents to establish his own home.[71] While Onkelos sees the verse in terms of the shift in physical domicile, the Midrash focuses on the emotional and psychic displacement: a man "leaves" much more than the physical environment of childhood when he marries.[72]

The stimulus for the midrashic comment is the remarkable verse that concludes the story of Isaac's marriage to Rebekah:

> Isaac then brought her into the tent of his mother Sarah, and he took Rebekah as his wife. Isaac loved her, and thus found comfort after his mother's death.
>
> (Genesis 24:67)

The Midrash notes the personal, psychological suggestiveness of the episode and reflects, as well, upon its universal insight:

> R. Jose said, "Isaac mourned his mother Sarah three years. At the end of three years he married Rebekah and stopped mourning his mother. Thus we see that until a man takes a wife, he directs his love toward his parents. Once he marries, he directs his love toward his wife, as we read, 'Therefore shall a man leave his father and his mother, and cleave unto his wife, so that they become one flesh.' Does a man leave his parents in the sense that he is free of the obligation to honor them? Rather, his soul's love cleaves to his wife. . . ."[73]

Expounding the Isaac-Rebekah episode, the Midrash is explicit where the Bible only hints. Isaac found, in loving his wife, consolation for the love he could no longer bestow upon his mother. But the Midrash then generalizes from Isaac's compensation for the love of his dead mother by the love of his wife, to the substitution of the love of one's wife for the love of one's living parents. In the process, the meaning of Genesis 2:24 is deepened. It is not only a physical displacement that is described but, more significantly, an emotional one. Filial love (though not filial respect!) is supplanted by love of one's mate.

Nahmanides read these verses from a similar perspective:

> . . . a man wants his wife to be with him always, as it was implanted in his nature for the males to cleave to their wives; they leave their fathers and their mothers, and see themselves one flesh with their wives. . . . Man . . . sees that his wife is closer to him than

his parents. . . .

When Isaac saw Rebekah he brought her to that tent to honor her, and there he took her, and this is the meaning of "he loved her and found comfort," which hints at his great, inconsolable sorrow over his mother until he was consoled in his wife, in his love of her, for otherwise, why would the Torah mention the love of man for his wife?[74]

Both Midrash and Nahmanides see in Genesis 2:24 a classic formulation of the new personal reality that is presented by marriage and the love it reflects. But this reality, while affecting filial love, need not affect filial responsibility of service and reverence. Indeed, the Midrash firmly rejects the notion that these responsibilities are terminated by marriage: "Does a man leave his parents in the sense that he is free of the obligation to honor them?" Yet, while the emotional development need not affect filial concern, and the Midrash insists it should not, the shift in physical arrangements and the new focus of responsibility cannot help but affect the dimensions of filial service and involvement.

The Talmud does not, to my knowledge, fully confront this problem either from the point of view of the conflict of the two norms or, even presuming a normative preference, from within the human reality that requires guidance and ethical wisdom even after a norm has been established. Thus, even after we have assimilated the claim of filial responsibility to its inevitable limitation when confronted by another *mitzvah*, in this case that of marriage, we search in vain for the ethical and psychological insight that would mold a reality hospitable to both claims. For what is wanted, ultimately, is not only the kind of normative decisiveness that presupposes irremediable conflict, but rather the happy balance that, while not compromising the normative axiology, nonetheless cultivates both values. The Talmud—and for that matter the bulk of the literature—seems most reluctant to offer explicit prescriptions; ethical maturity, it implies, must recognize the diversity of each situation, and can at best educate toward a responsible attentiveness to the basic values of the tradition.

A minimum of talmudic teaching can, however, be garnered. The most concrete statement is that of the following *baraita:*[75]

"You shall revere every man his father and his mother. . . . " We hear here only about a man. How do we know that a woman is also commanded? Since the verse speaks in the plural ["revere" is found in the plural form], we see that both are included.

Why then is "man" specifically spoken of? Because it is within

the man's power to act on his parent's behalf, but it is not in the
woman's power to do so, because she is in the control of another.

R. Idi b. Abin said in the name of Rav: If she is divorced, both
(man and woman) are equal.[76]

Men and women are equal in respect to filial piety; a daughter is
obliged to serve and revere her parent as much as is a son.[77] A married
woman, however, is limited in her ability, and hence her responsibility, to fulfill this imperative, for her energies and her very physical
residence are at her husband's disposal.[78] A wife, as another *baraita*
teaches, must honor her husband;[79] the *baraita* before us reflects both
that honor and the concrete obligations of marriage. These obligations
obviously restrict devotion to filial service, and this fact is readily
accepted.[80] At the same time, there is little suggestion that a married
woman is *ipso facto* released from those aspects of filial piety that are
within her power to achieve—that would surely be perverse.[81] Nor is
the husband's arbitrary whim law. The Mishnah, for example, lists a
variety of activities with which a husband cannot interfere, and among
them are periodic visits by his wife to her parents.[82] Probably, though, a
father would visit his married daughter more often than she would visit
him, reflecting precisely those domestic responsibilities assumed by
our *baraita*.[83]

Marriage, then, limits the filial responsibility of a *daughter*. But the
husband is not restricted by these factors, the very point of the *baraita*
being that his opportunities for filial service are not affected by his responsibilities toward his wife, or, more accurately, by his wife's
control.[84] This would not mean, then, that he is expected to neglect his
domestic responsibilities so as the better to serve his parents; indeed,
he is probably not entitled—either ethically or halakhically—to do so.
Rather, the *baraita* recognizes the fact that a husband is free (at least
formally) to order his affairs, and can structure his physical and emotional resources so as to accommodate both marital and filial responsibilities. But ability is identical with responsibility, and so it is fair to
say that this *baraita* requires the son to order his affairs with his parents' welfare in mind. The significance of this source is dual: it indicates that when a daughter becomes a wife, the focus of her responsibility shifts (this is both a descriptive and normative statement) from
parents to spouse[85] but a son who becomes a husband retains something of his prior responsibilities toward his parents even as he adds
new, and doubtless overriding, ones towards his wife.[86] (The contrast
with Genesis 2:24 is marked—there, it is the *husband* who "leaves" his
parents!)

The Honor of In-laws

The rabbis expect, as does the Bible, that both husband and wife honor their respective in-laws, and their dishonor is considered a gross evil. The day of God's redemption of His people is preceded, in the prophecy of Micah, by an evil time when "the son dishonors the father, the daughter rises up against the mother, the daughter-in-law against her mother-in-law"(7:6), and this verse is repeated by R. Eliezer in describing the signs heralding the coming of Messiah.[87] The bulk of the rabbinic discussions discloses, however, that this respect, over and above the respect owed to age *per se,* is more an expression of honor for one's spouse, whose parents are one's mother- and father-in-law, than the reflection of a new "filial" bond linking the extended family.[88] Functionally, though, the ethos of filial piety does include this extended parental pair.

The laws of bereavement and mourning (*avelut*) offer a useful example. (These structures must be explored quite sensitively, as we shall see, and with due regard for their specific perspective and assumptions, or they will mislead and confuse; nonetheless, this casual reference is instructive.) The talmudic discussion concludes that both husband and wife must personally mourn the death of the parents of the other.[89] This does not derive, however, from a filial relationship (indeed, *avelut* recognizes only biological filiation) but rather from participation in the sorrow of one's mate. Similarly, "A man rends his garments at the death of his father-in-law or mother-in-law, in respect for his wife."[90]

This analysis is at least partially corroborated by the mishnaic provision that a man may divorce his wife and deprive her of the divorce settlement if "she curses his parents to his face."[91] Such behavior, called a transgression of "Jewish practice," clearly violates the respect owed a husband—the detail, "to his face," is most revealing—and is, therefore, reason for divorce in its most punitive form. Indeed, the role of the son or daughter is so central to this dynamic, that *Seder Eliyyahu Rabbah* can declare that, "if a man marries a woman who does not herself honor his parents in their old age, it is as though he were an adulterer all his life."[92] As the characteristic vehemence of *Seder Eliyyahu* reveals, the normative analysis reflects the personal and psychological dynamic operating in the marriage, where the behavior of the son- or daughter-in-law is often merely an explicit demonstration of the attitudes implicit in the behavior of the son or daughter.

A number of aggadic passages do develop the concept of the autonomous honor of in-laws. The *Mekhilta* comments on Moses' bowing before his father-in-law Jethro (Exodus 18:7), "Hence they said, 'A man should always honor his father-in-law.' "[93] Similarly, David's addressing King Saul as "My father" occasioned the observation that "A man should honor his father-in-law as he does his father."[94] But these statements, while doubtless reflecting a sentiment that has endured in the Jewish ethos, were often argued at their source[95] (the Targum clearly sees in the Davidic expression, rendered, "My master," normal fealty to the king), and their integration into the conceptual framework of filial piety proved a difficult problem. Thus, the ruling of both *Tur* and *Shulhan Arukh*—if we may skip a millennium—that "a man is obliged to honor his father-in-law," is understood by most commentators to derive its warrant, not from the structures of filial piety, but from those of the marital relationship. There is no doubt, though, that the Jewish experience often took both aggadah and *Shulhan Arukh* at their word, expecting and achieving filial respect and service for in-laws. An ingenious solution to the problem was worked out by the author of *Sefer Haredim:* Inasmuch as husband and wife are considered (for certain legal purposes) "one body," a woman's father is to be considered her husband's father too! Certainly, this solution is more revealing as ethos than as legal concept.[96]

Wives and Mothers-in-Law

The Jewish ethos requires the honoring of mother- and father-in-law. But both law and lore recognize that the living situation often does not imitate the ideal projection, as is evident from the mishnaic citation given earlier, and that of *Seder Eliyyahu.* Both these sources focus on the hostility that exists between the daughter-in-law and the parents of her husband. A late midrash asserts with all-inclusive certainty, "If a lamb can live with a leopard, so can a bride live with her mother-in-law."[97] The clearest acknowledgment of the extent and depth of this hostility is the mishnaic ruling that since both mother- and sister-in-law are apt to perjure themselves in attempting to injure their daughter- and sister-in-law, their testimony is therefore to be disqualified in certain cases;[98] the bulk of both tannaitic and amoraic opinion is that a daughter-in-law is similarly disqualified from testifying in cases involving her mother-in-law.[99] It is significant, though, that the Talmud understands the hatred of the wife to be a response to that of her mother-in-law. The hatred of the mother-in-law, in contrast, is seen to derive from the "predatory" presence of her son's wife,[100] and while the Talmud itself interprets this as based on economic considerations ("she is eating us out of my hard-earned house and home"), may we not recall the primal tension implicit in "Hence a man leaves his father and his mother, and cleaves to his wife, . . ." and its midrashic articulation: "Until a man marries, he directs his love toward his parents; after he marries, he directs it toward his wife"?

A new problem comes to the fore in the medieval period. Talmudic law, which banned even the innocent but private closeting of mothers- and sons-in-law, fathers- and daughters-in-law, doubtless placed theoretic obstacles in the way of the common householding of both families.[101] But the responsa literature of gaonic and later medieval times reveals—and this may very well be true for talmudic times as well (cf. notes 125–127)—that the extended family of husband, wife, and in-laws often shared a common domicile. Indeed, Louis Epstein notes that mediéval marriage settlements often required the wife to care for her mother-in-law, or at least "to tolerate her in her house."[102] These arrangements reflect the economic and social realities of the time, as well as filial responsibilities. And, while the families concerned experienced both the difficulties and rewards of such arrangements in the privacy of the home, halakhists were consulted when problems became acute, and conflicts could no longer be resolved by patience and good will.

A common problem concerned the wife who claimed that she was persecuted by her mother- and sisters-in-law, and who refused to continue living under one roof with them. These difficulties may have been stimulated by child-marriages, which encouraged continued parental intimacy and control of a young couple.[103] What was the husband to do?

A number of answers were given to this question. Some terse gaonic responsa declare that the husband must either move his wife to another domicile, or grant her a divorce and pay the marriage settlement (*ketubah*).[104] The single axiological statement used is the talmudic "she [the wife] is given in marriage for a good life, and not for a life of pain";[105] clearly the husband's prime responsibility is toward his wife. Regretfully, the responsa in question are most brief and do not adequately describe the situation or the solution. We wonder, for example, whether the mother-in-law challenged her daughter-in-law's account, but was simply not believed in the face of the younger woman's version? Or did the husband testify to the accuracy of his wife's tale? Furthermore, we note that the mother is allowed to remain in the house, and the daughter-in-law is moved out: Is this a reflection of filial piety? And what if the husband cannot afford to maintain two residences—does he then evict his mother? Or do our responsa reflect a sit-

uation where the house is owned by the mother (perhaps making the
conflict easier to picture), giving the son no choice but to provide
another residence for his wife? These questions are all unanswered;
nonetheless, the basic thrust of these responsa is clear: it is the wife
who is to be protected.

A different response is reported by R. Alfas (11th century), who declared that the normal procedure in these cases was to station a female
investigator-conciliator in the home to ascertain where the root of the
trouble lay, the court then making its recommendations on the basis of
her report.[106] Both daughter-in-law and mother-in-law are to be observed, "and if it is clear that harm is being done, let the person causing
it be pushed away." It is quite clear here that the wife cannot be the
cause of friction and at the same time demand that her husband abandon his mother. While we are ignorant, again, of the concrete situation
being discussed, it is safe to say that filial responsibility is here no less
significant than domestic happiness or, more accurately, domestic happiness is not to be purchased unethically. If, however, the wife is in fact
being persecuted by her mother-in-law, she must be protected. No hierarchy of loyalties is presumed; the duty of the husband and son is decided by reference to the facts as reported by a disinterested third party.
The claims of mother and wife are evenly balanced.

A responsum written by R. Joseph ibn Megas, a student of R. Alfas,
represents a new departure as well as a broader focus.[107] The questioner told how Reuben owned a house in partnership with his parents and
wished to make his home in that house. His bride objected, however,
saying that she feared her husband's father and mother would vex and
distress her; rather, she urged, let her husband make their home in *her*
parents' house. . . . R. Joseph was firm in his reply: The woman must
follow her husband's desire. He had, after all, a financial stake in the
house he owned together with his parents, and moreover, his bride had
never actually experienced any discomfort from her new in-laws, but
was, at the most, apprehensive. She ought to try the arrangement de-
vised by her husband, and if her in-laws did in fact harass her, there
would be adequate opportunity to move out.

The responsum continues, however, to note that a different reply
would be in order if the husband had no financial commitment to the
arrangement described. If that were the case, the husband ought to respect his wife's apprehensiveness, and not attempt to have her share a
home—even on a trial basis—with his parents: "The choice is
hers. . . ." R. Joseph has articulated a posture that clearly views the
husband's prime responsibility as being toward his wife, and goes so
far as to demand that the wife's anticipation of psychological distress

(of apparently malicious origin, to be sure) be honored as sufficient reason for not living near his parents. It is of course clear, as it was for all the responsa already cited, that no financial consideration can justify a husband's compelling his wife to live with his parents if they in fact persecute her.

The rulings of Maimonides reflect these responsa, but are based primarily on principles of civil law rather than on considerations of domestic tranquility. In essence, he rules[108] that both husband and wife can exclude from their home the parents of either.

> If a man says to his wife, "I don't want your father or mother, brothers or sisters, coming to my home," he is listened to, and she must go to them . . . they may not come to her, unless something untoward, such as sickness[108a] or childbirth, occur. For we do not force a man to admit others to his property. Similarly, if she says, "I don't want your mother or sisters coming in to me, and I do not wish to live in one court with them because they harm me and pain me," she is listened to. For we do not force someone to allow others to live with him on his property.

Maimonides increases the scope of the power enjoyed by husband and wife. No provision is made for the gaonic "disinterested observers," or for any court involvement for that matter.[108b] Both husband and wife are free to allow their likes and dislikes free sway, and to exclude whom they would.[109] (Of course, Maimonides is here the legist, not the moralist or the counsellor.) A distinction is made, nevertheless, between husband and wife: The husband can exclude his in-laws for no reason at all, while the wife must claim—and her claim is accepted— that her in-laws cause her harm before they are excluded from the home.[110]

The bulk of the Maimonidean passage describes the legal power of a spouse in preventing access of his or her in-laws to the home, and does not concern itself with the possible exclusion of parents who already live in the house, though both "I will not live with them in one court" and the general halakhic underpinning for the ruling suggest that this latter situation is included as well. R. Abraham b. David (Rabad), however, argues that the two situations warrant different responses; in his gloss to the Maimonidean ruling he writes:

> When does this apply? When they "came into her domain"; but if she "came into their domain" we do not move them from their place for her sake, even though the house is his [the husband's] and

they have no rights in it, since he wishes them to stay. But we do ask them to so arrange matters that their dwelling in the house causes the wife no distress.

The schematization that emerges from this note is quite complex. It is clear, first, that distinctions are drawn only in regard to the wife's ability to exclude her husband's parents from the home; his ability to restrict her parents' access is total and uncompromised, based as it is on his property rights. But even his property rights—and hence his ability to engage in this particular expression of filial responsibility—are balanced, in part, by the personal rights of his wife. She will be sustained in her objections if he wishes to open their home to his parents. On the other hand, if it is the wife who is the newcomer to the household, the husband may continue to house his parents in his home despite her objections. The opposed claims of the personal rights of the wife and the property rights of the husband are thus weighted to preserve the status quo.

Though Rabad claims merely to have interpreted Maimonides, it would seem that the two do in fact differ over the extent of the wife's ability to declare her home off-limits to her in-laws. While Maimonides discriminates between the rights of husband and wife by ruling that the wife must produce a substantive objection to the presence of her in-laws, he does allow the wife the unrestricted exercise of her personal rights. Rabad, on the other hand, limits the wife by denying her the right to object to her husband's continued domiciling of his parents in the home after his marriage. Considering the final open-minded comment of Rabad, however, it is quite possible that his statement should not be read as a last word on the matter but as an interim suggestion; to put this in another way, perhaps the court and its law can do no more, can go no further in imposing a legal solution to the problem, which must thence be tackled in other ways—by love, or compromise, or acquiescence.[111]

Subsequent discussion moves along the path plotted by the gaonic responsa and the rulings of Maimonides and Rabad. Filial piety, by and large, does not enter into consideration as a normative category, although the husband's personal exercise of his property rights could doubtless be motivated by this concern. The one striking exception to this observation is the statement of Rashba—cited from a manuscript responsum by R. Jacob Castro (Egypt, d. 1610) but not found in our printed editions of the responsa of Rashba—that ". . . a woman must live with her father-in-law and mother-in-law, for her husband is obliged to honor and fear them, and may not depart from them."[112]

Some respondents did take this citation into account[113] but they remained, on the whole, in the minority.[114] Both points insisted upon here—the absolute duty of the son to dwell with his parents, and the requirement that the wife submit to this arrangement—are rejected, in greater or lesser degree, by the corpus of the Halakha. Indeed, it is R. Solomon ibn Aderet himself who gave us a responsum vigorously arguing the right of the wife to demand that her husband leave his parents' home:

> You have asked: "If a woman does not wish to continue to live together with her mother-in-law because she pains her and causes quarrels between herself and her husband, may she force her husband (to move)?"
>
> (Response) A wife can certainly tell her husband, "I refuse to live with people who pain me," for if her husband may not pain her, she certainly need not live among others who pain her and occasion quarrels between herself and her husband.[115]

Though Rashba concludes in this responsum that the husband need not move to another neighborhood but need only move to another house, it is clear that this opinion places him firmly in the Maimonidean camp, thus making the opinion cited in his name by R. Jacob Castro quite problematic. R. Joseph Karo, too, reproduces the Maimonidean ruling verbatim in his *Shulhan Arukh*. R. Moses Isserles appends, however, a gloss combining the views of both *Maggid Mishneh* (see note 109) and R. Alfas: "This is only when it appears to the court that there is substance to her claim that they harm her and are the cause of contention between herself and her husband; otherwise, she is not listened to . . . and it is the custom to place a reliable man or woman in the house, until the source of contention is clarified."[116]

Halakhic sources and decisions, valuable as they are both axiologically and historically, can of necessity offer only a fragmentary view of the whole. We are dealing, after all, with the stuff of love and hate, responsibility and its evasion, in a human structure that is often not given to quantitative objectification or even normative ruling. Moreover, even those rulings and halakhic discussions that do exist must be seen against the backdrop of the ethical and personal norms by which a society is constituted. The tradition of life itself is doubtless more potent that its literary reflection, and even that literary reflection is to be sought equally in the words of moralists and sermonizers, genres much less worked by scholars than the talmudic and halakhic sources. The aforementioned genres present their own characteristic difficulties, too: The texture and timbre of hortatory material differ from those of legal material; furthermore, inasmuch as halakhic decisions are subject to the close scrutiny and evaluation of succeeding thinkers, who must either accept or reject given decisions and postures, it is easier to discover in that genre principles of representative continuity and to discriminate between fervent piety and common standards. But if the moralists are liberated from the constraints of reality in a way that halakhists are not, they also grapple with a fuller cross-section of reality, for they are legitimately concerned with all the human aspects of a particular situation and structure, not only with those problems that can be solved by recourse to the halakhic model or are presented to the halakhist for his solution.

Sefer Hassidim (the greater part of which dates from the 12th century in Germany) both contributed richly to the formation of a Jewish ethos and reflected one already in existence, and we have on more than one occasion cited passages from that work. In the following paragraphs we see an attempt to balance the competing claims of filial piety and marital fulfillment:

> Parents who command their son not to marry so that he might serve them make an inadmissible request; let him marry and live near them. But if he cannot find a wife in the town in which his parents live, and his parents are aged and need him to support them, let him not leave the town. And if he can earn only enough to support his parents, and would be forced—should he marry—to end this support, let him obey his parents. But if the son is wealthy and can have someone else serve his parents, he may then go to another town to take a wife.[117]

The problems confronted in this citation are, indeed, fit for halakhic analysis. But *Sefer Hassidim* is an apodictic, not an analytic work; it announces rather than argues its code. The basic thrust of its opinion and value is clear: while parents are expected to sacrifice a measure of the filial service owed them by their son so that he may marry, the son cannot marry if he would thereby be forced to end totally the service his parents need. Obviously, most situations lie somewhere in the middle between absolute inability to care for parents and virtual continuity of the previous pattern. But the extremes are certainly not uncommon, and here *Sefer Hassidim* clearly gives priority to parental needs (when coupled with a parental command), requiring the son to forego marriage so as to ensure their satisfaction. This is a potent expression of an attitude (found elsewhere in *Sefer Hassidim*) that significantly enlarges the range of filial responsibility.

Another paragraph of pietistic advice counsels the son to enter into an unhappy marriage if he can thus please his parents. The father and mother are vigorously condemned for their brutality, but the exemplary son will nonetheless fulfill their desires:

> If the father commands his son to marry . . . a woman he does not want, and the son fears that if he marries her he will hate her, or he fears that he might sin with other women, it is best that he not marry her. But if he can withstand this temptation, though he will hate her, he does a great thing for his father and mother, but his parents sin in forcing him to marry a woman he does not love. And if the father knows that his son is very depressed, and that he will not fail to do whatever he is commanded by his father, the father sins by forcing him into the act.[118]

If, however, it is not merely the subjective feelings of the son that are injured, but it is clear that his parents want him to marry a woman "of wicked family," the son ought to refuse even if by doing so he angers his parents, for "they are treating him improperly." Union with wickedness cannot be countenanced, for the parents, too, are obliged to strive for good; but an unhappy marriage is of less moment. In all fairness, we must note the conflicting judgment of our author: on the one hand, "it is best" that he not marry the woman whom he will hate (even if he will not be unfaithful to her); on the other hand, "he does a great thing" if he does marry her!

A slightly different attitude is taken toward problems that arise to threaten an already existing marriage:

> If one's parents constantly argue with one's wife and if he would tell his wife to be silent she would become quarrelsome with him and refuse intercourse with him, let him keep silent himself. "There is a time to speak," when his words are hearkened to, and "a time to keep silent," when they are not. . . . Don't place yourself between two hot tempers.[119]

The ideal is the silent submission of both son and daughter-in-law to parental pique; the son, moreover, ought ideally to be able to control his wife's response. When this is impossible, or would lead to a breakdown of *shalom bayyit* (domestic peace) or perhaps worse (*Sefer Hassidim* specifies only refusal to continue sexual intercourse), the husband is advised to retire. Filial piety can prevent a marriage, in short,

but ought not to wreck one. Despite this concession to domestic survival, it can be said, as we pointed out at the beginning of this chapter, that
the medieval moralist has a more rigorous vision of filial piety than that
projected by some earlier sources, and tends to enlarge its scope in a
world of values at cross purposes.

Succeeding generations of moralists turned to these perennial dilemmas. Again, we find that the responsibility of the son in assuring the
honor of his parents is stressed, even at the price of marital tension.
Thus, we read in *Peleh Yo'etz* of R. Eliezer Pappo (an early 19th-centu-
ry moralist living in Bulgaria):

> There are sons who are on very good terms with their fathers and
> mothers until they marry; but when they marry, the bride rises
> against her mother-in-law [cf. Micah 7:6] and incites her husband
> to quarrel (with his parents). The God-fearing man . . . should
> scold his wife and silence her reprovingly, so as to soothe his par-
> ents' minds. And afterwards, when they are alone, he should pacify
> her, and he should rebuke her and show her the right way. . . .
> Therefore a man should "armor himself for combat" with his wife
> and seek to maintain the honor of his father and mother. But the
> "collar of responsibility" is also tied around the necks of the par-
> ents, that they not cause strife and hatred between a man and his
> wife. . . . [120]

Although his opening shot is fired at brides who tear husbands from
their parents and promote such alienation for their own purposes, R.
Eliezer Pappo's conclusion indicates he knew well that the reverse was
often true, as well. (In any event, the contrast with the talmudic
assumption that the mother-in-law and not the daughter-in-law is the
source of contention is most revealing.) The pendulum-like quality of
the prose betrays the complexity of both the situation described and the
feelings of the author himself. But what is of overriding significance is
his conclusion, and that establishes—in consonance with much general rabbinic theory (see Chapter V)—that whatever the parental share in
the creation of the painful situation, the son must assure their honor
and reverence.

A number of different sources have touched upon the expectation
that a son remain physically near his parents. While this expectation
may be most severely challenged by marriage, its relevance to our exploration is not restricted to this one situation, and it merits an inde-

pendent survey.

IV.
The Responsibility of Proximity

The issue of continued filial proximity to parents has been with us from Genesis 2:24 ("Hence a man leaves his father and his mother. . . .") on; we have heard it, too, in many of the medieval writings. Actually, though, the rabbinic sources do not discuss the matter as an "issue" at all, leaving it—at the most—a corollary of other, more basic responsibilities and attitudes. Filial proximity is viewed, on the whole, in functional rather than sentimental terms.

The apocryphal Jewish sources explicitly teach the son to remain ever at his parents' side. Ben-Sira advises: "My son, be strong in the honor of your father, and do not leave him all the days of your life."[121] And in the "longer version" of *Tobit*, the old Tobit commands his son to remain with his mother "all the days of her life."[122] These straightforward dicta appear in the context of concrete parental need: Ben-Sira goes on to speak of the service and honor to be rendered the aging and senile parent. While Torbit's wife is as old as her spouse, he himself is contemplating his own death and commands his son not only to remain with his mother for the rest of her life, but to bury her together with her husband. This is not to say that the son is bidden to remain only with his aged parent, rather that the controlling factor in filial proximity was the consciousness of the real parental needs that the son could and should meet.

The rabbinic sources do not to my knowledge contain such explicit instructions. One version of the testament of R. Judah the Prince to his sons includes the charge that they "be careful concerning the honor of [their] mother,"[123] but nothing as detailed as Tobit's behest of Tobias is found. The fullest source that deals with reverence and honor—the *baraita*—speaks, as we have seen, of the personal service owed the parent by his son.[124] It is probable that filial proximity is considered both so normal and necessary that explicit mention of it would be superfluous: service, after all, presupposes presence. (From a purely historical point of view, mobility in the ancient world was minimal; at the same time, both *Ben-Sira* and Tobit indicate by their mention of the problem that the continued presence of the son could not be assumed: in a world of little mobility, even separation by a relatively small distance looms large.) But the fact remains that the *baraita* itself is silent on this point. And if we do extrapolate the assumption of filial proximity, it is once again in the service of parental need, a need that must be met by the personal involvement of the son.

We have seen earlier that the son was expected to "leave his father and his mother" (Genesis 2:24) and that this verse was translated by Onkelos to include a shift in physical domicile. In mishnaic times, though, many married sons doubtless remained quite near the parental hearth, a tendency explicable on economic as well as social grounds. Parents would sometimes provide a "a bridal house for their son" in the immediate vicinity of their own home; if we may judge by its name, this was a temporary dwelling.[125] On the other hand, the rabbis disapproved of the new couple's living with the bride's parents,[126] though it was an old Judeaen custom for the son-in-law to "live-in" at the bride's home for the period separating the betrothal (kiddushin) and the completion of the marrige (nissu'im), and economic and personal considerations doubtless led to many similar situations throughout the country.[127]

There was, of course, one pursuit that did compel its devotee to travel far from the parental home for great lengths of time: the study of Torah. The student of Torah was encouraged by the rabbis to spend years at the academy (yeshiva), far from mother and father; as the rabbis won the loyalty of greater numbers of Jews, more and more young men doubtless left their homes to study at the central academies. Rav himself declared,

> The study of Torah is greater than filial piety. For Jacob was not punished for all the years (of study) in the academy of Ever. . . .[128]

Rav's illustration is most revealing: the student of Torah must, of necessity, go to the "place of Torah," he must leave parents and find his master. It is significant that the ethos of Jewish filial piety was in large part constructed by men who themselves had once chosen between a commitment to the study of Torah and the nearness of the parental home.

The richest midrashic reflection on the problem of filial proximity and service concerns God's command to Abraham to leave his father's house and go to the land that God would show him:

> Now the Lord said to Abram: "Get thee out of thy country, and from thy kindred, and from thy father's house, unto the land that I will show thee" (Genesis 12:1).
>
> What is written in Scripture just prior to this? "And Terah died in Haran" (Genesis 11:32). R. Isaac said, "Terah actually lived sixty-five years more after Abraham left! But, firstly, we infer that the wicked are called dead even while they are alive; for Abraham was

apprehensive, saying, 'When I leave, men will profane the name of God because of me, as they will say, "He left his aged father and went off." So God said to Abraham, "I release you from the obligations of honoring your father and your mother, but I will release no other from this obligation; furthermore, I will inscribe his death [in the Bible] before I inscribe your departure.' "[129]

The command to leave "thy father's house" was, the Midrash claims, a most literal one: Terah, Abram's father, was alive to bid his son a final farewell. How could Abram leave his "aged father"? Was this a beginning for a life of faithfulness to God? Readers in ancient times could be expected to show immediate distress at such behavior, just as the rabbis did themselves. The Book of Jubilees, for example, claimed that Abraham left with his father's consent and blessing.[130] Indeed, we are struck by Abraham's own equanimity, his preoccupation with what "men" will say; but Abraham speaks out of the experience of the divine charge—nor does Abraham object to the command to slay Isaac years later. The midrashic solution (indeed, our text telescopes two literary and conceptual units, and contains *two* solutions)[131] suggests that the wicked parent has forfeited his son's fealty and, fundamentally, that God uniquely and teleologically suspends His command of filial piety in this case (note the shift from the *ethical* formulation of Abram's imagined taunters and God's citation of the scriptural imperative: "Get thee out . . . from thy father's house").[132] We may note that this is typological rather than unique: the young prophet leaves the home of his parents for the company of Elijah, the student of a sage chooses academy over home and prefers the service of his master to that of his parent,[133] and the proselyte (Maimondes claimed), "who is a newly born babe," is in a most radical way loosed from the imperative, if not the ethic, of filial piety, much as was Abraham—father of proselytes.[134] All this reflects, of course, an evaluation of the religious-moral priorities present in the situation. But it is clear from this midrashic source that, in general, the son should not leave his father and will be condemned by both man—indeed, the Midrash must defend Abraham—and God for so doing. Yet the taunt anticipated by Abraham is certainly revealing: "He left his *aged* father. . . ." Again, the parental need provides the focus for the filial responsibility.

A second midrash explains a hidden but potent factor in the life of Jacob:

Joseph left his father Jacob for twenty-two years, just as Jacob left his father, Isaac, for twenty-two years.[135]

The Midrash here points out one of the many ironic balances in the life of Jacob. Just as he left his parents for twenty-two years—during which time he lived with Laban—so was he deprived of his son for twenty-two years—those years when Joseph, mourned by his father, was actually alive in Egypt—*middah k'negged middah* [measure for measure]. Yet, while the talmudic text cited above speaks in general terms of "leaving" one's parents, parallel sources are more specific; some versions of *Seder 'Olam*, for instance, tell of the "twenty-two years in which Jacob did not serve his father,"[136] focussing once again on concrete filial service.

Yet it will not do to speak of concrete service as "functional" and to dismiss all else as "sentimental." Loneliness *per se* is painful, and the pleasure of children's presence is very real. These too are "needs," or better—opportunities for honor; and the honoring child, we shall see (Chapter IV), will not want to be the cause of parental pain and sadness. The sixteenth-century R. Solomon Luria assumed, therefore, that—all things being equal—a son ought not leave a father when his departure "would be bitter as death."[136a]

Thus the vision of father and son dwelling together meant something deeper, too. Explaining his desire to possess a sanctuary amidst His people, God declares (according to the Midrash):

> You are my sons, and I am your father. . . . It is an honor for sons to dwell with their father, and it is an honor for the father to dwell with his sons. . . . Make, therefore, a house for the father in which he can dwell with his sons. . . .[137]

Clearly, filial piety had developed here beyond its minimal criteria; continuing the metaphor, the medievals see in this view of the Sanctuary an adumbration of a time when "the hearts of fathers will be turned to the children, and the hearts of the children to their fathers."

So much for both normative and midrashic material. The talmudic literature also contains a small number of relevant incidents. The first is actually less an incident than a parable:

> [R. Kahana, an emigre to Palestine from Babylon, received a hostile reception from the Palestinian students and used the following parable before R. Yohanan:] "If a man's mother insults him, and his father's wife honors him, to which should he go?" "Let him go where he is honored." R. Kahana left Palestine. . . .[138]

A second incident is better known, serving as it did to initiate medieval discussion on filial responsibilities to the mentally disturbed parent:

> R. Assi had an aged mother. Said she to him, "I want ornaments." So he made them for her.
> "I want a husband as handsome as you."
> Thereupon he left her and went to Palestine. On hearing that she was following him, he went to R. Yohanan and asked him, "May I leave the land?" "It is forbidden," he replied. "But what if it is to meet my mother?" "I do not know." Shortly, he came before him again. "Assi," he said, "you have determined to go; may the Omnipresent bring you back in peace." Then he went before R. Eleazar and said to him, "Perhaps, God forbid, he was angry?" "What then did he say to you?" he asked. "May God bring you back in peace," was the answer. "Had he been angry, he would not have blessed you." In the meantime he learned that her coffin was coming. "Had I known," he exclaimed, "I would not have gone out of the land."[139]

Though both incidents touch on the question of filial presence, they are quite peripheral to our problem; in both cases, filial absence is excused by exceptional circumstances. We are interested, however, in the unexceptional situation. As to that, we find little direct discussion.

The nonsystematic nature of the talmudic enterprise allowed certain dimensions of experience to remain untouched by explicit talmudic mention, and our immediate topic is one of these. In our case, this may be due to the nature of the literary sources available for elaboration, the belief that other sources—such as the imperative of filial service—adequately presented the proper posture, or the tacit acknowledgment that not all ethical and personal paths can be adequately mapped in a work both didactic and universal. Surely it is noteworthy that the medieval codes—Maimonides, *Tur, Shulhan Arukh*—all follow the talmudic program closely, not one inserting any reference to an expectation that the son remain at the parental hearth. Upon reflection, though, it is quite clear that the *baraita* of filial service (and the medieval codes, too) implies filial presence, which is thus not only an aspect of the culture of talmudic times and lands, but a component of its imperative as well. At the same time, filial presence must be integrated into the competitive hierarchy of values and commitments of which we spoke earlier.

As we have seen, the major medieval codes do not provide any data beyond that found in talmudic sources. That parents and children did live together is a patently obvious fact whose reality resounds in the literature. Occasionally, other discussions of filial piety are broadened by this realization; thus R. Sa'adiah Gaon writes:

> . . . the reward for filial piety is "length of days" . . . because it is destined to occur that parents will sometimes live for a long time with their sons, and become a heavy burden upon the sons, who weary of this "honor." Therefore, the reward specified for this *mitzvah* is "so that your days be long"; in other words, you must honor your parents *and live with them,* and if you occasionally regret their longevity, know that you regret your own life."[140] (My italics.)

But even here the normative component is blended with the circumstantial. The citations from *Menorat ha-Ma'or* (see Chapter II) similarly reflect a situation where parents and son live together. So, too, in a 20th-century author:

> . . . when the father is aged, and the son takes him to his house and table, (the son remains) seated at his normal place at the head of the table as previously, but . . . the father nonetheless is to perform the (ritual) washing of hands first, and to receive the first portion of food, as well as all other designations of honor at the table. This is our practice, and there should be no deviation from it.[141]

Some medieval sources do speak in normative terms on this matter: we have seen Rashba cited to the effect that the son (and his wife) are always to remain with his parents.[142] *Sefer Hassidim* similarly required that the son return to the vicinity of his parents with his bride, so as to minister to their needs.[143] But the nonsentimental quality of this filial proximity is startlingly illustrated by the allowance—despite the normally personal character of this service—that the "wealthy" son may leave his parents to marry as long as he arranges for the satisfaction of their needs.

Curiously, it is *Sefer Hassidim* that takes fullest cognizance of the problem of filial incompatibility with parents:

> It is best that a father and a son separate if they quarrel with each other, for much pain is caused; and I do not mean only the pain of the father or teacher, but even the pain of the son.[144]

A radical shift indeed from the patterns of thought predominating in discussions of filial responsibility. First, the category of pain and distress within the relationship is itself legitimatized, and second, the son is allowed psychological rights that override, in practice, the responsibilities of filial piety. Significantly (though perhaps typically, for our author), *Sefer Hassidim* does not attempt to defend his advice ("it is best") in standard halakhic categories.

Discussions of such conflict are noticeably absent in the responsa literature; it is, again, curious that we found the most explicit note of such situations taken in a moralistic tome. Indeed, despite the certain prevalence of such situations, and the suggestive precedent set by R. Me'ir of Rothenberg when he rejected all personal contact with his father (behavior explained on purely normative grounds by his major disciple, R. Asher: see Chapter VI), it is to a later moralist that we must turn for further discussion of this subject.

R. Eliezer Pappo wrote:

> And inasmuch as the Sages have said that a man should not dwell near his master if he cannot accept his authority, we may infer that if a man cannot honor his parents as they should be honored, then . . . it is best that he no longer share his father's board, provided his father agrees to this. It is also best that a man—if he can— send his children from his table, lest he be guilty of placing a stumbling block before them . . . and thus there shall be peace in your home.[145]

R. Eliezer Pappo clearly knows it is best that the son leave his parents, but he does not feel himself as free as *Sefer Hassidim* directly to so advise his reader. (So, too, he relies on an argument from analogy to *Berakhot* 8a rather than on the appeal to filial pain recognized by *Sefer Hassidim*.) The son, on the contrary, is always bound by the parental will, but that will should be supple and constructive, as, indeed, the talmudic precedent to which our author refers urges ("lest he be guilty of placing a stumbling block before them"; see Chapter V). The 19th-century moralist, then, is fully in touch with the dynamic of filial duty and parental responsibility and in a sense he is enmeshed in it. Ironically, this very matrix produces the rare assertion that the father ought to recognize that the welfare of his son is better served by the separation of parent and child than by their continued endurance of each other, and that the parent ought to encourage such separation.

V.

The Sick Parent

Parental incompetence or senility does not pose a profound conceptual problem to the rabbinic ethic. The needs of the sick parent are usually greater than those of the healthy one, and so the filial responsibility and response should each correspondingly grow; obviously, the Jewish ethic will not sanction the abandonment of a parent in such straits. But these conditions do raise disturbing behavioral problems even, or perhaps especially, in the context of an ethic of filial responsibility. What, for example, is "abandonment" in these circumstances? And how is the filial responsibility best expressed? Should the filial response change if the child—because of the nature of the situation—no longer achieves much through the normal patterns of filial piety? And is there a legitimate limit to filial endurance and patience? It is true, no doubt, that an increased lifespan and the atomization of the family have, in our day, expanded the dimensions of the problem; yet, as a moment of reflection teaches, it is a universally human one. We recognize an all-too-familiar urge in the legendary treatment of parents in Biblical Luz: "What would they do with their elderly? When a man became fed up with his mother or father, the parent would be taken to another city, where he immediately died." The inhabitants thus guaranteed that "the Angel of Death never entered the city."[145a]

Treatment of this problem in pre-Maimonidean times is generally restricted to brief apodictic *dicta*, or the edificatory narration of specific instances. The pre-talmudic *Ben-Sira*—a work in which we have often found the first literary evidence of certain specific concerns in the area of filial piety—exhorts its readers: "My son, be strong in the honor of your father, and do not leave him all the days of your life. And even if he loses sense, let him do all that he wishes[146] and do not shame him all the days of his life."[147] The post-talmudic *Seder Eliyyahu* teaches much the same thing: "Even if your father's spittle is running down his beard—obey him promptly."[148] Explicit talmudic discussion—even of an anecdotal nature—is rare, though. We can press into service Dama ben Netinah's equanimity when publicly humiliated by his mother, an equanimity displayed, according to one midrashic narrator, in the face of a senile parent.[149] (Indeed, one wonders whether more normal circumstances would have, or should have, elicited this response. The tosafists, whose attitude toward the "wicked parent" we shall explore in Chapter V, would probably have thought not.) [150] Furthermore, some modern scholars understand the declaration of R. Eliezer, that filial reverence goes so far as to allow one's father to throw one's wallet into the sea, as describing a disturbed parent.[151] One cannot agree immediately here, though; we remember R. Hunna, who deliberately tested the temper of his son by tearing his clothes to his face.[152] Finally, the behavior of R. Ishmael's mother, who insisted on washing the feet of her illustrious son and drinking the water thus used, suggests mental disturbance, though this too is far from certain.[153]

All these dicta and incidents converge on one central point: filial reverence is to accompany a parent throughout his life and its fluctuations. Old age and sickness are, indeed, spurs to devotion. Yet the post-talmudic authorities do recognize the fact that senility and mental incompetence can render the conventional response meaningless or impossible; they grapple with the conflicts born of the commitment to reverence and service, on the one hand, and the inadequacy of these structures in the situations described, on the other.

There is little talmudic material at our disposal here. The citations above simply and unequivocally demand personal devotion. One bit of talmudic biography was marshalled, however, by the medievals who opened the question for fuller discussion: the story of R. Assi and his mother (cited above, section IV, n. 139).

R. Assi, alarmed by the indecency of his mother's request, leaves his aged (and widowed or divorced) parent in Babylon and makes his way to Palestine. One suspects that the mother was not impelled by wicked lust but was rather the victim of advanced years;[154] nonetheless, R. Assi, convinced that he could not respond constructively to her situation, left. Is there remorse in his subsequent eagerness to take to the road to greet her as she pursued him?[155] Whether or not this be the case, the departure of R. Assi from Babylon has been read as a legitimate response to the situation and was taken, especially by Maimonides, as reflecting a normative judgment.

Thus it was Maimonides who initiated the separate categorization of the mentally incompetent parent. He wrote:

> If one's father or mother should become mentally disordered, he should try to treat them as their mental state demands, until they are pitied by God. But if he finds he cannot endure the situation because of their extreme madness, let him leave and go away, deputing others to care for them properly.[156]

To which Rabad responds: "This is an incorrect teaching. If he leaves, whom will he depute to supervise the well-being of his parents?"

Most analysts of these passages focus on the view of Rabad, questioning its propriety in the light of R. Assi's presumably normative behavior.[157] For our study, though, concerned as it is with the rabbinic ethic as it in fact crystallized, the opinion of Maimonides deserves scrutiny. In bridging the gap between the talmudic incident, on the one hand, and the codified ruling, on the other, Maimonides brings to bear a number of methodological and ethical tools. First—assuming that our story is Maimonides' precedent—the incident is assumed to reflect a legitimate and normative option. Maimonides is hardly forced to see the occurrence in this light, inasmuch as other talmudic incidents could compel filial endurance of parental senility. Second, he understands the crucial element in the situation to be, in fact, parental senility and not the moral deterioration of the relationship: the mental-health aspect alone is decisive in the Code. Third, it is made clear that the son is not released from the responsibilities that are his—although he does not care for his parent personally, he sees to it that others do. This detail is lacking in the talmudic story; Maimonides adds it as part of the integrative process by which anecdote becomes authority. (Furthermore, it is realistically consistent with his view that the son should expend "whatever money he is able" for the welfare of his parent.)[158] Fourth, he defines the crucial breaking point: "If he cannot endure . . ."; the focus being on the evaluation by the son himself of his own situation as determinative.[159]

The ethos that crystallizes here by no means reflects an abandoning of either principle or parent. The son is expected, despite the difficulties created by his parent's incompetence, to remain with him and personally attend to him. Yet it recognized that filial endurance has its limits (curiously, this seems to be the only instance where "filial endurance" is a legitimate factor), and when these are reached, the son may leave, relegating the care of his parent to others. Personal concern, though, remains alive, and the son remains responsible for the welfare of his parent. Filial responsibility does not lapse—but its personal intensity is attenuated. It has been suggested, in explanation of Maimonides' ruling, that the parent can be treated more effectively when the unique stimulant and irritant embodied in the son is withdrawn.[160] Clearly, though, the main consideration for Maimonides is the welfare of the son.

The specific objection of Rabad to the Maimonidean schematization can be explained in a variety of ways.[161] The major thrust of the glossator is quite clear, though: the son is not to leave his parent but must shoulder the emotional burdens that are the price of effective, personal, filial care. The "endurance" of the son is not a viable rationale for tampering with the objective norms of *kibbud av*.

The statement of Maimonides was taken, virtually verbatim, into the

Shulhan Arukh.[162] Though some later commentators do side with Rabad,[163] the opinion of Maimonides seems regnant, accepted as it was by R. Joseph Karo.

One obvious implication of the Maimonidean passage is that—barring the kind of mental difficulty that makes filial care exceptionally trying—the son should personally be involved in the care of sick parents. Furthermore, while senility may be a reason for transferring the attention needed by the parent to other eyes, old age and the difficulties it raises are not. Old age is expected to stimulate additional contact with parents rather than their abandonment. Jewish filial ethic focusses on filial fulfillment of parental needs, and these needs normally increase as the parent grows older and as the child can become, parentlike, the sustainer of those who once sustained him. Thus, the normative sources stress the duty of man to remain with his aged parents, who do, in reality, need him, rather than the more sentimental idea that children ought generally to stay with or near their parents, although this has also doubtless been expected by some. In any case, the aged parent is not to face his growing need, psychological as well as economic, alone. Abraham, we have seen, does leave his aged father Terah, but through him the Midrash emphasizes the duty of all others: "I release you from the obligations of honoring your father and mother, but I will release no other. . . ."

Indeed, it is this period of the relationship that is perhaps the most difficult and, at the same time, the most significant; here Judaism stresses that the parent-child relationship is a key relationship in one's entire life and is not exhausted in childhood and in its elementary challenges. For when parents reach advanced years, their children are generally in their vigorous prime, less inclined to be diverted from their own involvements, and unwilling to subordinate themselves and their concerns to their parents. Now the child must not only succeed to the parental role of sustainer, but must infuse this role with emotional as well as economic meaning. Finally, it is just this situation, with all its obvious indicators of parental dependence, that must be filled with a sense of parental worth and even centrality. The Midrash points to these needs:

"(Now these are the names of the sons of Jacob who came into Egypt) with Jacob" (Exodus 1:1):
R. Simeon ben Halafta said, "It is the way of the world that when a man is in his prime, his sons are subordinate to him, but when he

ages he becomes subordinate to them. But here, even in Jacob's old age and after his death, his sons are subordinate to him, as it is written, 'with Jacob.' ''

Another interpretation: Though all his sons were mature men, engaged in raising their own children, they did not attend to their own affairs until they first attended to the affairs of their father, and so it says, "with Jacob," and then concludes, "every man came with his household."[164]

The Bible clearly subordinates the role of the children of Israel to that of their father. Why? Was Jacob not well past his prime, and were not his sons the vigorous bearers of the Jewish future?

The first answer of the Midrash speaks of the centrality of Jacob to God and to Jewish history, a centrality reflected in the biblical phrase. Yet the motif of the subordination of children to parent is continued in the second explanation as well; here, however, it is the subordination expressed in daily affairs, in the common concerns of life. The sons of Jacob did not accept the normal pattern, the "way of the world," in which primacy is mediated by power. Rather, mature men themselves—ironically, yet deliberately rearing their own chidren—they placed their father's affairs before their own.[165]

Another midrash portrays the positive potential that maturation holds for the relationship of parents and sons, a potential that includes not only the care of children for parents, but also the parental recognition that his sons are men, that they are all "brothers":

> "And Jacob said to his brothers,[166] 'Gather stones' '' (Genesis 31:46): How many brothers did Jacob have? But one, and that one wished him dead and buried! Rather, he called his sons "brothers" in Hebrew. Said R. Hunya, "They were mighty as he was, and as righteous." Said R. Yudan, "When a man wears the clothes of his father, he is as his father."[167]

The father acknowledges the mature son as "brother," an acknowledgment born of objective achievement. A later midrash is both more sentimental and more personal: " . . . a man will not refuse to call his sons 'brothers,' for when a man's son matures he becomes as his brother."[168]

Plucked from its context in an ethic that vigorously differentiates between parents and children and rigorously insists upon the legitimate roles of each, this homily might be understood as a flabby surrender of parental worth. Within its native ethic, however, it is nothing of the sort; rather it reflects the growth within the relationship, as son becomes comrade and "brother."

V
Parental Initiative and Filial Response

From any point of view, even the purely normative one, filial responsibility is only part of an overarching structure binding parents and children. The responsibilities of children toward parents are, in a sense, balanced by the responsibilities of parents toward children. This latter area itself constitutes a broad aspect of the Jewish ethos, and we can only refer to it cursorily. The most basic enumeration of parental duties reads:

> The father is obliged to circumcise his son, to redeem him [if a first-born; cf. Numbers 18:15-16], to teach him Torah, to have him wed, and to teach him a trade. Some say he must also teach him to swim. . . .[1]

In more general terms, the father is expected to "guide his sons and daughters in a straight path,"[2] and both the more obviously "spiritual" and the seemingly "physical" concerns of the above list all contribute to this goal. Filial piety must be seen, then, in the balanced perspective provided by a knowledge of this complementary parental responsibility. The seriousness with which the Jewish ethos has approached the former is in many ways—experiential as well as normative—matched (and perhaps fueled) by the extent and depth of the commitment to the latter.[3]

But parental responsibility does not only complement filial piety. The parent is seen—and not only through his educational role in *talmud torah*—as a vital component in the son's ability to fulfill his filial responsibilities; he is an active participant in the process and not merely a passive recipient. Rabbinic law knew full well that filial relations were not a one-way street but rather a dynamic, enclosing both parent and child. Often the child, despite the code to which he is responsible, can in reality do no more than respond to the parental initiative. The parent can so structure the relationship that the normative responses of reverence and honor are either apt expressions of filial sentiments or are virtually eliminated, humanly speaking, as possible filial options. Yet—and this is a crucial point—the son is never, except, possibly, in the case of the "wicked parent," freed of his normative responsibilities. Rather, two different—but related—stresses emerge:

The *son* remains responsible to maintain the norms of filial respect and service. Yet, precisely because the parent had created a situation where the son was forced, psychologically speaking, to reject the norms of respect and service——

The *parent* is morally and legally culpable in the future deterioration of the relationship. Curiously, this moral culpability can be said to exist only where normative responsibility is retained by the son.

These judgments bear significant behavioral and ethical fruit. The parent's role is not a passive but an active, formative one; moreover, his success is not only measured by the quality of filial regard he in fact enjoys, but is judged by normative standards of responsibility. The son is presented with the ethical proposition that his responsibility of filial respect and service remains constant, irrespective of the merit of his parent. The son is not—at least with regard to his filial responsibilities— his parents' judge. Nor is the father his son's "partner" in filial piety in the sense that the son can shift this responsibility to parental shoulders.

I.
The Risk of Parental Assertiveness

The *locus classicus* for this problem is *Mo'ed Katon* 17a:

A maid-servant of the House of the Patriarch saw a man strike his mature son. She said, "Let that man be placed under the ban, for he has violated [the command of Scripture, Leviticus 19:14] . . . 'you shall not place a stumbling-block before the blind. . . .'" As the *baraita* says, "You shall not place a stumbling-block before the blind"—this refers to one who strikes his mature son.[4]

The verse condemning the placing of a stumbling-block before the blind is understood by the rabbis—the powerful image underscoring the degree of ethical reprehensibility felt—as describing the act of misleading a man blind to the realities of a given situation, or of irresponsibly placing the spiritually immature in an overly seductive situation.[5] (This rabbinic rubric—a recurrent one in the literature, by the way— merits sensitive analysis in its own right as a category of Jewish ethical thought and behavior.)

The action of the father is described by the "stumbling-block" metaphor because it contributes to the son's subsequent rejection of the norms of filial respect and service. It can be presumed that the behavior of the father will have a corrosive affect upon the son;[6] even, apparently, within the context of a patriarchal Oriental society, he who strikes his mature son can expect no kindness in return.

Maimonides expanded the insight and prescription of the talmudic source:

> 8. Although children are commanded to go the above-mentioned lengths [of filial piety], the father is forbidden to impose too heavy a yoke upon them, to be too exacting with them in matters pertaining to his honor, lest he cause them to stumble. He should forgive them and shut his eyes; for a father has the right to forego the honor due him.
>
> 9. If a man beats a grown-up son, he is placed under ban, because he transgresses the negative command, "Nor put a stumbling-block before the blind."[7]

The *baraita* given in the Talmud and the maid-servant's act are formally codified in paragraph 9; the insight and program implicit in the talmudic sources are articulated by Maimonides in paragraph 8. The father ought not only to avoid specific aggressive acts, but should also—and this is obviously the more significant and total demand—see his "right" to filial piety as relative to his son's ability to tender reverence and honor.[8] It ought to be kept in mind, though, that Maimonides stresses the avoidance of excessive demands; he does not focus on the parental responsibility for positive growth. This same ethos is found in *Sefer Hassidim,* which is more explicit as to the extent to which filial behavior can be purely a response to parental initiative: ". . . the father and mother should not so enrage the son that he cannot restrain himself but must rebel against them."[9]

Neither author, however, indicates that the conditioning parental behavior licenses filial disrespect from a normative point of view. Indeed, the halakhic logic of the "stumbling-block" motif presupposes filial responsibility; for it is precisely because the filial behavior is culpable that antecedent blame is to be fastened upon the parent. In certain instances, as we have seen, some sources recommend that the son leave his parents so as to escape a growing incompatibility. But these reflect extreme situations. By and large, the son's responsibilities remain unchanged. This lack of normative reaction may seem overly harsh from a psychological point of view. But as we have seen, the rabbinic sources are quite aware of the psychological dimension and indeed integrate it, in their demands upon the parent, into the normative structure. It does not, however, constitute a factor qualifying the son's responsibilities, for that would distort the basis of filial piety and dilute its functional thrust as an imperative.

Both the *baraita* and the incident involving the maid-servant of R. Judah the Patriarch condemn, specifically, the beating or striking of a *grown* son. This detail should not be taken casually. In general, both Bible (e.g., Proverbs 23:13-14; 13:24) and Mishnah (*Makkot* 2:2) are favorably disposed to the rod: "He who spares the rod, spoils his son." And the Midrash, noting David's overly permissive treatment of Adonijahu and the latter's subsequent revolt against his father (I Kings 1), urges a more disciplined approach and concludes, "If one vigorously disciplines his son, the son loves him all the more and honors him."[10] The idea that parental love and involvement are displayed by firm parental guidance is well understood.[11] The aggressive father of our sources is condemned, then, not because he struck his child, but because he struck his *adult* child, an act likely to produce, not obedience, but its opposite.

This point is discussed at greater length by the medieval scholars. Rashi insists that the sources are to be taken at their word, literally: it is only the mature son who is not to be struck.[12] Maimonides strikes an interesting balance. In paragraph 9, where he rules on the specific offense of corporal punishment, he speaks of the "grown-up" son; but in paragraph 8, where he propounds the principle of parental caution, he speaks of "children" in general. Parents are, of course, decisive factors in the development or retardation of filial piety, particularly before their children reach maturity. A most open approach to our text is taken, though, by Ritba: "It would appear that 'mature' *(gadol)* is not to be taken literally, but according to the temperament of the child—i.e., if it is to be feared that he will react violently in either speech or deed. For even if the child is not yet *bar-mitzvah* [13 years old], it is not right that he be incited to strike or curse his father. Rather, he ought to be spoken to and won over. The Talmud speaks of the "mature" son only because it is more common for the mature son [to be angered by being struck]."[13] Thus Ritba introduces a more urgent note of relativity and goal-orientation. The law, he argues, presents guidelines and articulates the ethic of the situation; it does not provide rules.

R. Joseph Karo *(Yoreh De'ah* 240:19-20) reproduced the Maimonidean formulation verbatim, "He who beats his grown-up son is placed under the ban . . ." to which R. Moses Isserles added, "A person is not called 'grown-up' for this purpose until he is twenty-two or twenty-four years old." If Ritba, on the one hand, relativized the talmudic text beyond its apparent meaning, R. Moses Isserles firmly rejects any such

fluidity; basing himself on other talmudic sources, as interpreted by
Rashi, Ramah allows corporal discipline till that age.[14] At least one
contemporary of Ramah introduced a demurring note, though: R. Solomon Luria (Maharshal) agreed that in most cases a son "grew up" at
twenty-two, but pointed out that a married son of whatever age was
considered a man by the townspeople, and ought to be treated as such.[15]

These rulings by Ramah and Maharshal—based upon commentaries
cited by R. Joseph Karo[16]—are revealing in another way, too. The talmudic term *gadol* ("mature") is itself ambiguous. In certain legal discussions, *gadol* is understood as denoting a child who has reached
puberty, it often being assumed that this includes a boy at thirteen and
a girl at twelve. A careful reading of Ritba, above, shows that this was
his understanding of the literal meaning of *gadol*. Another meaning is
also possible: elsewhere, R. Yohanan argues that *gadol* means a child of
whatever age who is economically independent of his father.[17] Indeed,
the Talmud accepts this definition in its discussion of *baraitot* concerning the liability of a father "who injured his grown-up son," i.e., the
identical situation and idiom of our case.[18] Yet despite both these common meanings of *gadol*, late-medieval decisors took *gadol* to mean a
full adult—a man already married or in his 20s. Certainly they extrapolated their opinion from Rashi (see note 15). But the words of Rashi are neither unambiguous nor definitive; surely, they are outweighed by the normal uses of *gadol* sketched above. Rather, it is clear
that a tendency existed to permit the use of corporal punishment in the
case of one's own children till as advanced an age as possible.

II.

The Scope of Mehila

Maimonides urged the parent to mold his child's filial piety through
the wise use of *mehila:* ". . . a father has the right to forego the honor
due him." This structure is a talmudic one, though it was not until medieval times that it was seen as a positive instrument of parental policy
rather than as a way of reacting to filial initiative.

The prime talmudic source is the terse statement:

> R. Isaac b. Shila said in the name of R. Mattenah, who said in the
> name of R. Hisda: "A father may forego the honor due him."[19]

No illustration of the type of behavior contemplated is given by R. Hisda himself. (Actually, this amoraic generalization had been adumbrated in the tannaitic teaching that the parent of a *ben sorer* ["rebellious

son"] could waive his rights, thereby freeing the boy.[20] The developing talmudic discussion, though, applies this rubric to the question of whether a son may accept the service of his parents or, to be more precise, whether a disciple may accept the service of his master [the original source having also considered the *mehila* of the latter]. And elsewhere we read:

> R. Jacob b. Abuha asked Abaye: "What should I do?—When I return from the academy my father brings my cup and my mother fills it."
> He answered: "Accept it from your mother but not from your father. Since he is a sage, he would feel humiliated."[21]

Though the term *mehila* is not used in this exchange, Abaye's answer integrates well into the other discussions in which *mehila* plays a role. Parenthetically, we may note the practical insight of Abaye, who taught R. Jacob to probe beyond his father's verbalized (and even concretized) *mehila* and discover his parent's true feelings.

An earlier incident illustrates the lengths to which parental rejection of the customary expressions of honor could go; so extreme was the self-humiliation of R. Ishmael's mother in the service of her son that acceptance of such a service in itself became a heroic act of filial piety. We read:

> The mother of R. Ishmael came to complain about her son to the rabbis, and she said, "Rebuke my son, Ishmael, for he does not show me honor." The faces of the rabbis grew pale, and they said, "Is it possible that R. Ishmael should not show honor to his mother? What has he done to you?"
> She said, "When he goes to the House of Study, I want to wash his feet and to drink the water wherewith I have washed them, and he will not permit it."
> They said, "Since that is her wish, honor her by permitting it." [Lit.: "Her will is her honor."][22]

And so R. Ishmael is directed to accept his mother's ministrations, unwelcome as they obviously were, for to refuse them would distress and therefore dishonor her. There is no objectively binding criterion of "honor" or of "humiliation." Rather, "her will is her honor." This somewhat folkish formula is more positive than the amoraic *mehila*, and can therefore stress the breadth of parental latitude by designating as acts of "honor" behavior that would normally be insulting and scandalous. Furthermore, "her will is her honor" is better applied to behavior that is welcomed by the parent, despite its scandalous quality, than to the overlooking of behavior that the parent, in fact, considers offensive, which is the connotation of *mehila*.

While this anecdote illustrates the extremes of parental acceptance of humiliation, the earliest post-talmudic authority limited that prerogative. Drawing out the implications of other talmudic sources, R. Ahai noted in his *She'iltot:*

> The rule that "a father may forego the honor due him" applies to his honor. But he may not allow himself to be struck or cursed. [23]

Presumably, R. Ahai distinguished between the objective acts, specified by the Pentateuch, of striking and cursing a parent, on the one hand, and affronts to his honor, on the other; the former are always banned, the parent's sentiments notwithstanding, while behavior involving the honor of parents—either the neglect of the positive acts of honor due them or even the perpetration of acts dishonoring them—is within the scope of parental *mehila*. Azulai (Italy, 18th century) cites manuscripts of the *She'iltot* that deny the parent the right to *mehila* even of distress (*za'ar*) caused him by his son, however.[24] This version, difficult as it may be to reconcile with the talmudic sources, does reflect a tendency in the medieval treatment of the topic. Thus, Rabad is cited by R. Isaac b. Sheshet (Ribash; North Africa, 14th century) as writing that a father can certainly not waive insults and taunts; Ribash accepts this distinction himself, as do other respondents.[25]

Maimonides, as we have seen, expands the role of *mehila* until it is not merely a possible parental response to a filial slight, but an instrument by which the parent shapes the dimensions of the filial honor according to the potential of his child. This doctrine is taken up in *Sefer Hassidim*, which also speaks to the question of the limitations built into this instrument:

> A person's will is his honor, even with respect to filial honor. For were this not so, even a perfect saint could not escape sin in this area. Why? Of necessity, his father or mother would give him a cup, or fill it for him—there are things a person cannot avoid. Therefore it is best that all God-fearing men waive the honor due them, even without expressly telling their children of it. . . .[26]

> If a man's sons constantly fight with each other . . . he may not say, "Hit me," or "Hit your mother," and the same applies if they curse each other. And even though the father would be happier if

he were the object of the curses, he may not say that to them, and they may not strike or curse their parent.[27]

Though the father may forego the honor due him, this frees the son only in the eyes of the "earthly court," but not in the sight of the "heavenly court."[28]

In the first citation, *Sefer Hassidim* expresses the indispensability of parental *mehila,* focussing on a different aspect of the problems inherent in filial piety than Maimonides did. Although the talmudic sages had, in effect, declared that even a perfect saint would fall short when measured against the ideal standard of filial piety,[29] *Sefer Hassidim* maintained that without parental *mehila* the failure would be grotesque; daily life itself compels the surrender of filial piety. This fact is not met by the simple abandonment of those parts of the structure that present unrealistic demands but, characteristically, by a redeployment of the elements that must seemingly be surrendered: they are not conceded but are consciously waived, and only thus is the son released from their claim. But, *Sefer Hassidim* stresses, they must be waived. And by specifying that the *mehila* should not be verbalized, our author implies (as Maimonides had as well) that what is crucial is not the spoken, formal *mehila,* but the quality of a relationship erected on a foundation of parental understanding and flexibility.

Mehila is, at times, merely making the best of a shameful situation. The third citation above apparently concerned a rich son whose humble father continued to labor at a demeaning occupation. The son does nothing to ease the lot of his father or enable him to leave his unpleasant job; the father, for his part, bravely "waives" the consideration he might expect from his son. The formal requirements of filial piety have all been satisfied, but surely, such *mehila* does not deceive the heavenly judge. . . .

Is the dynamic of *mehila* outlined above merely a formal device by which certain insoluble problems are evaded, or is it a creative component in the growth of a genuine filial piety? We have, on more than one occasion, referred to its potentially decisive role in fashioning the actual dimensions and quality of filial piety—whether in a discussion of the limits of filial argument or of the bounds of filial service.[30] But is *mehila* only a casuistic bowing to the inevitable, or does it possess some content of its own? To the degree that a parent can refuse to waive his rights—not only verbally but, of course, in the quality of his relationship with his son—he demonstrates that *mehila* is a real force. But is this true only in a negative sense?

There is one important sense in which it is not. In the teaching of filial respect and honor, it makes all the difference in the world if a given standard is simply discarded, or if its validity remains precious, though at the moment undemanded. This approach retains a lively awareness of the presence of filial responsibility even as the parent is engaged in the process of foregoing the fruits of that responsibility. Hence, it is crucial that this new departure be the prerogative of the father alone. The son can neither expect it nor demand it. It is true that the father ought to take this step, but the very fact that he alone is empowered to construct the bridge means that the gulf between the generations remains its basis. The formal externalizing of reverence is waived while reverence itself is achieved. This is not accomplished by a denial of the externalizations, however, but by building upon and beyond them a structure faithful to these foundations.

It is also most significant that the forgiveness of God is consistently described—from biblical times on—as the forgiveness of a father toward his children. "As a father has mercy on his children—so have mercy on us, O Lord" is a frequent liturgical refrain modeled on Psalms 103:13. The Midrash constantly returns to the parable of the king (God) who is also father to the disrespectful prince (Israel), and who welcomes him back because He is father. This pervasive recognition that God's forgiveness is an expression of fatherhood is surely representative of the Jewish ethos of parenthood, and helped mold it.[31]

III.
The "Wicked Parent": the End of Responsibility?

In the previous section we focussed on the role of the parent in shaping filial piety. Another, equally crucial question concerning the parental role may be raised: Is the parent inalienably the object of filial reverence and service? Does his very person require responses irrespective of his own behavior and character, or are the responses dependent in some way upon his virtue? Can a father, his biological paternity notwithstanding, become undeserving of a son's honor? In rabbinic literature, this is the "problem of the wicked father."

Epictetus thought that a father never forfeits his right to filial care and submission: "Duties are universally measured by relations. Is a man a father? The precept is to take care of him, to yield to him in all things, to submit when he is reproachful, when he inflicts blows. But suppose that he is a bad father. Were you then by nature made akin to a good father? No, but to a father. . . ."[32] For Epictetus, then, "nature" is the origin of filial piety and its final court of appeal.

The rabbis, too, agree that filiation is rooted in biology. But they also maintain that "nature" is subject to the judgment of other standards, though they disagree on the extent to which these other norms may reshape or curtail the imperative of filial piety.

The Talmud, to be sure, is aware of the ease with which zealous youth discovers its parents' clay feet and the abuse of filial piety that could result from frequent and enthusiastic discovery of "wicked parents." Thus, even when a father must be corrected by his son, there is no slackening of the respect owed the father by the son; the son must be meticulously careful not to pain his parent by condescending or arrogant instruction.[33] Nonetheless the "wicked parent" does exist, and he is recognized as such. We recall that the reverence and service owed a father is superseded by the reverence and obedience owed by both father and son to God: the father who demands immoral or impious behavior of his son is to be disobeyed. A substantial body of rabbinic opinion maintains that this judgment may be made not only of specific parental requests, but of the person of the father as well. Others argue that the parental status is not to be violated, although the gravity of filial impiety is recognizably diminished.

This issue was developed by the medieval scholars on the basis of limited but suggestive talmudic material. The following sources were probed for their relevance to this problem:

(a)

Mishnah: If one has any kind of a son, that son exempts his father's wife from the levirate marriage [Deuteronomy 25:5-11], is liable to punishment for striking or cursing his father, and is deemed to be his son in every respect. . . .

What does "any kind" include? R. Judah said: "It includes a bastard. . . ."

And "is liable," etc.: But why? One should apply here the Scriptural text, "Nor curse a ruler of thy people" [Exodus 22:27], only when he practises the deeds of thy people! As R. Phineas in the name of R. Pappa said elsewhere, "When he repented," so here, also, it is a case when he repented. . . .[34]

(b)

Where the [deceased] father left them a cow or garment or anything which could be identified, they are liable to restore it in order to uphold the honor of their father. . . . But why should they be liable to restore it in order to uphold the honor of their father? Why not apply to them, " 'Nor curse a ruler of thy people'—only when he practises the deeds of thy people" [and their father was a thief]? As R. Phineas in the name of R. Pappa said elsewhere, "When he repented"; here also we suppose that the father made repentance.[35]

(c)

Come and hear: If one was going forth to be executed, and his son came and smote and cursed him, he is liable; if a stranger did this, he is exempt. . . .

    . . . a tanna of the school of R. Ishmael taught: "For no offense may a son be appointed an agent to smite or curse his father, exempting if the father is a *mesit* [he who incites people to worship idols]. . . .[36]

The tannaitic elements of these citations do not bear heavily on our problem, though they clearly contain the seeds for future thinking. The Mishnah in (a) is primarily concerned with the status of the son, and establishes that biological filiation endows father and son with all the responsibilities and powers that legally inhere in the relationship; practically speaking, the Mishnah doubtless intends to rule that the *mamzer* is fully a son.[37] This doctrine, which was in certain respects a matter for quizzical discussion in the early second century,[38] runs counter to Greek and Roman legal and ethical thought, which releases the illegitimate son from filial obligations.[39] Consistent with this contrast is the fact that Roman law recognized adoption as constituting legal paternity, while Jewish law did not.[40] For the Romans, paternity was established by the fulfillment of given legal requirements, in cases of both natural and adopted children, while for the Jews, paternity was established biologically. Legal structures—whether adoption or *mamzerut*—can neither create such a fact where it is absent, nor dissolve it when it is present.

The dominant impression given by the tannaitic components of these sources is the inviolable sanctity of the parental status. Thus, (c): a son may not be the agent to punish his father, even when such a punishment is required by law. Clearly, the criminal's fatherhood is sacred.[41] Even the thief's honor (b) must be salvaged by his children.

But the rabbis, characteristically stimulated by other, suggestive tannaitic comments, further explore and clarify the state and significance of parental virtue, modifying the original tannaitic concept in the process.

The Talmud forces the clarification of the character of the parent involved in (a) and (b) by questioning the assumption that all men, and all parents, are protected by law from abuse. Tannaitic exegesis had understood " . . . nor curse a ruler of thy people"[42] to refer only to the ruler who lived in harmony with the ways of his people; as this verse is then taken to protect not only the ruler but all men, the proviso that the wicked do not share in this protection is a natural extension of the original idea.[43] This restriction upon Exodus 22:27 is extended to include Exodus 21:15 and 17, which ban the striking or cursing of a parent.[44] Thus, the Talmud asks, why should the father of a *mamzer* be protected by the law from the assault of his son, when his very fathering of the child placed him beyond this protection? The answer given, that the Mishnah assumes that the father had repented of his sin, leaves us with the clear dogmatic position that the unrepentant father ought, in fact, to suffer the blows and curses of his son.[45] And in the citation (b), the Talmud concludes that the son need not act to defend the honor of his father, an acknowledged and unrepentant thief. Thus the talmudic discussion, by confronting our primary tannaitic statements with other tannaitic material, has brought about a fundamental shift in the status of "the wicked parent." Medieval scholars read these talmudic discussions in two contrasting ways.

Both Rashi[46] and R.Tam[47] read these sources as completely releasing the son from the rubrics of filial piety. But R. Alfas, followed by Maimonides, disagree; they read *Yevamot* 22b very closely, and concluded that the son is not to be *penalized* for his action, but is not permitted to strike or curse his parents.[48] Indeed, Maimonides rules that the son must continue to honor his father whatever the moral or religious degradation to which he has sunk:

> If one's father or mother were completely wicked, and violated the commands, even if they had been condemned to death and are on their way to execution—he must not strike them or curse them. If, however, he curses or strikes them, he is not punished. But if they have returned to God he is culpable, and is put to death. . . .
>
> The bastard is obliged to honor his father and stand in reverence of him, though he is not punished for striking him or cursing him unless he has returned to God. Even if his father is a wicked man and a violator of the law, he must honor him and revere him. . . .[49]

While hermeneutics may be responsible for the differing opinions of Maimonides and the French-German scholars, clear conceptual and human implications flow from the two postures (and, of course, may be responsible for them).[50] For Maimonides, the reverence and honor due a parent are not functions of the objective worth or virtue of the parent. Rather, they inhere in his status or person. (Does this echo the Maimonidean notion that filial reverence and honor do not presuppose filial love?[51]) As a related talmudic citation has it, "But after all, his father is his father and his mother is his mother!"[52] A parent is guaranteed (ideally, at least) that however he may be judged by both his fellows and God, he never forfeits the minimal loyalty of his son. The biological fact written in the fibre of both beings is not altered; the createdness with which the son is blessed, the acknowledgment and gratitude with which he must respond, are unchanged. Can one revere or honor the man who is, by all standards available to the son as to everyone else, a doer of evil? Maimonides, apparently, thought one could—as a son.

The tosafists, on the contrary, argued that one could not—or, better still, need not. They, too, agree that filial reverence and honor are not generally subject to the fluctuations of parental virtue. Yet there is a chasmlike point where the path of filial reverence falters and, quite abruptly, ends. There are some to whom none—not even children— owe regard: biology alone cannot constitute an imperative to honor the unrepentant murderer—indeed, there is something immoral about honoring him even if you are his son. It appears, then, that just as the son must reject the specific desire of the father when its fulfillment would run counter to Torah, so, too, may he reject the person of the father when the latter embodies a testimony to evil and wickedness.

The subsequent code of Karo and Isserles embodies both opinions, R. Joseph Karo reproducing the view of Alfasi and Maimonides, and R. Moses Isserles, apparently that of Rashi and R. Tam. Thus we find:

> *Code:* A bastard is obliged to honor and fear his father; even if his father is an evil-doer and a violator of the law he must honor him and stand in awe of him.
> *Gloss:* And some say that one is not obliged to honor one's wicked father unless he repents.
>
> (*Shulhan Arukh* 240:18)

> *Code:* If one's father or mother are completely wicked and violated the commands, even if they have been condemned to death and are on their way to execution, he must not strike them or curse them. And if he strikes them or curses them, he is not punished. But if

they have repented, he is punished for his guilt and is killed, although they are going to be executed themselves.

(241:4)

The code, indeed, reproduces the very words of Maimonides, while the gloss seemingly presents the other opinion. Later commentators, however, doubtless puzzled by the omission of a similar gloss to the second passage above (241:4), see the crystallization of a third position here.[53] Utilizing a distinction between positive acts of honor and the avoidance of acts of dishonor—already debated by *rishonim*, to be sure, but in different contexts[54]—they argue that Isserles glossed 240:18 so as to indicate that the son is released from the expectation of positive responsibility, while agreeing—through his silence–with the ban on actions likely to pain one's parents described in 241:4. We can readily see the human and broadly ethical sense of this approach. The son need not exert himself in positive acts reflecting the worth and esteem implied in filial honor; at the same time, he must retain the elemental sensitivity to the father-son relationship that restrains and, indeed, prevents acts of overt hostility. Needless to say, this line is difficult and, at times, impossible to detect; the omission of the expected expression of honor is often, in reality, a source of pain and even shame. Yet with all its imprecision it remains a useful guide.

There is little guidance, on the other hand, in establishing the criteria by which a parent is categorized as "wicked." The great medieval authorities contented themselves with generalities, on the whole, and there are few specific questions raised in the responsa literature on the subject that would have compelled discussion of the topic. Certain offenses, it is true, do carry with them the denomination of "wicked parent" or "he who does not do as thy people do" in talmudic and later literature, but the rejection of parental authority thus generated usually concerns the specific area of parental delinquency, and so offers no guide for general halakhic policy (see note 46).[55] It is fair to say, I believe, that halakhists were wary of mobilizing either of the two categories just mentioned, and were reluctant to label a father or mother as "wicked parents" unless they were confronted by a totally depraved person.[56]

The aggadah tells a curious tale of sympathetic involvement in parental peccancy: A man was so given to drink that he would sell his household effects to support his habit. His sons, disgusted with this squandering of their eventual patrimony, abducted their father and left him in a cemetery. Simultaneously, some wine merchants, fearing government confiscation of their merchandise, deposited full wine-skins in the same place. The father delightedly discovered the treasure and daily became drunk. Some time later the sons returned, only to discover their father drinking away to his heart's content. "Inasmuch as God Himself supplies you with drink, we must behave accordingly," they said; and so "they resolved that each son should supply his father with drink one day (a week)."[57]

VI

Fathers and Teachers:
Faithfulness and Growth

I.
When Master is Father, and Disciple, Son

> And it came to pass, when the Lord would take up Elijah by a whirlwind into heaven, that Elijah went with Elisha from Gilgal. And Elijah said unto Elisha: "Tarry here, I pray you." . . . And Elisha said, "As the Lord lives, and as your soul lives, I will not leave you." . . .
>
> And it came to pass, as they still went on and talked, that behold, there appeared a chariot of fire, and horses of fire, which parted them both asunder; and Elijah went up by a whirlwind into heaven. And Elisha saw it, and he cried: "My father, my father, the chariots of Israel and their horsemen!" And he saw no more; and he took hold of his own clothes, and rent them in two pieces.
>
> (II Kings 2:1–12)

"My father" and the devotion it embraces pour from a distraught and mourning disciple, not from a dutiful son; they are addressed not to a father but to a master.[1] Indeed, the induction of Elisha as disciple-prophet had already hinted that the young man would not only include his master in his filial devotion, but would rather transfer the heart of his dedication from his father to his mentor:

> So he [Elijah] . . . found Elisha the son of Shaphat, who was plowing . . . and Elijah passed over to him, and cast his mantle upon him. And he left the oxen, and ran after Elijah, and said, "Let me, I pray thee, kiss my father and my mother, and then I will follow you." And he said unto him, "Go back; for what have I done to you?" . . .
>
> (I Kings 19:19-20)

That master becomes father and disciple becomes son is also assumed by the Book of Proverbs, where the teacher of wisdom often turns to his student as, "My son." This vocabulary and attitude persist

137

in the rabbinic period, too, as the rabbis address their students as "My son."[2] But the rabbis not only participated in this transformation or expansion of the meaning of fatherhood, they also described it, integrated it into an axiological structure, and discussed its various experiential crystallizations.

The most general presentation of this idea emerges in the treatment of the command to teach Torah: "And these words, which I command you this day, shall be upon your heart; and you shall teach them diligently to your children" (Deuteronomy 6:6-7):

> "Your children"—[by this is meant] your pupils. You see that pupils are always called sons, as we read, "You are the children of the Lord your God" (Deuteronomy 14:1). Thus, "And the sons of the prophets . . . came forth" (I Kings 2:3)—were these the prophets' sons? They were only their pupils! Hence we see that pupils are called sons.
>
> And so too Hezekiah, king of Judah, taught the entire Torah to the people of Israel, and called them sons ("My sons, be not now negligent . . . . " (II Chronicles 29:11).[3] And just as pupils are called sons, so is the master called father. . . .
>
> (*Sifre*, Deuteronomy 6:6–7, and Rashi)

Since "children" now means "pupils," the command to teach Torah to one's own children is broadened to include a responsibility toward all the children of the people: since they can all become your pupils, they are all potentially your sons; indeed, it is precisely through this teaching and receiving that they do become your sons. From a purely pragmatic point of view, the effective reach of the educational structure is massively enriched by this exegesis and its halakhic translation. And, while the exegesis of "the sons of the prophets" may be artificial, other biblical idioms point to a similar transformation on a linguistic level at least,[4] while the historic Jewish drive to teach the whole people Torah and make it a public heritage must certainly have implied a broad construction of verses like Deuteronomy 6:6–7.

But the Midrash also hints at the ideological basis or model for this new understanding of paternity, an understanding rooted, not in biology, but in the spirit. It cites, as its very first proof-text, the fact that Moses called the people Israel the "sons of God." Certainly, no biological kinship is intended; the mythological origins of the phrase had long since been transcended.[5] The relationship between God and His people was established through the covenants binding the two, and the prime covenant is Torah itself: the Torah that God revealed and taught the people, through which He is their teacher and father. Just as filial respect for parents has as its model man's reverence and devotion to the God Who created him, so too does devotion to one's master have as its model devotion to God, He Who endows man with spiritual, or meaningful, life: "You are the children of the Lord your God. . . . "

Human growth, the long process in which man moves beyond the biological situation to a more total fulfillment, is thus affirmed. Its model is the movement of mankind from creation to the revelation at Sinai. God is now known not only as Creator but as Teacher. But whereas the variety of God allows man to grow by discovering new facets of the divine or by being addressed by them, the growth of man in his human environment is different. Here, the son will discover that the master who can give him the meaning demanded by his own maturity may in fact be, not his biological father, but another man. Paternity in human society, then, includes the separate persons of both father and teacher, much as human maturity implies both physical and spiritual growth. Therefore, Jewish tradition sees the flowering of paternity in the master from whom one acquires Torah.

This growth is reciprocal; if the disciple discovers a new father, the master discovers a new son. The master is considered to have fathered his disciple: "He who teaches his comrade is considered to have conceived him, formed him, and brought him into the world."[6] Such paternity is not merely an ethical concept, it is emotional as well. When Moses died, the Midrash tells, Joshua mourned him thus: "My father, my father! My master, my master! Father who raised me, master who taught me Torah."[7] Surely, the author of this midrash belonged to a society in which teachers might demonstrate genuine paternal care for their disciples.

The Palestinian Talmud explains the fact that Resh Lakish accepted ritual consolation for the death of his student R. Hiyyah b. Addah: "A man's disciple is dear to him as his son."[8] An aggadic bit of exegesis conveys the same ethos: Isaiah, the Talmud says, speaks of "the children whom the Lord has given me"(8:18); "but were these his children? They were in reality his disciples! Hence we see that they were so beloved to him that he called them, 'My children.' "[9] The paternity of the master is achieved, then, not by the intellectual act alone, but by the growth of affection and paternal love. As the incident of Resh Lakish indicated, the love of the master for his disciple equals that of the father for his son, and this is expressed in triumph as well as in sadness: "A man envies the success of all others, except that of his son or of his student."[10] Indeed, Maimonides unequivocally demands such development on the master's part: "A man should take care with his pupils *and love them,* for they are the sons who benefit one in this world and the next."[11] Just as discipleship opens the heart of the younger man to the service and reverence by which his new filial relationship is expressed (and we note, incidentally, that the disciple is not expected necessarily to love his master), so, too, the master learns that his sons are not his biological offspring alone, but those in whom he has fathered wisdom and the love of God. The true master must love his disciples as a father. And it is instructive that in regard to the laws of a "common court" (*eruv*) there are only two pairs of which the Talmud can say without question that the individuals fuse into a single legal person: father-son and master-disciple.[12]

When we reflect upon the seriousness with which Judaism endows the filial relationship, this expansion of paternity amply demonstrates the significance of the growth described above. For, as is by now obvious, parents are not outgrown in the Jewish perspective, the relationship is not ephemeral or a fixture of one's childhood. The acceptance of the teacher into this order of honor and reverence is no facile gesture, but is rather a well-considered and important choice.

II.
When Responsibilities Conflict

The student of Torah, we recall, was expected to leave home for the academy. Though the personal claims of teacher and parent may not often have conflicted, they could do so, and the tradition undertakes to plot the course of such conflicts. Moreover, the positing of competing claims is in part a literary device through which hierarchies of value can be articulated.[13]

The valuation essential to any resolution of this tension was expressed by R. El'azar b. Azariah, when as a youthful disciple of the ailing R. Eliezer he tried (unsuccessfully, by the way) to assuage the pains of his master by telling him that he "is more precious to Israel than a father and mother; for father and mother are of this world, while you are of this world and of the world to come."[14] The terms in which R. El'azar offered his consolation ought to have been most significant to R. Eliezer, who had once ridiculed disciples leaving his lecture on a holiday as men "who neglect the life of the world to come and busy themselves with the life of this world."[15]

This valuation provides the perspective within which the normative halakhic texts discuss the problem. Master is to be given preference over parent because "one's father brought him into this world, while one's master who taught him wisdom brings him to the future world."

Two Mishnahs teach clearly that the responsibility to one's master takes precedence over that to one's father. This halakhic resolution could, quite reasonably, be taken as evaluative of the depth and significance of the two relationships:

(a)

If a man's own lost article and his father's lost article need attention, his own takes precedence. His own and his teacher's—his own takes precedence. His father's and his teacher's—his teacher's takes precedence, because his father brought him into this world, whereas his teacher, who instructed him in wisdom, brings him to the future world. But if his father is a sage, his father's takes precedence. If his father and his teacher were each carrying a burden, he must first assist his teacher to lay it down, and then assist his father. If his father and his teacher are in captivity, he must first redeem his teacher and then his father. But if his father is a sage, he must first redeem his father and then his teacher.[16]

(b)

Everywhere Scripture speaks of the father before the mother. Does the honor due to the father exceed the honor due to the mother? But Scripture says, "Ye shall fear every man his mother and his father" (Leviticus 19:3), to teach that both are equal. But the sages have said: "Everywhere Scripture speaks of the father before the mother because both a man and his mother are bound to honor the father." So, too, in the study of the Law, if the son gained much wisdom while sitting before his teacher, his teacher comes ever before his father, since both he and his father are bound to honor the teacher.[17]

Both Mishnahs direct the disciple to prefer the needs and honor of his master to those of his parent, should the two conflict.

Mishnah *Keritot* [b] bases such preference on the premise that the father, too, owes the master reverence, and so should not be honored at the master's expense (an idea reminiscent of the priority of the fulfillment of a *mitzvah,* or the avoidance of its violation, over filial respect: "Both you and your father must observe My Sabbath").[18] Mishnah *Baba Mezia* [a] is more fundamental. The growth of the individual from biological to spiritual being is clearly articulated and conclusions as to halakhic and personal reorientation are drawn. These conclusions—the precedence of teacher's life and property over those of the parent—no doubt mirror, in normal circumstances, an emotional and personal reorientation (growth is actually a better word) as well.

Despite the clear valuational priority projected by the Mishnah, we cannot overlook some of the subtler elements of the text.

First, the Mishnah assumes that in all situations other than the conflict situation it constructs, the imperative of filial reverence and service is undiminished. Spiritual maturity and growth do not—as chronological and physical growth do not—diminish the commitment to that imperative; the filial relationship and responsibility are not ended by the new relationship that transcends it. "Honor your father and your mother" is not outgrown. Responsibility to master takes priority *in cases of conflict*—it does not cancel filial responsibility pure and simple. It cannot: the reality of life and physical being are never denied in Judaism, nor are the ethical imperatives that are rooted in that reality.[19] Indeed, the very priority bestowed upon the master becomes more significant because it must transcend the still vital filial relationship, than it would be if it shattered it. Master is added to father as the scope of paternity is enlarged and its meaning enriched.[20]

Second, our Mishnah stipulates that "if his father is a sage, his father takes precedence." The father thus retains his priority even if he is not the equal of his son's master and, apparently, even if he did not contribute to the education of his son (though one may argue that the father who is a sage doubtless did, and such contribution is assumed by the Mishnah).[21] The status of *Hakham* (sage, probably an "ordained scholar") alone entitles him to priority over one's master.[22] Coming at these teachings from a different methodological posture, one might almost say that, in general, the "scholar class" asserts its claim to the youth, whom it tears from his natural moorings; thus this claim need not be made when the father is himself a member of that class. Yet the fact that no generalized diminution of filial responsibility is attempted speaks powerfully against such an interpretation. In the last analysis, whatever construction is put upon these norms, the crucial fact remains that there is no across-the-board usurpation of the paternal rank by the master.

After these considerations have been stated, we must return to what is surely the heart of the matter. The basic point being made is, of course, the primacy of master over father, and that should not be obscured. One may not agree with all the nuances of Fromm's presentation, but in the main he captures the essence of the teaching: "The paragraph quoted here demonstrates how the Jewish tradition has developed . . . to a position where the blood relationship to the father has become secondary to the spiritual relationship to the teacher. The spiritual authority of the teacher has superseded the natural authority of the father, even though the biblical command to honor one's parents has not been voided."[23] Or in the terse but no less generalized words of the 8th-century *She'iltot:* "The honor of one's master is greater than the honor of one's father."[24]

The radical nature of this stance can be seen in the following discussions:

"If his father and his teacher were each carrying a burden, etc."— Our Rabbis taught: "The teacher referred to is he who instructed him in wisdom [i.e., the dialectical understanding of the Mishnah, such as is found in the Talmud—Rashi], not he who taught him Bible and Mishnah [the knowledge of the Mishnah-text alone—Rashi]." This is R. Me'ir's view. R. Judah said: "He from whom one has derived the greater part of his knowledge." R. Jose said: "Even if he enlightened his eyes in a single Mishnah alone, he is his teacher. . . ."

Samuel rent his garment for one of the rabbis who taught him the meaning of "One was thrust into the duct, etc." [M. *Tamid* 3:6].

'Ulla said: "The scholars in Babylon arise before each other and rend their garment for each other in mourning; but with respect to a colleague's lost article, when one has one's father also to attend to, he returns a scholar's first only in the case of his teacher *par excellence* (*rabbo muvhak*). . . ."

It has been stated: R. Isaac ben Joseph said in R. Yohanan's name: "The *halakha* is as R. Judah." R. Aha son of R. Hunna said in R. Sheshet's name: "The *halakha* is as R. Jose." Now, did R. Yohanan really say this? But R. Yohanan has said: "The *halakha* is as the anonymous Mishnah," and we have learned, ". . . . his teacher who instructed him in wisdom!"—What is meant by "wisdom"? The greater part of one's knowledge.

(*Baba Mezia* 33a)

Here we find a group of mid-second century tanna'im debating the definition of "master." R. Judah argues that one's master can be only that teacher who has been the disciple's major mentor and exemplar.

For R. Jose, on the other hand, any teacher who makes a genuine contribution to the pupil's education, enlightening him, say, as to the meaning of a single Mishnah, becomes his master.[25]

This discussion involves far more than terminology, however. The acknowledgment of a man as one's master has broad implication. As the behavior of Samuel indicates, one must concretely mourn the passing of a master; one must certainly render him other gestures of esteem ("the scholars in Babylon rise before each other"). But these responses (concretizations, in a sense, of the *dictum:* "He who learns from his associate one chapter, one *halakha,* one verse, one saying, or even one letter must show him honor")[26] ought not to becloud the issue. In context, the question is not, "For which master do I mourn?" rather, "Which master takes priority over my parent?" For it is the master whose lost article and, indeed, whose freedom takes precedence over the identical needs of the parent who is the subject of the Mishnah and of the subsequent *baraita.*

In this context, one can trace a debate that winds down the centuries. R. Judah, as we have seen, argues that only that master who has truly formed the person of his disciple can claim so overriding a commitment.[27] R. Jose, on the contrary, argues that priority must be given to any single link in the educational process, no matter how quantitatively small it might be. This latter posture is most radical, both in its reading of the Mishnah (which had, after all, characterized the master as one "who brings him to the future world"[28]), in its immediate halakhic effect, and most broadly, in its general judgment as to the relationship of the maturing son to his parent, on the one hand, and to the body of his teachers, on the other. Clearly, R. Jose would shift the balance of loyalty most substantially away from the biological center. We are reminded of R. El'azar b. Matya, who argued that the fulfillment of any *mitzvah* took precedence over filial responsibility.

As we continue to read our passage, it becomes clear that the broader definition of "master" was accepted in the areas of mourning and personal courtesy. But as 'Ulla reported, the same Babylonians who would mourn for their colleagues in acknowledgment of the learning that men derive from their peers would not prefer their peers to their parents, nor would they so prefer any but their true master. Finally, we read of an ongoing debate on this question: R. Yohanan declared for R. Judah, and R. Sheshet for R. Jose. It would appear, then, that the latitude of loyalty transference in situations of conflict was a matter of disagreement among the sages. The debate of R. Judah and R. Jose shows how far the principle of the transcendence of the biological loyalty by the spiritual bond could be taken.[29]

Subsequent medieval discussion and codification decided the issue
of priority in favor of R. Judah, as one might expect. Taking their cue
from the Babylonian practice recorded in the Talmud, virtually all authorities ruled that while a teacher is to be granted priority over one's
parent, this expression of honor is reserved for one's master *par
excellence.*[30] But both the pragmatic and conceptual implications of
this priority-in-conflict are clear: it is expected that every man will
grow in Torah through attachment to, and guidance of, a *rav muvhak,*
and with this growth comes a new maturity and a new hierarchy of responsibility and loyalty.

This reasonably clear pattern is complicated, however, by an observation of *Sefer Hassidim* that was taken (in large part) into the *Shulhan
Arukh* by R. Moses Isserles:

> When does a master . . . take precedence over the father? Only
> when the father has not hired the master to teach his son. But if the
> master was hired by the father for that purpose, and would other-
> wise not have taught the son, . . . then the father . . . takes prec-
> edence. Similarly, if an individual or group of Jews paid the wages
> of the teacher, they take precedence.[31]

The sense of this observation is patent. If the master deserves priority as
an expression of gratitude for his bringing the disciple into "the life of
the world-to-come," then the father who employed the teacher is in reality the son's benefactor. This insistence doubtless restored many a devoted father to his position of greatest honor. We may well imagine that
it also taught many a budding scholar, eager to transfer his loyalties
from dull father to luminous master, a lesson in ethics.[32] Interestingly,
this analysis of the gratitude owed parent and teacher applies, too, only
in situations of conflict. Surely *Sefer Hassidim* does not suggest that
the salaried teacher deserves no respect or—speaking experientially—
that he is not involved in the personal growth of his student. Despite
the apparent inconsistency, the distinction between the salaried and
non-salaried teacher is mobilized only when one is faced with a conflict of responsibilities between the competing claims of parent and
teacher.

One final caveat. Without displacing the value scheme outlined
above, one tannaitic teaching displays a flexibility not to be over-
looked: "If he and his father and his mother and his master are all captives, he sees to his own redemption first, and that of his master before
that of his father, but that of his mother precedes them all."[33] The rigors
of captivity press harder upon his mother than upon the men and so

she is to be redeemed first (as, indeed, women are to be freed before men). But this teaching contains the seeds of an important ethical and halakhic judgment that, if broadened, adds a significant new dimension to the entire discussion. For now the halakhic ethic in this area consists of two elements: first, the formula of priority to which we have devoted much attention; but second, the variety implied by the context. The teaching that master precedes father can, it seems, be seriously reshaped where the parental stake is objectively deeper than that of the master. The individual human dimension thus becomes a meaningful variable in the equation. Or, put another way, context and norm may function as coordinates.

Other talmudic sources also illumine this concern for the relative status of parent and master. One such discussion focusses on the right of each to forego the honor that is normally his due.

> R. Isaac b. Shela said in the name of R. Mattena who said in the name of R. Hisda: "If a father foregoes the honor due him, his honor is waived; but if a master foregoes the honor due him, his honor is not waived."
> R. Joseph said: "Even a master may forego the honor due him, for Scripture says, 'And the Lord went before them' (Exodus 13:21). . . . "[34]

Superficially, it might seem that the crux of the argument is the relationship of the honor due a parent with that due a master: R. Hisda claims that the honor of a master must be more profound than that of a parent, and R. Joseph claims that the two are identical. But on second thought it appears more likely that the two disagree about the quality and nature of the honor due a master (as the continuation of the talmudic discussion indicates), and this debate is quite independent of the standards of filial honor. Nonetheless, the literary structuring of the discussion, which presents a parent-master sequence, focusses our attention on the relative strength of the honor due each.

Another such contrast emerges from a discussion of *hesebah* (the reclining position that symbolizes freedom and ease) during the Passover seder. The question is, To what degree do certain social roles conflict with *hesebah*?

> A woman in her husband's house may not recline, but if she is a woman of importance she must recline. A son in his father's house

must recline.

The scholars asked: "What about a disciple in his teacher's presence?" Come and hear, for Abaye said: "When we were at the master's house, we used to recline on each other's knees. When we came to R. Joseph's house, he remarked to us: 'You should not do it: the fear of your teacher is as the fear of Heaven.' "

An objection is raised: A man must recline with all people, and even a disciple in his master's presence?—That was taught of a craftsman's apprentice.[35]

It is agreed by all that a son must recline in his father's presence, but the posture proper to a disciple in the presence of his master is a matter of debate. R. Joseph considered such reclining disrespectful, and notified the disciples of that. On the other hand, the practice at the home of Rabbah b. Nahman ("the master's house") and the simple sense of the teaching that "a man must recline with all . . . even a disciple in his master's presence" both require the disciple to rank the Passover posture of freedom ahead of the respectful mien normally assumed in his master's presence. Again, the discussion concerning the extent of the respect owed a master is probably not derived from the relationship of that respect to filial respect. Nevertheless, that relationship clearly emerges: for some, the presence of neither father nor master ought to prevent the son from reclining as a "freeman" at the *seder;* for others, the respect owed a master is greater than that owed a father and does inhibit *hesebah.*[36]

III.

No Mourning for a Master

The area of mourning provides another opportunity to compare—and contrast—the parent-child and master-disciple relationships.

The Talmud prescribes norms of bereavement and mourning upon the death of one's parents, child, wife, brother, or sister. For the initial seven-day period of mourning one stays at home, to be consoled by relatives and friends ("sitting *shiv'ah*"); one is forbidden, among other things, bathing, shaving, sexual intercourse, the study of Torah, the wearing of shoes, and, of course, banquets or other festivities. The mourning continues—its rigor and requirements much abated—for thirty days, and in the case of parents, for twelve months.[37]

Does the "filial" relationship with one's master integrate the latter into this pattern? Does a disciple mourn his master as he would his father? By and large, he does not.

The disciple does, as we have seen, rend his clothes at the death of his master; this rent is never mended (as that torn for his father is not), and according to Maimonides resembles that torn for his father in all other ways as well—for example, the disciple tears through all his clothes until he bares his breast.[38] Furthermore, he observes the regimen of bereavement for one day.[39] Yet neither the one-day bereavement nor the rending of garments is more than the exception that proves the rule, which restricts mourning to those bound by ties of blood.

The unmendable rending of garments is, in fact, prescribed for a wide range of calamities: for the death of parents, one's master, the king, and the Nasi, as well as for the destruction of the Temple, evil tidings, the sight of Jerusalem in her desolation, and the burning of the Torah.[40] Thus, the master is included, not by virtue of his assimilation to "paternal" rank, but by his autonomous significance as a center of value (much like the Temple or the Torah). Furthermore, the Talmud hints that "rending of garments" (keriah) is a structure that stands apart, in various ways, from the procedures of mourning (avelut), thus suggesting other rationales for keriah upon the death of a master.[41] Similarly, one-day bereavement is obviously a symbolic gesture, and in fact denies the master "filial" mourning. Indeed, the source attesting to this practice objects to the expansion of this one-day bereavement into the seven- and the thirty-day pattern: "When R. Yohanan died, R. Ammi 'sat' seven and then thirty days. R. Abba b. R. Hiyya b. Abba said, 'What R. Ammi did—he did for himself alone. For R. Hiyya said in the name of R. Yohanan, "Even for the master who has taught one wisdom—one sits in mourning for only one day." ' "[42]

Disciples, then, were certainly grief-stricken at the death of their master, and often expressed this grief in deep and even extreme gestures; to some of these we shall turn shortly. But what is at present significant is that the normative patterns of mourning and bereavement were, on the whole, restricted to one's physical family. Although mourning for parents is the most protracted and intense of these patterns, it is, perhaps, not an expression of kibbud av, but rather part of a generalized response to death in the family. In any case, one does not mourn one's master as one mourns one's parent.

Halakha reflects experience; the death of relatives and, especially, parents, strikes and shocks the individual at a level of kinship which, precisely because of its biological moorings and their psychic implications, rarely admits even the most intimate of masters. The components of this bond between parents and children, the expressive function served by the objective experience of bereavement, the support provided the individual confronting this rupture in his continuity and existence by the unwavering structures of mourning and by his integration into the community—these are all psychological and phenomenological questions clearly beyond the competence of this essay. Yet it is clear that though master becomes father in many respects, the bestowal of life and the web of experiences that are inexorably woven out of the matrix of origins bind parents and children in a unique way. It is these bonds and their roots in physical kinship that invoke the structures of halakhic mourning.

This absence of a formalized routine leaves the disciple free either to respond minimally or to express his emotions as an individual and in singular ways. Thus we have seen how some disciples voluntarily undertook the seven- and thirty-day periods of mourning for their masters. A more dramatic paradigm is afforded by R. Akiba's grief for his master R. Eliezer:

> Now it happened that when R. Eliezer died, R. Akiba bared both arms and beat his breast, drawing blood. And thus he spoke, "My master, my master, 'the chariot of Israel and the horsemen thereof!' A multitude of coins have I, but no money changer to sort them."[43]

The public sobriety with which R. Akiba confronted the death of his father provides an instructive contrast: "Now it happened that when R. Akiba's father died, strangers bared their arms for him, whereas he did not."[44]

It would seem that it was his status as a master of Torah that inhibited R. Akiba from "baring the shoulder" at the death of his father.[45] Such behavior, it was felt, would be unseemly in this aristocrat of the spirit of the second century, when men clearly knew what nobility ought and ought not to do. Once again, though, we are brought back to our earlier concern: the conflict or contrast of the claims of the master and the parent. Here, the situation is complicated by the coincidence of master and son in the person of R. Akiba. The Talmud, however, offers another instance of conflict between the requirements of filial mourning and the disciple's sensitivity to a master's honor:

> For all other dead, if he desires, a man bares his shoulder and if he does not desire he does not bare it; for his father or his mother he must bare his shoulder.[46]
>
> It happened once with a certain "great man of the generation" whose father had died that he desired to bare his shoulder, and another "great man of the generation" desired to bare his too, and on that account he [the mourner] refrained and did not bare his

shoulder. Said Abaye: "The 'great man of the generation' referred
to was Rabbi, and the other 'great man of the generation' was R. Jacob b. Aha. .. . ."[47]

The first sage does not bare his shoulder for his parent when it becomes clear that his companion also intends to join him in what was no
doubt a demeaning procedure. The son then refrains from his own filial
response, preferring to honor the Torah of his comrade though he must
neglect thereby the full range of mourning for his own father. Of
course, the dimensions of the specific embarrassment caused one's
comrade must be weighed against those of the omission of a ritual gesture. But, on balance, it is quite fair to see here another instance of the
value judgment consistently demonstrated in these rabbinic texts. As
Nahmanides concluded, " . . . a disciple ought not to demean himself
in the service of his father."[49] Indeed, R. Akiba refrained from baring
his shoulder at the death of his own father, apparently mindful of his
station as a master of Torah.

We thus see that the dynamic of father-son, master-disciple relationship is a complex one, and cannot be reduced to a simplistic formula. It
is clear, on the one hand, that the master-disciple relationship infuses
new meaning born of growth and maturation into the seemingly static
paternity, and that master becomes father with this new thrust of personal development. Master shares in filial reverence and service, and at
times takes precedence over the natural father. On the other hand, the
significance of physical paternity is, in itself, never diminished; one
does not outgrow the imperative of reverence and service of one's natural parents, despite the attachment to one's master and the quality of
that relationship. What is more, certain sectors of Jewish experience—
such as mourning—remain firmly bound to the biological kinship pattern. There, inclusion of the master would distort the primal stuff of human experience molded by the halakhic structure.

The sensitivity of our topic and its complexity are mirrored in a
query reportedly put to R. Me'ir. The great tanna was himself a student
of R. Elisha b. Abuyah, and faithfully sustained their relationship even
after his master defected from Judaism. After the death of "Aher" ("the
other," as Elisha was called after his defection), the disciples of R. Me'ir
asked him: "Master, if they ask you in the world-to-come, 'Whom do
you want—your father or your master?' what will you say?" The questioners apparently wanted to learn whether after all that had happened
(including signs of heavenly disapproval of Aher) R. Me'ir still considered himself the disciple of his erstwhile master. The story is told in
two sources, and each preserves a different reply. According to the Pa-

lestinian Talmud, R. Me'ir replied, "My master first, and then my father."[49] But according to *Kohellet Rabbah,* he answered, "First father, and then master."[50] From a critical point of view, the former reply seems the more authentic, the latter probably reflecting a pious emendation.[51] But in either case, the story—and the very existence of two versions—reflects an unwillingness to prefer one at the total expense of the other; R. Me'ir takes neither horn of the dilemma, but attempts to capture them both—he would take both men with him into the world-to-come. When both master and father are precious, it is not an easy matter to choose between the two.

IV.

When Son Is Master

R. Akiba, sensitive to his status as a master of Torah, did not "bare the shoulder" in mourning for his father. A new element is now added to our discussion of the conflicting claims of master and parent to filial service and honor: When the son is himself a master of Torah, should he demean himself in the service of his parent, or should the parent honor the son with all the honor due a master of Torah? The question is clearly an unsentimental one, and the Talmud does not solve it by appealing to the feelings of filial concern normally present in the most distinguished of offspring.

In considering the problem of the son who is the Torah-master of his father, the Talmud presents, in the most radical way possible, the full autonomy of that spiritual paternity of which we spoke earlier. Can a relationship so transcend the biological that father becomes son, and son father? The fact that this question is posed is itself evidence of the possibility of standing paternity on end. R. Akiba acted, indeed, as Torah-master of the man who was his father.

Yet, let us beware of taking the instance of R. Akiba as our only model. A different ethos is revealed in the following narrative about R. Eliezer (the master whom R. Akiba mourned so violently and deeply) and his father, a narrative that touches our inquiry at a number of points. This ethos, too, is represented in the talmudic discussion and is in fact codified by Maimonides. The story is told that, already a man in his twenties, Eliezer thirsted to study Torah and was attracted to the school of R. Yohanan ben Zakkai in Jerusalem; he left his home over the strong objections of his wealthy father, who followed the son to Jerusalem with the intention of disinheriting the "prodigal." The arrival of the father, Hyrcanus, coincided with the first, astoundingly masterful lecture of the son. But Hyrcanus did not realize that the young master was in fact his son:

> R. Yohanan ben Zakkai approached [his student] and kissed him on his head, saying: "Praised are Abraham, Isaac, and Jacob, for this man is descended of their loins."
>
> Asked the father of R. Eliezer: "About whom do you speak thus?" "About your son Eliezer."
>
> He said to them: "Is it right that you should say, 'Praised are you, Abraham, Isaac, and Jacob, that this man is descended of your loins?' What should be said is, 'Praised am I, that he has descended from my loins!'"
>
> R. Eliezer continued to teach and remain seated; his father rose before him. He said: "Father, I cannot continue to sit and teach Torah while you stand on your feet." And so he rose and sat his father next to him.[52]

Hycranus rises before his son, acknowledging him a master of Torah, renouncing any claim to filial reverence. But it is at this point that R. Eliezer can—and must—reestablish his filial relationship with his father. He refuses to sit while his father stands, though these contrasting postures do correctly reflect the proper respect to be shown a master of Torah. R. Eliezer does not maintain the prerogatives of the Torah-master, but himself renders the fealty worthy of a son. And so we see that the son, even when he has become his father's master, does not expect the gesture of a disciple from his father. The story of R. Eliezer and his father is a record of relationship in process, and an account of the exemplary consideration of a son for his father's honor. It is not a normative halakhic discussion. Yet, as we have had occasion to see, a norm is often clarified by reference to individual piety; historically, much of the Halakha in the area of filial piety is in fact extrapolated by making of imitation a norm. So, too, in the question of the son who is both son and master, the Talmud atempts to elicit a norm from reasoned observation of events in the lives of the masters. The tale of R. Eliezer is the seed from which a talmudic discussion could have grown.

Sons always do discover that they are wiser than their parents; this discovery is often made more rapidly by the budding scholar. The Talmud warns, of course, against this common arrogance of the schoolhouse, which, perhaps, is intensified when the scholar in question is also a young spiritual virtuoso:

A favorite saying of Raba was: "The goal of wisdom is repentance and good deeds, so that a man should not study Torah and Mishnah and then despise [lit., "kick at"] his father and mother and teacher and superior in wisdom and rank. . . ."[53]

The discussion we are about to consider, on the other hand, presumes recognized filial mastership, and not its semblance.

The scholars propounded: What if his son is his teacher; must the father stand up before him?

Come and hear: For Samuel said to R. Judah: "Keen scholar! Rise before your father!"

R. Ezekiel (father of R. Judah) was different because he had many good deeds to his credit, for even Samuel too stood up before him. . . .[54]

The scholars propounded: What if his son is his teacher; must the father stand up before him?

Come and hear: For R. Joshua b. Levi said: "As for me, it is not meet that I should stand up before my son, but that the honor of the Nasi's house demands it."[55] Thus the reason is that I am his teacher but, if he were my teacher, I should rise before him.[56]

No. He meant thus: As for me, it is not meet that I should stand up before my son, even if he were my master, seeing that I am his father, but that the honor of the Nasi's house demands it.

The questions are asked in ascending order: First, ought a son, who is his father's mentor, to rise in deference before his father?[57] Second, ought the father, in fact, to rise before the son? The second question logically derives from the first, spinning out its possible implications to their fullest. Does the Torah of the son so outweigh his filial responsibility that the father should indeed tender the gesture of respect toward his son, much as he would to any other master?[58] Yet our neat and precise putting of the question and spelling out the conceptual roots of the alternatives, the movement of the logic, does not do justice to the dramatic impact of a father's rising before his son—not only foregoing the honor normally tendered a parent, but bestowing it upon his son. This, as we have pointed out in a number of contexts, in a non-egalitarian society that did not easily waive expressions of filial respect. Torah as value is decisive here, both in the formation of the personal ethos, with its psychological and emotional resonances, and in the articulation of social teaching. Inasmuch as neither query is resolved unambiguously, one cannot say that the Talmud decisively decides the issue.

Yet the fact that the questions were raised is itself most significant.

With respect to the first question—ought a son who is his father's master to rise before his student—the Talmud cites the charge of Samuel to his pupil R. Judah. R. Judah (who was elsewhere urged by Samuel to to be more mindful of his father's feelings) is told to rise before his father, though he was the latter's master.[59] But the Talmud rejects the attempt to generalize from this incident: Samuel himself (and here the Talmud recalls concrete historical data) would rise before R. Judah's father, and so R. Judah was not being urged to filial piety alone.[60] Thus, the incident is not decisive; the Talmud is wary of ruling on the basis of this source that the son must rise before his parent.

The second citation is no less ambiguous. There, however, the initial impression is that some fathers ought generally to rise before their sons. This reading of the ambiguous (and slightly bitter?) comment of R. Joshua b. Levi is then rejected; it is possible, the Talmud argues, to understand his declaration as, in fact, implying that no father should rise before his son, at least not because of the spiritual merits of the latter. Respect for the ruling house, though, is another matter, and prudence may dictate that which Halakha does not.[61] Interestingly, some sources disclose that R. Joshua b. Levi would rise as well before his grandson, R. Meyasha, who had been honored by the Roman administration. The family of R. Joshua, then, was a powerful one and held sensitive posts; the talmudic conclusion that R. Joshua reacted to a specific situation is a most realistic one.[62]

The talmudic discussion is stymied. No conclusion can be reached as to the precedence of the Torah of the son, or his filial status. R. Asher (13th-century Germany) summarizes the situation, and comments upon it:

> "What if his son is his master—must he rise before his father?" This question was not resolved. "What if his son is his master—must the father stand up before him?" Neither was this question resolved. Since these uncertainties concern laws of the Torah, let each rise before the other.[63]
>
> It was said of R. Me'ir of Rothenberg that, from the day he achieved stature, he did not visit his father, nor did he wish that his father visit him.[64]

Inasmuch as the talmudic discussion is indecisive, the priority of neither son nor father can be established, and so R. Asher counsels that each must honor the other.

R. Me'ir of Rothenberg solved the problem by not allowing it to arise—son and father remained apart.[65] R. Me'ir—who was sensitive even to the honor of his students—would doubtless have risen before his father, but (as E. E. Urbach points out[66]) he could not accept homage *from* his parent; and so neither ever visited the other. This rather severe course was doubtless the solution of an individual, an act of personal piety alone; R. Asher, the great pupil of R. Me'ir, prescribes a course of conduct different from the tack taken by his master, and does not even pause to argue his position. But acts of piety become models and then norms: What is a master for, but to inspire our grasp to achieve our reach? In the 16th century, one finds scholars wrestling with the conduct of R. Me'ir, now understood as a halakhic precedent.

The two major discussants were R. Soloman Luria (Maharshal) and R. Moses Isserles (Ramah), and they questioned both the propriety of R. Me'ir's own behavior and its usefulness as a precedent. Ramah focussed on the narrower halakhic questions that could be raised, while Maharshal emphasized the broader implications. As might be expected, the resolutions achieved by these two thinkers reflect the scope of their respective problems.

R. Moses Isserles is troubled by R. Me'ir's failure to simply waive the honor due him (*mehila,* while not cited in our context by the Talmud itself, which maintained an ideal, unsentimental, posture, is cited elsewhere) and thus continue a normal relationship with his father, and his choice of the much more radical break with his father. For Ramah, the solution, which requires some biographical speculation, is a conceptual one, and lies in a necessary restriction of the scope of *mehila* and its applicability:

> . . . Why did R. Me'ir not forego the honor due him? . . . It appears to me that R. Me'ir reasoned that . . . in public, one must consider those people who do not recognize his father. But it seems to me that where the father is known to the townspeople, the son is permitted to forego the honor due him[66]

Thus the behavior of R. Me'ir assumes normative dimensions; in certain circumstances the son is expected to avoid the presence of his father, as R. Me'ir did. Ramah adds the proviso, however, that the son may waive his honor to his father when the latter is known by the townsfolk.

R. Joseph Karo recorded the opinion of R. Asher in his code, and R. Moses Isserles added the following note:

> If the son wishes to waive the honor due him and serve his father,

he may do so, for a teacher's honor is his to waive. But this only applies in intimate situations, or to public situations where the master's father is well-known to the townspeople as his father. If, however, the son is a Torah-scholar of great renown and the father is not known to the townspeople as such, one must consider the possible degradation of Torah if the son demeans himself before his father; and so, the two ought to place some distance between themselves so that neither may show disesteem of the other. . . .[67]

Maharshal was also perplexed by the neglected option of *mehila,* as his closing comments will indicate. But his chief concern in considering the behavior of R. Me'ir and projecting it as a norm, is the difficulty in assuming that filial respect could be constructively achieved by filial absence; such conduct, he argued, wins the battle but loses the war, as the honor thus tendered is more than offset by the pain that is its price. And so he, too, is forced to restrict the implications of R. Me'ir's conduct; but in contrast with Ramah, the determining factor is not the possibility of *mehila,* but an evaluation of the total situation and the causes and dimensions of parental hurt:

> It would appear to me that such conduct [is proper] for one in the situation of R. Me'ir of Rothenberg, since they [father and son] were not living in the same place. But one for whom this is impossible, need not leave his father's home. This is especially true where the father is very much attached to his son, whose departure would be bitter to him as death. Rather, let the son rise before the father, and let him forego [*yimhol*] the honor due him [as a master of Torah], though the father should indicate respect of the son.[68]

The discussion thus concluded outlines the approach of the German and Polish schools in medieval times. Distinctly different is the tack taken by Maimonides. He apparently felt that the talmudic material lent itself to a more decisive reading, and so recorded the following in the *Yad:*

> If the father is the student of his son, he does not rise before his son; rather, the son rises before his father, though the latter is his student.[69]

Maimonides interprets Samuel's charge to R. Judah at face value, and rejects the Talmud argumentation as indecisive.[70] Such evaluation of talmudic material for codificatory purposes is not at all rare.[71] Furthermore, the ethos thus articulated is endorsed by the numerous instances of service and honor rendered by talmudic sages to their parents; indeed, these stories, perhaps more than the generalized norms, characterized rabbinic filial piety and served as its models. No doubt these sages were their parents' superior in learning, yet this fact was irrelevant. Thus the commentators point to the episodes of filial service and self-demeaning activity on behalf of the sages' mothers —certainly not their sons' equals in learning and probably not in piety either.

Maimonides declares firmly that a son who is his father's master remains in all respects and responsibilities a son—bound to the same expressions of loyalty and reverence as any other child. The father is, of course, expected to render due homage to any master of Torah and, as we saw, any son must honor his own master before his father. But the honor due a master is transcended by the filial reverence of a son for his father when son and master are one and the same person. A father ought never to rise for his son; it is doubtless significant that the instance of R. Joshua b. Levi, who rose before his patriarchally connected son, is not cited by Maimonides. Apparently he felt that while prudence may have urged such respect for the Patriarchate, the Jewish ethos should have nothing of it.

It becomes clear in analyzing the Maimonidean posture (and to the degree that it is ambivalent, the talmudic posture as well) that a delicate and meaningful balance has emerged. The honoring of one's parent can conflict with the honor due a master of Torah in two contexts: when the master of Torah is a third person and when the son is himself the master. In the former case, the son is taught to prefer his master to his father: he will, say, retrieve his master's loss before his father's, or even redeem his master from captivity before his father. But when the son is himself his father's master, his responsibility to his father outweighs the esteem he might normally expect as a master of Torah: thus, the son rises before his father, not the reverse. Apparently, the personal element is decisive. It is not Torah alone that is primary, but its crystallization in a concrete individual—another individual. A gesture of recognition of the other is essential; a son can prefer only his master to his father, not himself. Reverting to the idiom of the Mishnah, his master bestowed upon him "the life of the world-to-come," just as his father bestowed upon him the "life of this world." Alone, he could have achieved neither. Thus, the spiritual-personal growth that may set up centers of personal loyalty and valence which transcend the filial ones is not to be understood as growth away from the filial nexus, but more significantly as growth toward a new, deeper center of meaning and value.[72]

Notes

1 See, e.g., Deuteronomy 32:6, 14:1; Hosea 11:1; Psalms 68:6, 89:27, 103:13; Exodus 4:22; Jeremiah 31:18,35:14; Isaiah 62:13,64:7,63:6.

2 Malachi 1:6.

3 *Sefer Ben-Sira ha-Shalem,* ed. M. Z. Segal (Jerusalem: 1953), pp. 13–14.

4 *Ibid.,* p. 13; M. D. Cassutto, "Kibbud Av ve'Aim," *Enzyklopedia Mikra'it,* IV. p. 78.

5 Sibyllene Oracles 3:594 (*Ha-Sefarim ha-Hizoni'im,* ed. A. Kahana [Tel-Aviv: 1936–1937], II, p. 402).

6 Josephus (*Antiquities,* IV, 262 [Loeb Classics, trans. H. Thackeray, IV, p. 603]) imagines the parents of a rebellious son (*ben sorer*) saying, ". . . God is Himself distressed at acts of effrontery to a father, since He Himself is father of the whole human race and regards himself as a partner in the indignity done to those who bear the same title as Himself, when they obtain not from their children the honor that is their due." Compare this passage with the rabbinic teaching, *Kiddushin* 30b, cited *infra* n. 7. Josephus's version is characteristically depersonalized. Elsewhere, Josephus describes Isaac as "showing a devoted filial service and a zeal for the worship of God" (*Ibid.,* I, 222 [IV, p. 110]). In the *Contra Apion,* he echoes Aristaeas: "Honor to parents the Law ranks second only to honor to God. . . ." (II. 205; Loeb Classics, I, 377). Cf. nn. 39–43, *infra.*

Considering the ubiquity of the formula linking respect to God with filial piety, perhaps Jesus' statement (Matthew 22:39) that love of fellow ranks next to love of God ought to be read as a polemical response to the common Jewish hierarchy of God/parents. This would be consistent with other, related attitudes expressed in the Gospels; see Chapter VI, n. 19.

Philo, *The Special Laws,* II, section 235 (Loeb Classics, trans. F. Colson, VII, p. 453), and *infra.*

7 *Kiddushin* 30b.

8 H. Wheeler Robinson, *Inspiration and Revelation in the Old Testament,* (Oxford: 1946), 25–28, who cites other material as well. Since filial responsibility is not a specifically Jewish or revelational concept, it is most apt that the rabbis focus on God as creator of universal life, rather than on God as father of the people Israel. Cf. also Oliver Shaw Rankin, *Israel's Wisdom Literature* (Edinburgh: 1936), p. 10.

9 *Sifre Deuteronomy,* 32 (ed. Finkelstein, p. 54).

10 P. *Kil'ayim* 8:4; 31c; *Niddah* 31a; *Kohellet Rabbah* 5:10 (where it is discussed by R. Judah the Prince). These midrashic teachings are discussed at length by E. E. Urbach, *Hazal, Pirkei Emunot veDe'ot.* 190ff. The *baraita* was later applied to Job 2:10, which speaks of the preservation of life: see *Midrash Job,* par. 33 (S. Wertheimer, ed., *Batei Midrashot,* II, 172).

11 The passage cited is composed of a number of segments:
   (a) "Honor . . . against the Lord";
   (b) "All this . . . partners in the creation of a man";
   (c) "The rabbis taught . . . his mother";
   (d) "When a man . . . they would pain me."
The distribution of these segments in the sources at our disposal is as follows:

	Kid. 30b	Sifra ed. Weiss 86d	Mekhilta ed. Horowitz p. 232	p. Pe'ah 1:1; 15c	p. Kil'ayim 8:4; 31c	Niddah 31a
(a)	x	x	x	x		
(b)	x	x		x		
(c)	x				x	x
(d)	x					

There are minor stylistic variations even between those sources we have registered as identical. Despite these, it is clear that the first half of *Kiddushin* 30b draws upon *Sifra*, and that the basis for equating divine and parental honor in the sharing of the creative role among all three is already tannaitic, as our citation from Josephus (n. 6) confirms. (Other stylistic similarities further indicate the reliance upon the *Sifra-*, rather than the *Mekhilta*-source.) (c) is presented in expanded form in p. *Kil'ayim* 31c: "The white matter is of man—from that are formed the brain, the bones, and the veins; the red matter is of the woman—from that comes the skin, the flesh, and the blood; life, and the spirit, and the soul are of God. And they are all partners in him." This is further inflated in *Niddah* 31a, which concludes, "When man's time comes to depart from the world, God takes back his share, and leaves the share of the parents before them." (See L. Ginzberg, *Legends of the Jews*, VI, p. 42, n. 224.) With regard to later sources: *Mekhilta d'RSBI*, p. 152, is based on *Midrash ha-Gadol* mss.; *Pesikta Rabbati* XXIII, p. 122b, follows *Sifra Kiddushin* 30b. See also *She'iltot*, 56, and *Ha'amek She'alah*, n. 4.

12 A later midrash (*Pesikta Rabbati, op. cit.*) tells that the nations of the world were unimpressed by the Ten Commandments, until they heard the fifth, commanding filial piety: "According to our laws, if a man enrolls himself as a servant of the king, he thereby disowns his parents. God, however, makes it a duty to honor father and mother." In other sources it is clear that that duty itself redounds to the honor of God. My translation follows Ginzberg, *Legends*, III, p. 100; he adds, however, "truly, for this is honor due to Him," which is not in the text.

13 *Kiddushin* 31b.

14 M. Noth, *Exodus*, p. 165; M. Cassutto, *op. cit.*, and *Perush 'al Sefer Shemot*, p. 170. Cassutto adopts the Philonic-Nahmanidean exegesis, stressing the pivotal role of this command. See also G. Harrelson, *Interpreter's Dictionary of the Bible*, IV, pp. 569b, 571a.

15 *Mekhilta*, p. 233. See also p. *Shekalim* 6:1; 49c for other views.

16   Nahmanides, *Commentary* to Exodus 20:12–13 (*Perush ha-Ramban*, ed. C. Chavel, I, pp. 403–404). The dual character of this imperative is reflected in the contrasting stances adopted by Nahmanides in this long passage. There is no inconsistency here, however; see R. Isaac Abarbanel, *Commentary, ad loc.* A Halakhic reflection of this duality emerges in the question of the 19th century R. Joseph Babad: Is *kibbud av* to be categorized as a command "between man and man," or as one "between man and God"? See *Minhat Hinukh*, 33(end).

17   *On the Decalogue*, sec. 106–107, 120; *The Special Laws*, II, sec. 225 (*Philo, The Special Laws*, pp. 61, 68–69, 447).

18   *Laws*, trans. A. E. Taylor, XI, section 931a-d (*Plato, The Collected Works*, ed. E. Hamilton, pp. 1481–1482). Classical material paralleling the Jewish filial ethic is presented in I. Heinemann, *Philons Griechische u. Judishe Bildung*, pp. 231–261.

19   *Ethics*, trans. W. D. Ross, IX, Chapter 2, sec. 1165a (*Introduction to Aristotle*, ed. R. McKeon, p. 499). The equation of parent with God is a very old motif; the "the Mesopotamian is constantly admonished, 'Pay heed to the word of thy mother as to the word of thy god' (T. Jacobsen, in H. Frankfort, ed., *Before Philosophy* [Penguin ed.]. p. 217)": The idea remained a commonplace: Sempronius, a 2nd century C. E. Egyptian, wrote his brother that they should "worship her who bore us as it were a god. . . ." (A. Deissmann, *Light From the East*, p. 195).

20   See Heinemann, *op. cit.*; L. Ginzberg, *Legends*, VI, p. 42; Philo also states (II, 2, p. 307) that "parents are copies and likenesses of the divine power."

21   The Philonic formula was taken verbatim into the Catechism of the Council of Trent (1563), iii.5.1.

22   *Exodus Rabbah* 30:5.

23   For the correlation of God-king-father in Philo, see E. Goodenough, *The Politics of Philo Judaeus*, pp. 95–97.

24   From the ethical will of Eleazar of Mainz as translated by I. Abrahams, *Hebrew Ethical Wills*, II, pp. 207–218.

25   Many biblical texts speak of "the Lord who took you out of the land of Egypt," and while this warrants more than gratitude, it certainly includes it. See G. Mendenhall, "Covenant Forms in Israelite Tradition," *Biblical Archaeologist*, XVII, 3 (1954), esp. pp. 58, 63.

26   Y. Mansour, *Bar-Ilan*, III (1965), pp. 263–265.

27   On the verb *gamal*, here translated "requite" (as in both new and old JPS), see Brown, Driver, Briggs, *Lexicon of the Old Testament*, *s.v.* "gamal," p. 168, ic. See also Isaiah 1:2.

28   It is likely that God is seen not only as father, but as mother too: "You forgot God who brought you to birth" is a possible translation of Deuteronomy 32:18 (Oxford-Cambridge version). This is the "climax of ingratitude" (Driver,

I. C. C., p. 363–364), as the people reject in one figure both father and mother. Note *Sifre, ad loc.*, especially the comment of R. Me'ir (ed. Finkelstein, p. 365, line 15).

29 *Sifre, ad loc.*, sec. 309.

30 See especially Deut. 32:5, 6, 11, 13, 15, 18–20.

31 The Midrash telescopes two levels of the appeal for filial regard: first, gratitude for the good done the child by the parent, for his care and concern; next— implying that these moral considerations may not impress—fear lest he be disinherited. The rabbis, incidentally, were quite aware of the persuasiveness of inheritance and disinheritance; it is said that honor rendered to the dead parent is true, disinterested honor, for "they are honored in their lifetimes only because they are feared, and because of the inheritance. . . ." (*Semahot* 9:21, ed. Higger, p. 177. *Cf. Genesis Rabbah.* sec. 96 [in Vatican ms.], ed. Theodore-Albeck, III, p. 1239.). No illusions here, though the context—the desire to encourage proper funerals—doubtless contributed to the extreme formulation.

The rabbis do not complete the application of the parable by saying that God will reject Israel and "make another his heir" or his favorite (a more appropriate phrase). Is this due to general national loyalty, or is there a special sensitivity to the Christian's claim that *his* community in fact represents the "new Israel"?

32 M. *Baba Mezia* 2:11.

33 P. *Kiddushin* 1:7; 61a. I have taken *teman taninan,* which introduces the citation, to refer to M. *Eduyyot,* with the parallel to the *baraita* of filial duties (see Chapter II at length) being of amoraic authorship. It is possible, however, that the statement in its entirety is a late *baraita* (itself utilizing tannaitic material), as *teman taninan* can so function as well: see Y. N. Epstein, *Mavo le-Nusah ha-Mishnah,* pp. 888–891, esp. p. 891.

34 In *Midrash Numbers Rabbah* 17:1, five parental duties are listed, corresponding to the list of five filial duties.

35 This passage is found in two tractates of the Palestinian Talmud, *Pe'ah* and *Kiddushin,* but a slight variation—one letter—distinguishes the doublet. The former has, "an act that is the payment of a debt"; the latter has, "an act that is *like* the payment of a debt". Was the *kaph* ("like") dropped by a careless copyist, or was it added by one sensitive to the mercantile connotations of the vocabulary used?

36 P. *Pe'ah* 1:1, 15d; p. *Kiddushin* 1:7, 61b; *Pesikta Rabbati* XXIII, 121b.

37 *Exodus Rabbah* 32:5. Actually, God does not desire that His concern evoke gratitude alone, but that it bring forth the filial relationship in its totality; see below. This verbal acknowledgment was understood as an important indicator of the reality: see Jeremiah 3:19 and *Code of Hammurabi,* sec. 192 (Pritchard, *Ancient Near Eastern Texts relating to the Old Testament,* p. 175); Nahmanides to Exodus 20:12.

38 "And now we come to honor to be shown to parents while they are yet in

life. Here religion demands the due discharge of this earliest and heaviest debt, the most sacred of all our obligations. It bids a man count all he has and owns at the service of those who gave him birth and breeding, to minister to their needs to his utmost ability, first with his substance, then with his body, and then with his mind, in repayment of a loan of care and painful labor made so long ago on the security of his youth, and now to be made good to his elders in their age and sore necessity. Moreover, all his life through a man should observe particular reverence of tongue toward his parents, for light and winged speech brings heavy doom; right has her appointed messengers, Nemeses, to keep watch over the matter. So one should yield to them when they feel anger, and discharge it, in word or deed. . . .'' (Plato, *Laws*, IV, sec. 717b-d.) See also Aristotle, *Ethics*, VIII, 1163b (pp. 494–5), and IX, 1165a (pp. 498–9); *Oeconomica* I.ii.2, 1343b (pp. 331–3); see Heinemann, *op. cit.*

39   *Ben-Sira* 7:28–29.

40   *Letter of Aristaeas*, 228 (Kahana, *Ha-Sefarim ha-Hizoni'im*, II, p. 59).

41   *Tobit* 4:3–4 (*Ibid.*, p. 321).

42   Josephus, *Contra Apion* II, 206 (Loeb Classics, I, 377).

43   Josephus—like Philo—may betray here the influence of *patria potestas*. See Heinemann, p. 251, Chapter II, n. 2a (end); see also A. H. Freimann, "Ben Sorer," *Enzyklopedia Mikra'it*, II, pp. 161–162.

44   See also *Antiquities* IV, 261 (L. C., IV, 601).

45   Philo, *Special Laws*, II, sec. 229–231 (L. C., VII, 449–451).

46   Philo, *Decalogue*, sec. 112, p. 118; *Special Laws*, II, sec. 248 (L. C., VII, 63, 67, 461–463). Though the very nature of this monograph stresses the theme held in common by both the rabbis and Philo, the point ought to be made—as Heinemann and Goodenough, *Jurisprudence of the Jewish Courts in Egypt*, pp. 68–76, show—that the Philonic treatment, read as a whole, bears the unmistakable imprint of Hellenistic, rather than rabbinic thought. For example, Philo claims that "parents have received authority over their children," and not that alone, but also "the power of a master corresponding to the two . . . forms under which servants are owned. . . ." (*Special Laws*, II, sec. 231, 233.) The rabbis do claim that children should serve their parents in menial and even servile tasks, but to predicate the relationship on this analogy, even in part, would be alien to them. But see Belkin, *The Alexandrian Halakha in Apologetic Literature of the First Century C. E.*, pp. 55–57. Goodenough also cites Philo's suggestion that parents "upbraid their children and admonish them severely and if they do not submit to threats . . . to beat and degrade them and put them in bonds . . . (sec. 232)," as foreign in tone and substance to the Jewish ethos. Yet such suggestions could easily be read out of certain biblical passages (Proverbs 23:13-14; 13:24; Deuteronomy 21:18; 1 Kings 1:5-6) and is also reflected in rabbinic sources (see Mishnah *Makkot* 2:2). For the later development, cf. Chapter V; Chapter IV, n. 69.

47   *Sefer Emunot veDe'ot* (*Book of Beliefs and Opinions*), III, 2 (trans. Rosenblatt, p. 141). Rav Sa'adiah (cited in Ibn Ezra, Exodus 21:16) explains the ban on kidnapping and its positioning in the text as deterrents of situations where children will not know their parents. The Midrash (*Numbers Rabbah* 9:8) indicts adulterers similarly. Aristotle rejects Socrates' ideal community of wives because of the difficulties arising from the lack of clear paternal and filial identification, among them the "impiety" of quarreling or striking those who are (unbeknownst to us) our parents (*Politics*, II, Chapter 4, 1262a).

48   *Commentary* to Exodus 20:2. Cf. also at Deuteronomy 21:13.

49   *Sefer ha-Hinnukh, Mitzvah* 33.

50   *Sefer Emunot veDe'ot*, III, 1 (p. 139).

51   R. Bahya b. Asher (14th century Spain) is more bluntly explicit: "The imperative of *kibbud av* has as its goal the honor of the Prime Father . . . for His mercies to His creatures are greater than those of the natural father to his son" (*Kad ha-Kemmah* [Ostrau: 1793], *Kaf*, p. 53d). Note the utilization of the motif of gratitude as well.

52   As we have seen, gratitude is considered both rational and socially expected.

53   *Hovot ha-Levavot*, III, Introduction.

54   The rabbis will attribute selfish motives to prospective parents, but these statements are doubtless sermonic and one-sided. At any rate, I did not find the rabbis questioning the propriety of filial piety on that basis—perhaps because they never predicate it solely on gratitude! "Whoso curses his father or his mother, his lamp shall be put out in the blackest darkness" (Proverbs 20:20)—R. Judah b. Nahman and R. Levi. One said, it is like a man who bought a knife to cut meat. The knife fell on his finger and cut it. He said, "I bought this knife to enjoy it—did I buy it to cut my finger?" So too a man produces offspring only for his honor, and these curse him. . . . The other said, it is like a man who lights a candle so as to use its light, and it burned his coat. He said, "I lit this candle to enjoy its light, not to be burnt by it; so too a man produces offspring only to enlarge his honor, and not to diminish it" (*Midrash Samuel* VII: 1). Given an ethos of filial piety and concern, it was only natural for a parent to expect his children to provide for his old age. Talmudic law, in fact, allows a wife to claim both divorce and marriage settlement from her impotent husband on the grounds that she wants "a staff to lean on and a hoe to dig my grave" (*Yevamot* 65b).

55   *Avot* 4:29.

56   IV Ezra 8:5.

57   John Milton, *Paradise Lost*, X, lines 743–746; 762.

58   This attitude is rooted in the biblical account of creation: "And God saw everything that He had made, and behold, it was very good." See E. E. Urbach, *Hazal*, pp. 224–226.

59   Xenophon, *Memorabilia*, II.ii.

60   *Antiquities,* IV, 261 (L. C., IV, 601). Josephus merely replaces one form of self-gratification with another.

61   *Leviticus Rabbah* 14:10.

62   R. Israel b. Joseph Alnakawa, *Menorat ha-Ma'or* (ed. H. Enelow), IV, 18; *Orhot Zaddikim,* Chapter 5 (New York: 1946), p. 35. This last passage continues to say that a man should love his parents "because through them he fulfills the divine command to honor his father and mother." This extreme formulation is not necessarily a late-medieval phenomenon; compare the following talmudic passage: "For no relatives does a man rend [his clothes in mourning] so as to expose his breast, only for his father and mother. . . . This is because he now loses the *mitzvah* of honor [*kibbud*] (p. *Mo'ed Katon* 3:8; 83d)."

63   See Chapter V.

64   R. Abraham Danzig, *Hayye Adam,* 67:2. The author is obviously aware of the passage in *Hovót ha-Levavot* cited above, and attempts a stronger rejection of the claim raised therein.

It is most interesting to note that contemporaries of R. Abraham Danzig opposed to Hasidism (and perhaps the Gaon of Vilna himself) accused their opponents of rejecting the parental claim in precisely the same language: "They do not practice filial piety at all, for they say, 'Because my father wanted to satisfy his lust, was I born, similarly my mother. . . .'" *Hayye Adam* was published in 1810; the comment cited above, in 1800. Is the passage in *Hayye Adam* part of the same polemic? See M. Wilenski, *Hassidim u-Mitnagdim,* I, pp. 275–276.

65a   *What Is Political Philosophy?* [Glencoe, Ill.: 1959], pp. 12–13.

65b   Tannaitic opinion was apparently divided on the meaning of this promised reward. R. Jacob took it as a reference to personal well-being in "the world that is only good . . . the world that endures" (*Kiddushin* 39b). But another, earlier(?) tannaitic comment reads: "'. . . on the land which the Lord your God is giving you'—when you [plural form] are on the land, there is length of days, and blessing is found; but blessing is not found in the exile or in foreign settlements" (*Midrash Tanna'im.* ed. D. Hoffmann, p. 23). See M. *Kiddushin* 1:10, and H. Albeck, *Mishnah, Nashim,* p. 413; see also *Berakhot* 8a.

It has often been suggested that "length of days" is the qualitative enrichment of one's life by the enjoyment of the filial regard of one's own children, a trait they have acquired through imitation of their parents' filial piety. This reading may even be at the heart of the midrash (cited by M. M. Kasher, *Torah Shelemah,* XV. p. 97, n. 314, from *Bet ha-Midrash,* VI): "If you observe [the first part of the verse and] 'honor your father and your mother,' I will fulfill for you 'that your days may be lengthened,' but if you don't, I will fulfill 'in thee have they made light of father and mother (Ezekiel 22:7).'" The placement of punishment and reward in opposition suggests that the reward, too, is to be found in a modality of the parent-child relationship. Philo writes of the filial service of young storks, who "moved by piety and the expectation that the same treatment

will be meted to them by their offspring repay the debt that they may not refuse . . ." (*Decalogue*, sec. 117). As we shall see, analogous conduct is demanded by Philo of man.

66   M. *Pe'ah* 1:1, and *Commentary* of Maimonides *ad loc.* My rendering follows the Hebrew translation of Y. Kapah, *Mishnah 'Im Perush ha-Rambam*, I,
54.

67   *Code, Hilkhot Me'ilah* 8:8; see also *Commentary to Mishnah*, "Introduction to *Avot* " (*Shemoneh Perakim*), Chapter 6, and n. 62.

68   *Guide for the Perplexed*, trans. M. Friedlander, III, p. 41. S. Pines, *Guide*,
p. 562, renders the passage thus: " . . . destroying the good order of the
household, which is the first part of the city," identifying the crucial element as
"order." It is interesting, in this connection, that Maimonides includes the laws
of filial piety in the section of his *Code* called *Hilkhot Mamrim*, "Laws of Rebellion"; they are found there in Chapters 5 and 6, following four chapters that deal
with the "rebellious elder" (Deuteronomy 17:8–13). But there are adequate
structural reasons for this. Maimonides codifies the laws concerning the "rebellious son" (Deuteronomy 21:18–21) in this section (Chapter 7), and the general
expectation of filial piety and its conditions find their natural place as a preface to
these (in itself, an interesting juxtaposition).

69   *Laws*, 790b, p. 1362.

70   *Oeconomica*, I.i; II. i, etc.; *Politics*, I. xii. 1259b.

71   Maimonides, *Treatise on Logic*, trans. I. Efros, p. 63. See also Philo, Special Laws, II, 226–7, 234 (pp. 447–9, 453); L. Strauss, *Persecution and the Art
of Writing*, pp. 131–32.

72   *Commentary to the Torah* (Venice: 1547), p. 77c.

73   *Commentary to the Torah* (Warsaw: 1862). II, p. 38c. This theme remains
popular; see S. R. Hirsch, *Commentary to the Pentateuch*, II, pp. 274–6; J.
Hertz, *Pentateuch*, p. 299; R. Me'ir Simha of Dvinsk, *Meshekh Hokhmah*, p.
159a.

74   *'Ikkarim*, III, p. 26.

75   *Genesis Rabbah*, 87:7 (ed. Theodore-Albeck, III, 1073). The biblical text
(Genesis 39:7–18) ought to be consulted here, for the midrash is rooted in the
two attempts at seduction, with Joseph's response varying in each case. On vi-
sions of the "image of one's father" in preventing sin (as a psychological phenomenon), see J. C. Flugel, *Man, Morals, and Society* (Penguin ed.), pp.
67–68. Some mss. read, "The image of his *mother* (!) appeared to him," reflecting the view of R. Abun that "the image of Rachel" was also seen by Joseph (p.
Horayyot 2:6, 46d).

76   *Kitvei Ramban*, ed. C. Chavel, I, pp. 369–371.

77   For the broad periphery of the filial metaphor, see, for example, *Bezah* 4b;
Pesahim 50b; *Yalkut Shim'oni* to Proverbs 22:28; *Hovot ha-Levavot*, V, 5; the

Introduction—and very title—of R. Menahem ha-Me'iri, *Magen Avot* ("Defense of the Fathers"). For the metaphor as a sign of stultification, see *Hullin* 13b (R. Yohanan apparently utilized the idea with both significations). Many religious reformers will argue in their initial revolutionary periods that excessive respect for parental custom has corrupted the religion; it is so with Islam and Karaism, for example. The counterreaction will sometimes be a renewed stress on parental custom as a sactioning force. Generally, the polemic context ought to be kept in mind when interpreting certain passages; see, e.g., *Mishnat R. Eliezer* (ed. H. Enelow), p. 249; also Chapter IV, n. 25; Chapter VI, n. 19.

78   See A. C. Lovejoy. *Primitivism and Related Ideas in Antiquity*, especially pp. 11–15, 103–117, 447–456. On the modern Hebrew use of *tevah*, for "nature," see L. Zunz, *Synagogale Poesie*, pp. 634–6; L. Ginzberg, "Notes," in I. Efros, *Philosophical Terms in the Moreh Nebukhim*, p. 134; E. Ben-Yehudah, *Dictionary*, IV, p. 1842, especially n. 1.

79   The literature on this topic is truly voluminous. Two recent discussions are those of H. Wolfson, *Philo*, II, pp. 165–200, and H. Koester, "Nomos Fuseos," in *Religions in Antiquity*, ed. J. Neusner, pp. 521–541.

80   See n. 91.

81   *'Eruvin* 100 b. See also Ginzberg, *Legends*, I, 43, and Proverbs 30:24–28. My translation of Job 35:11 follows R. Hiyya's midrashic treatment; the verse is usually understood by translators and exegetes to mean just the opposite: "Who teaches us more than the beasts of the earth, and makes us wiser than the fowls of heaven?" See also V. Aptowitzer, "Rewarding . . . of animals, . . ." *HUCA*, III (1926), pp. 117ff., who concludes that the standard aggadic view endows animals "with the power of reason and morality."

82   *Ketubot* 49b.

83   *Sotah* 49a.

84   *Sanhedrin* 72b.

85   Elsewhere, however, we find talmudic affirmation of the ubiquity of filial concern and love even in the throes of conflict: " 'A Psalm of David when he fled from Absolom his son—'A Psalm of David'? He ought to have said: 'A Lamentation of David'! R. Simeon b. Abishalom said. . . . 'When the Holy One, Blessed be He, said to David, "Behold, I will raise up evil against thee out of thine own house," he began worrying. He thought: It may be a slave or a bastard who will have no pity on me. When he saw it was Absalom, he was glad, and therefore he said: "A Psalm." ' " (*Berakhot* 7b). Many mss. (cf. *Dikduke Soferim*, n. 2) add: "for a son has mercy on his father."

86   P. *Pe'ah* 1:1; 15d.

87   See *Ketubot* 49b, where the Talmud states (according to Rashi) that the white, immature ravens are not accepted by their parents, while the black, more mature offspring are accepted. The eagle is the classic rabbinic example of self-sacrificing parenthood, so solicitous of its young that it bears them aloft on its

wings, presenting its own body as a target to hunters below. See Rashi to Exodus 19:40.

88   For a more extended discussion of some of the texts noted here and the problem surrounding them, see M. Kadushin, *Worship and Ethics*, pp. 39–57, and S. Schwarszchild, "Do Noahides Have to Believe in Revelation," *Jewish Quarterly Review*, LII, 4 (April 1962), pp. 297–308; LIII, 1 (July 1962), pp. 30–65. A facile identification of Noahide law, *mishpatim,* and "natural law" is too often made.

89   Note, however, Maimonides (n. 91), who does, apparently, integrate filial piety into this category; and see R. Joshua, *infra* (n. 92–93), which may provide a source.

Generally, any medieval thinker who argued the social and ethical benefits of filial piety, as we have seen Sa'adiah and Maimonides do (see section 2 above), is of course urging the rationality of the imperative, and categorizing it either as a *mitzvah sikhlit* ("rational command") or as a universally conventional norm.

90   The *Book of Jubilees* (c. 125 B.C.E.) does describe the dying Noah as commanding his children to do justice, cover their nakedness, bless God, honor their parents, love their neighbors, and avoid sexual sins, impurity, and robbery (7:20–21), and these may represent elements of a list of common human duties; K. Kohler, "Jubilees, Book of," *Jewish Encyclopedia*, VII, p. 302. On the other hand, the author of *Jubilees* projects much of the Sinaitic legislation back to Patriarchal and even Noahide times; thus Noah continues (7:35–37) to command his children the laws of *'orlah* and *reva'i* (see Leviticus 19:23–25). It thus becomes difficult to speak of a Noahide law in *Jubilees* (C. Albek, Buch der Jubilaen, [Berlin: 1930], pp. 34–35).

91   The Seven Commands of the Noahides may be distinguished from the *mishpatim,* despite their many points of contact, and not only because the former contain two imperataves more than the list of the latter. The Noahide Laws are presented only as imperatives (the term *mitzvah* is significant here, as well as the statement that the Noahides "accepted the commands" [*Baba Kamma* 38a]), and never as the "internal law." *Mishpatim,* on the other hand, while "written" and deriving their authority from that fact, nonetheless are presented as "worthy of having been written even if they had not been written," or as being discovered by unaided humanity. Indeed, these different formulations ("seven commands," "worthy of being written . . . ") may represent different approaches or stresses in the question of morality and revelation-command. Interestingly, neither list includes elements of *hesed*—mercy, love, kindness. Some of the most weighty medieval authories did identify the two: Maimonides, of course, wrote that *"da'at* inclines" to the seven commands—but he insisted that they were *commands*, and should be observed on that rather than their rational basis (*Code, Melakhim*, 8:11, 9:1); cf. n. 88 *supra*. Surprisingly, it is among those not usually counted among the "rationalists" of Jewish thought that one finds the more thoroughgoing identification: R. Jacob Tam claimed that the "seven commands are among those things that 'were worthy of being written' " (cited in R. Bezalel

Ashkenazi, *Shittah Mekubezet* to *Baba Kamma* 87a in a passage that may otherwise be corrupt); and Nahmanides wrote,

> ". . . according to our masters the rabbis, antediluvian man was commanded concerning . . . the seven commands from the time of Adam, and they elicited from them Scriptural hints. . . . According to the plain-sense, these are "rational commands" and ought be heeded by every creature who knows his creator. . . . (*"Torat Hashem Temimah,"* in *Kitvei Ramban*, ed. Chavel, I, 173).

92   *Mekhilta, Vayassa* 1 (ed. Horowitz-Rabin, p. 156), to *Exodus* 15:25. My citation of biblical verses reflects the tannaitic exegesis. See the editor's notes for other rabbinic parallels to this view.

93   R. El'azar of Modi'im understood these terms differently: "*Hok*—these are the laws of forbidden sexual unions; *Mishpat*—these are the laws of assaults, and fines, and damages" (*Mekhilta, ad loc.*). Does R. El'azar disagree as to the *mishpat* quality of filial piety? Or is he simply pointing to the more usual uses of the term *mishpat* as designating civil law? We also note his assertion that *arayot* (forbidden sexual unions) are an instance of *hok*, in contrast to the *baraita Yoma* 67b that considered it *mishpat*. See Maimonides, *Commentary to the Mishnah, Introduction to Avot (Shemoneh Perakim)*, Chapter VI (ed. Kapah, *Nezikin*, p. 258, especially n. 14).

94   *Mekhilta, Massekhta de-Bahodesh*, 8, p. 232. The parallel, *Kiddushin* 30b-31a, lacks the significant phrase, "Where a deficiency exists—he filled it;" see below.

95   For bibliographic data, see S. Baron, *A Social and Religious History of the Jews* (2nd ed.), I, p. 310, n. 20.

96   It is indeed strange to find the very verses distorted in an attempt to impose a patriarchal pattern on biblical filial piety. Thus, Theodore Reik writes, "Judaism remained a father religion. The intense and revivified need to 'Honor thy father', . . .(!)" (*The Temptation*, p. 230). And Erich Fromm speaks of the "biblical demand of obedience to father" (*You Shall Be As Gods*, p. 75). The anayltical distinction between Judaism as a "father-religion," and Christianity as a "mother-religion" is not our present concern.

97   Heinemann, *Philons* . . . , pp. 250–252. There is another, more puzzling midrashic treatment of these verses: "Honor your father and your mother"—further on (Leviticus 19:3) the reverence for one's mother is mentioned before that of one's father, and here, in connection with honor, the father is mentioned before the mother. R. Joshua of Sikhnin said in the name of R. Levi: "In the Tent of Meeting (*Ohel Mo'ed*), where the gentiles could not hear, he mentioned father before mother to the exclusion of the gentile, who has no paternity" (*Pesikta Rabbati*, p. 123a).

The text, as it stands, is quite difficult; for it was at Sinai, where God spoke publicly and the whole world could hear, that "father" precedes "mother." Consequently M. Friedmann, the editor of the text, emended it to read, "In the Tent of Meeting, . . . he mentioned mother before father," to refer to Leviticus 19:3. Nonetheless, the sense of the passage is still unclear. See Friedmann, n. 17; the priority of "mother" would seem to accord well with gentile "non-paternity"! In any case, perhaps there is an oblique reference here to the Septuagint version as one more sensitive to gentile feelings, but less authentic for that very reason. Friedmann understands R. Levi to maintain that gentiles are commanded the law of filial piety, but see *Genesis Rabbah* 16:6 (ed. Theodore-Albeck, pp. 149–150) where R. Levi finds scriptural support for "the six commands" given Adam. Yet filial piety might be a later command to the gentiles. See n. 114. For R. Levi see also *Genesis Rabbah* 31:6 (I, p. 280).

98   *Sifra, Kedoshim* 1:9 (p. 87a); *Mishnah Keritot*, end (trans. H. Danby, p. 572). But see R. Levi b. Gershom, *op. cit.*

99   See *Enzyklopedia Talmudit*, IV, pp. 92–93, especially R. Hezkiah Medini, *Sedeh Hemed*, "Kaph," sec. 20.

100   *Kiddushin* 31a. The talmudic text itself is equally halakhic and playful:
> The son of a widow asked R. Eliezer, "What if my father asks me to give him a drink of water, and my mother makes the same request at the same time—which takes precedence?" He answered, "Leave the honor of your mother and honor your father, for both you and your mother are obliged to honor him." He came before R. Joshua and asked ". . . What if they were divorced?" R. Joshua said, "One can tell by looking at your eyelashes that you are the son of a widow. Put water in a bowl and call them as you would hens."

Obviously the answer is not fully clear. Some understand R. Joshua to be declaring a halakhic Buridan's ass.

101   R. Simeon b. Yohai is given as the author of this passage in *Tosefta Keritot* 4:15; see Bacher, *Aggadot ha-Tanna'im*, Vol. II, pt. 1, p. 74, n. 22. But the parallels in *Mekhilta* and *Genesis Rabbah* suggest that R. Simeon only discussed the relation of heaven and earth (indeed, the phrase "they are equal" with regard to these two is spoken by his son, R. El'azar, who probably heard it from his father; cf. *Mattnot Kehunah* to *Genesis Rabbah* 1:15), the other pairs being derived from an anonymous collection. Cf. L. Ginzberg, "Al ha-Yahas . . . ," *Studies in Memory of M. Schorr* (Heb.; ed. L. Ginzberg and A. Weiss), pp. 57–60.

102   Is it mere accident, then, that most sources (cf. n. 98 *supra*) list "father and mother" as the last of a series of balanced pairs, while *Midrash Samuel*, Chapter 5 (ed. Buber, 8a–b) omits the parental pair? Or does this source reflect a view that assigned priority to the father?

103   See E. Sachers "Patria Potestas," Pauly-Wissowa, *Realenzyklopadie der Klassischen Alteriumswissenschaft*, XXII, pt. 1, pp. 1046–1175, and especially pp. 1063–1065, 1130–1131; M. Kaser, *Das Romische Privatrecht*, II, pp. 142–145.

104   See Charles, *Apocrypha and Pseudepigrapha*, II, pp. 653–7; W. Frend. *Martyrdom in the Early Church* (Anchor ed.), p. 432, n. 46.

105   IV Maccabees 2:10.

106   See, e.g., *Yevamot* 5b. See Chapters IV–V.

107   IV Maccabees 15:10; 15:13.

108   *On the Decalogue,* sections 115–118. The stork is a common Hellenistic model of filial gratitude and service; see Colson, L.C., p. 612. Cf. also *On the Virtues,* 133 (L.C., VIII, p. 245).

109   See note 79.

110   See our discussion of the Noahide Law, and *Nazir* 61a.

111   Naturally, there were exceptions; R. Akiba says, "I saw a gentile bind his father before his dog, who ate him" (*Sifre Deuteronomy,* sec. 81; ed. Finkelstein, p. 147).

112   *Kiddushin* 31b, and elsewhere.

113   *Genesis Rabbah* 65:16.

114   *Tanhuma* (ed. Buber), *Kedoshim* 15 (p. 40a). *Midrash ha-Gadol,* cited by Theodore-Albeck (*Genesis Rabbah,* II, 728 [1:3]), relates these last two midrashic statements: R. Simeon ben Gamliel contrasts the behavior of Esau, who served his father in royal costume, with his own habit of attending to his father in ordinary dress. Hence, the descendents of Esau merited secular dominion in this world. *Middah ke-negged middah: kabod* is returned for *kibbud.*
  With the Muslim conquests, this theme is then applied (by isolated sources) to Ishmael; because he "feared his father a bit," he was awarded worldly dominion. See *Seder Eliyyahu Rabbah,* ed. M. Friedmann, Chapter 14, p. 65. The exact nature of Ishmael's meritorious conduct is not spelled out; Friedmann (n. 48) refers to the midrash that speaks of Ishmael's repentence during his father Abraham's lifetime; Ginzberg (*Legends,* V, p. 230, n. 114) understands the reference to be to Ishmael's dutiful burying of his father.
  Another biblical incident that clearly bodies forth the ethos of filial piety is the covering by Shem and Japhet of Noah's nakedness in Genesis 9:20-28. The behavior of these two sons is assimilated to the imperative of filial piety by some rabbinic teachers (note the terminology used and the literary sources implied!): " 'But Shem and Japhet took a cloth . . .'—R. Yohanan said, Shem initiated the fulfillment of the command (*mitzvah*), and Japhet followed him . . . they placed their hands over their faces, and walked backwards, so as to observe the proper honor, as befits the reverential obligations of a son toward his father [cf. M. *Kiddushin* 1:7]."—*Genesis Rabbah* 36:6, ed. Theodore-Albeck, I, pp. 339-340. See also *Exodus Rabbah* 30:5.

115   The rabbis differed on the interpretation of this verse. For some it showed Esau's solicitousness toward his father; for others it indicated his eagerness to see his father dead. See *Genesis Rabbah* 67:8 (p. 764), and notes.
  I. Heinemann, *Darkhe ha-Aggadah,* p. 33, claims that the rabbis knew all along that the filial piety of Esau (and more important, of Rome) was only skin deep, and hence valueless; in this regard he cites *Midrash Tehillim* 14:3, which notes Genesis 27:41 (see paragraph above). However, this does not adequately

account for the many contrary rabbinic statements, nor does it adequately evaluate the significance of behavior *per se,* apart from its intention. Generally speaking, both tannaim and amoraim disagreed on the worth of Roman moral and social achievements; see, for example, *Baba Batra* 10b, and S. Lieberman, *JQR, XXXVI,* 4 (April 1946), pp. 357-359.

116   Heinemann, *Philons* . . . , p. 257.

NOTES FOR CHAPTER II

1   The translations that follow are largely those of the 1917 Jewish Publication Society (JPS) version. The 1962 version gives for Exodus 21:17, "He who insults (or 'reviles'). . . ." and for Deuteronomy 27:16, " . . . he that insults . . . " as well. According to Brown, Driver, Briggs, *Lexicon of the Old Testament,* the verb *k-l-l* can mean, "lightly esteem, curse, make contemptible" (p. 886), and *makleh* means to "treat with contempt, dishonor," and is the opposite of *kabed* (p. 885).

Jewish tradition has understood Exodus 21:17, which does, after all, impose the death penalty, to refer to the cursing of parents (see *Mekhilta, ad loc.*); Deuteronomy 27:16 is understood to be referring to the slighting of parental dignity (see Pseudepigrapha—Jonathan, Sa'adiah [*Commentaries,* ed. J. Kapah, p. 148], and Rashi, among others). Compare Ezekiel 22:7. The entire list of curses in Deuteronomy 27:15-26 does not impose judicial penalties, but the curse of God; the majority of sins listed are described as "secret," and, perhaps (as in our case), not given to objective quantification. See also D. Hoffmann, *Commentary to Deuteronomy* (Hebrew), II, p. 509, and Y. N. Epstein, *Mavo le-Nusah ha-Mishnah,* I, p. 87.

Philo, on the other hand, apparently did not distinguish between the two. He writes (*Special Laws,* II, 248; Colson, p. 461): " . . . if . . . he uses abusive language to those to whom good words are owed as a bounden duty, or in any other way does anything to dishonor his parents, let him die." Imposition of the death penalty clearly takes us to Exodus 21:17 (though how does one quantify for judicial purposes—indeed, purposes of the death penalty!—"anything" that dishonors parents?), which is understood not as "cursing" but as "insulting."

S. Belkin (*Philo and the Oral Law,* pp. 150-151) notes: "According to Philo, the punishment for dishonoring one's parents . . . is death. The Pharisees, however, who were lenient in punishing offenders, imposed the punishment of death for cursing parents only if the curse was invoked in the name of God. No punishment was set for the dishonoring of parents. . . . [See, also, on this point E. Goodenough, *Jurisprudence,* p. 73, n. 151.] Like Philo, the LXX, Matthew xv. 4, and Mark vii. 10 convert the biblical phrase, 'he that curses his father,' into 'he that speaks evil of his father.' It may be that all these represent an earlier tradition which considered speaking evil against parents, without cursing by the name of God, included under Leviticus xx. 12." (For references to the Samaritan and Karaite exegesis of this verse, see B. Revel, *JQR*, III [1913], pp. 372-373). Interestingly, R. Aha, *She'iltot*, 60, apparently derives the ban on paining parents from Exodus 21:17 rather than from Deuteronomy 27:16, but see R. Naftali Berlin, *Ha'amek She'alah*, n. 6. A sixteenth-century work cites Targum Yerushalmi to Ex. 21:17 as rendering *mekalel*—abuse (R. Abraham Rappoport, *Minhah Belulah* [Verona, 1594], p. 83b) but this version is unattested elsewhere. An anonymous geonic epistle (published by S. Assaf, *MiSifrut Ha-Ge'onim* [Jerusalem, 1933], p. 173) does treat Ex. 21:17 much as did R. Aha, too (cited by M. Kasher, *Torah Shelemah*, XVII, p. 94, n. 326). Medieval Jewish moral exegesis thus returned to the broadest understanding of *makleh*: R. El'azar Azkari (*Sefer Haredim*, Chapter 1, sec. 35) writes that the verse refers not to the cursing of parents but to thinking of them as unworthy of respect.

2   The biblical text is itself somewhat ambiguous on this point. The son is accused of the dishonor of his parents and disobedience to them, but also of violating accepted social norms ("He is a glutton and a drunkard"); see Deuteronomy 21:18—21. So, too, in rabbinic tradition both elements are present; the son must disobey his parents and also be a thief and drunkard. But inasmuch as the rabbis allowed the parents the right of *mehila*, or pardon (*Sifre, ad loc.*, and *Sanhedrin* 88b), the parental component remained primary, even though the son could not be condemned by his parents but only by the "elders of the city." See also Chapter I, nn. 43–44; Cassutto, *Enzyklopedia Mikra'it*, IV, p. 78.

3   An examination of the ancient Near–Eastern material is of interest here; regrettably, we have few texts to use. A Mesopotamian hymn describes the "coming golden age as "Days when one man is not insolent to another, when a son reveres his father . . . in a general restoration of authority" (T. Jacobsen, in H. Frankfort, ed., *Before Philosophy* [Penguin ed.], p. 217; and cf. Micah 7:6); we recall that a Mesopotamian son "ought to heed the word of thy . . . mother as . . . the word of . . . god." The following from the 14th century B.C.E. Ugaritic *Tale of Aqhat* (in the translation of H. L. Ginsburg, in J. Pritchard, ed., *Ancient Near Eastern Texts*, p. 150, col. A, lines 26–37) is more specific:

> A scion . . .
> Who sets up the stelae of his ancestral spirits,
> In the holy place the protectors of his clan;
> Who frees his spirit from the earth,
> From the dust guards his footsteps;
> Who smothers the life-force of his detractor,
> Drives off who attacks his abode;
> Who takes him by the hand when he's drunk,
> Carries him when he's sated with wine;
> Consumes his funerary offering in Ba'al's house;
> Even his portion in El's house;
> Who plasters his roof when it leaks,
> Washes his clothes when they're soiled. . . .

As A. van Selms (*Marriage and Family Life in Ugaritic Literature*, pp. 100–103) reads this passage, the major filial duties listed are the ritualistic funerary actions; support of the parent in quarrels with fellow citizens (Van Selms translates lines 6–7 above differently than does Ginsburg, and refers to Psalms 127:4–5: "As arrows in the hand of a mighty man, so are the children of one's youth. Happy is the man that has his quiver full of them; they shall not be put to shame when they speak with their enemies in the gate''; note also the rabbinic "and does not contradict him"); care of the parent when drunk (Ginsburg, n. 8, brilliantly refers to Isaiah 51:17–18: "Awake, awake, stand up, O Jerusalem, you have drunk at the hand of the Lord the cup of his fury; you have drunken the beaker, even the cup of staggering, and drained it. There is none to guide her among all the sons whom she has brought forth; neither is there any that takes her by the hand of all the sons that she has brought up.''); repair of the roof in winter; and the washing of soiled clothes. A comparison of this list, fragmentary as it doubtless is, with the Jewish materials discloses the omission of ritualistic concerns from the latter as well as a concern with different needs (though this should not be pushed, given the literary context of the Ugaritic document, and the detection of Hebraic parallels by scholars, *supra*).

An indirect but exceedingly valuable source for the study of pre-Mosaic filial piety are the bills of adoption that have been preserved from the ancient Near East. It can be assumed that the rights acquired by the adoptive parents when they bought the child from its natural parents reflect the rights and expectations of those parents themselves. Thus, if an adopted son takes upon himself the obligation "to serve and provide for his parents as long as they live," as an Assyrian bill of adoption, translated by I. Mendelsohn, *Slavery in the Ancient Near East,* p. 22, puts it, we may assume that the boy's natural parents could expect to be served and provided for by their son as long as they live.

Indeed, this very point is made explicit in an Aramaic document of adoption written in the Jewish garrison town of Elephantine in the 5th century B.C.E., as translated by Emil Kraeling (*The Brooklyn Museum Aramaic Papyri*, p. 181, 11. 11–12): "Tpmt and Yohoyishima, her daughter, say: We will serve thee as a son or daughter provides for his (or her) father. . . ." The stability of cultural norms is demonstrated for this period as well; the very vocabulary of the 5th-century Aramaic document is quite similar to that of the mid-Assyrian documents (both use forms of *p-l-h:* contrast the translations of Mendelsohn and Kraeling with that of M. David, *Die Adoption im Altbabylonischen Recht,* p. 92, 101, who renders the term by "honor," which is, according to Prof. B. Eichler, a less satisfactory translation than "serve"). See also Chapter III, No. 4, *infra.*

Van Selms continues to say that the "father had far reaching powers over his children. He orders them about, even when they have reached years of discretion. They, on their part, call their father their *adn,* 'sire,' and their mother their *adt,* which is the feminine form of *adn* . . . even the kindest father remains his son's sire.'' (Other literary material cited by van Selms reminds us that children loved as well as served their parents.) And E. Neufeld (*The Hittite Laws,* p. 123) asserts that the absolute power of the father over children was common throughout the East. Yet he carefully distinguishes between this power and the Roman *potestas patrias:* the latter extended not only over sons and daughters but also over the children of the sons and the more remote descendents through males (n. 48, Neufeld), which was not true of the former.

It is indeed instructive to compare the rabbinic list with the Roman requirements of filial piety, specifically those associated with *obsequium* and *officium*, terms which bear some resemblance to the Hebrew *morah* and *kibbud*. The earliest Roman records of "royal laws" (*leges regiae*) attributes to Romulus regulations that determined the character of all subsequent Roman thinking on the subject of filial piety: ". . . he gave virtually full power to the father over his son during his whole life, whether he thought proper to imprison him, to scourge him, to put him in chains and keep him at work in the fields, or to put him to death. . . . And . . . he even allowed him to sell his son . . . as often as three times. . . ." (As translated in N. Lewis and M. Reinhold, *Roman Civilization*, I, pp. 60–61.) The Twelve Tables (c. 450 B.C.E.) allowed the father—indeed commanded him—to "quickly kill . . . a dreadfully deformed child," but limited the number of times he might sell his son to three (Lewis and Reinhold, 104).

Patria potestas ("Our children . . . are in our power": *Institutes of Justinian*, Bk. 1, Title ix; trans. T. C. Sandars, p. 29) bestowed upon the father many important powers. The son could—at any age, as only the death of the father or the emancipation of the son terminated this relationship and its rights—be punished corporally by his father, sold into slavery, or killed by him legally. Furthermore, the value of all services performed by the son, and all property he acquired, belonged to the father (cf. Chapter I, n. 103). The evolution of Roman law, particularly in the period of the Empire and in the Christian era (see Chapter I), limited many of these disabilities. The extent of this evolution, though, is shown in the successive revisions of the stipulation that a son can hold no property. Augustus, apparently, allowed the son to retain all he earned or plundered while a Roman soldier (*castrense peculium*). Some centuries later, this was extended to anything acquired in the civil service of the state (*quasi-castrense peculium*). The *Institutes of Justinian* (Bk. II, Title ix; Sandars, pp. 157–158) retained these concessions and added that what the son acquired in any other way also belonged to him, but that the father owned the use and enjoyment (usufruct) of that property. Similarly, Justinian stipulated that when a father emancipated his son he should not deduct a third of those things over which he had no right of acquisition (as had been the practice), but should merely retain the usufruct of one-half of that property. Clearly, the son remained in many important ways a stunted legal person, limited in his rights of person and property. Furthermore, the basic operative concept derived from the "power" of the father, not the duty of the son.

These same characteristics inform the code of *obsequium* and *officium*. Though one might be tempted to identify the rabbinic *morah* with the first of these institutions and *kibbud* with the second, the contrast between the Jewish and Roman concepts is more striking than the similarities. The Romans stipulated that "by freedman or son the person of patron or father should always be honored and held sacred" (*Justinian, Digest*, xxxvii, xv. 9). The actual duties involved were "never formulated" fully (A. M. Duff, *Freedmen in the Early Roman Empire*, p. 36), but we do know of some stipulations attached to *obsequium* and *officium*. *Obsequium*, in particular, is most revealing; it forbade the son from bringing a civil lawsuit against his father unless he received special permission to do so, and limited his rights to criminal suits severely (Duff, pp. 37–40). Once again, the legal person of the son is diminished in conceptual harmony with *patria potestas*. The Roman *owns* his son; the Jew doesn't.

Indeed, were one to search for rabbinic points of contact with the Roman system—an unnecessary quest, incidentally; *morah* and *kibbud* are both biblically rooted and indigenous concepts—one might claim that the rabbinic definitions of *morah* stand in deliberate contrast with the Roman *officium*. In general, it must also be remembered that Roman law was not always identical with the law of the provinces. Thus R. Taubenschlag (*The Law of Greco-Roman Egypt in the Light of the Papyri*, pp. 97–99) points out that though *patria potestas* represents within "the Roman orbit" a genuine power, "as far as the Greeks and Egyptians are concerned . . . *patria potestas* is in the historical era nothing but a kind of guardianship," and even Roman practice was (in the 2nd and 3rd centuries C.E.) more liberal than Roman law on filial possession of property (pp. 110–111).

4   Parallels to this citation (with some variation) are found in *Sifra, Kedoshim* 1:10; p. *Pe'ah* 1:1; *Tosefta Kiddushin* 1:11; *Peskita Rabbati* xxiii (-iv) (p. 122a). The most significant variation in the wording of this *baraita* is found in the version of the *Sifra* and Palestinian Talmud, which reads: ". . . he must not sit in his place or speak in his place."

5   Mishnah *Kiddushin* 1:7.

6   This Mishnah is recognized to be part of an ancient source: see Y. N. Epstein, *Mevo'ot le-Sifrut ha-Tanna'im*, pp. 52–54; and A. Weiss, "Haza'at ha-Homer, . . ." *Horeb*, XII (1956), pp. 70ff.

7   See *Commentary* of R. Yonah to *Avot* 4:12. A discussion of this point can be found in Rabbi J. Perlow, *Sefer ha-Mitzvot Le-R. Sa'adiah Gaon*, I, p. 193.

8   Maimonides, *Commentary to Mishnah, Kiddushin* 1:7 (ed., Kapah, *Nashim*, p. 197).

9   R. Eliezer of Metz, *Sefer Yera'im*, sec. 221–2; R. Menahem ha-Me'iri, *Bet ha-Behira, Kiddushin*, p. 181.

10   Mishnah *Pe'ah* 1:1 lists, among those things which have no limit, "*gemillut hasadim*," usually defined as acts of personal charity, giving of self (see *Enzyklopedia Talmudit*, VI, pp. 149–153). R. Samson, in his commentary to *Pe'ah* (*ad. loc., s. v. vehabikkurim* [end]), inclu:des honor and reverence of parents in this category. (This, despite the fact that the latter part of Mishnah 1 lists "*gemillut hasadim*" and "*kibbud av*" as two distinct areas.)

11   *Tosefta Megilah* 3(4): 24; *Sifra, Kedoshim* 7:14. For later sources and discussion, see Prof. S. Lieberman, *Tosefta Ki-Fshuta*, V, p. 1202. *Halakhot Gedolot* (Berlin, p. 646), cited by Lieberman, states expressly: "These norms apply to parents, to one's teacher, and to the sage." Cf. also Josephus, Antiqui-

ties 18:12 (L. C., IX, 11): "[the Pharisees] do not rashly presume to contradict their elders."

The *baraita* concludes, "(they are to come first) in business and in entering and leaving, and they take priority over all others." These latter demands are not normally found in the context of filial piety, though see paragraph, *supra*.

12 See Philo, *The Special Laws*, II, pp. 237–239 (Colson, p. 455). Compare *Laws* 600A (pp. 1284–5).

13 See n. 4, and S. Lieberman, *Tosefta, op. cit.*

14 It is curious that the *baraita* chose to express itself with the male singular (*his*, i.e., the *father's* place), when Leviticus 19:3 states clearly, "You shall each fear your mother and father." Certainly, rabbinic law demanded reverence of both parents (see Chapter I); at the same time, some medieval explications of our *baraita* (see on) filled in with details appropriate to the father's situation only. In *Midrash Aseret ha-Dibrot* (ed. A. Yellinek, *Bet ha-Midrash* I/i, p. 76), though, we read: "How must a man honor *them?* . . . How must a man reverence them? By not sitting in *their* place, etc." For another instance of such sensitivity on the part of this author, see Chapter III, n. 55.

15 So too the *baraita* of *hiddur* (n. 11, *supra*). Does "in his place (*bimkomo*)" mean "in his presence," or "out of sequence"? Hillel, in his commentary to *Sifra*, explains: "A son ought not to speak before (*le-fanav*) his father." See also Rashi to Leviticus 10:19.

16 *Avot* 5:7. The texts in *Avot* (and *Avot de'Rabbi Nathan*, ver. A, ch. 37; ver. B, ch. 40) vary from *be-fanav* and *le-fanav:* both mean "in his presence" (the latter form does not mean, "before he speaks"). See Y. N. Epstein, *Mavo le-Nusah*, pp. 1127–1128, and A. Bendavid, *Leshon Mikra u-Leshon Hakhamim*, p. 197. I do not know how the medievals used *le-fanav;* see note 15.

17 *Kiddushin, ad loc.* See also *Tosafot Ri ha-Zaken* (R. Isaac b. Samuel), who stresses the literal meaning of "place."

18 Cited by R. Yeruham, *Sefer Adam veHavah, Sefer Adam*, 1:4; 15c. So too in *Tosafot Ri Ha-zaken. Shulhan Arukh, Yoreh De'ah*, 240:2.

19 *Bet ha-Behira, Kiddushin*, p. 184. The editor assumes (n. 3) that Me'iri had a variant text. It may be, though, that *'omed bimkomo* was interpreted to mean, "to stand—to remain—in the presence of one's parent." The Maimonidean parallel (and, I believe, source) is *Code Hilkhot Talmud Torah* 5:6: "The student should not sit in his master's presence until he has been told to sit, nor should he rise to take his leave until he has been told to rise, or he has received permission to rise." Cf. also I. Abrahams, *Jewish Life in the Middle Ages*, p. 123.

20 Cited in *Sefer Adam veHava, op. cit.* The thrust of the argument of R. Me'ir Abulafia is that "tip the scale" could not refer to support of the father's adversary, since that would be no better than "contradicting him." Rashi may have held, though, that the additional clause is necessary, lest one distinguish between unilateral opposition to one's parent and agreement with another sage who

disagrees with one's father.

21   The ideal portrait of father as teacher of Torah implies, of course, the full range of intellectual intercourse. "R. Hiyya bar Abba said: 'Even the father and son, the master and student, who study Torah together become hostile to each other [Rashi: since they sharply question each other, and one does not accept the other's answer], but do not quit the field until they come to love each other' " (*Kiddushin* 30b). Thus, the common quest creates a bond deeper than the disagreements along the way; there is no indication that the disagreements need be resolved and in one direction only.

22   R. Israel b. Joseph Alnakawa, *Menorat ha-Ma'or* (ed. H. G. Enelow), IV, p. 19.

23   The extent to which filial silence was expected should not be underestimated. Torah provided an exception, not a rule. And even Torah discussions could be limited; thus, R. Me'ir Abulafia (*op. cit.*) distinguished between substantive argumentation (which he would allow) and purely personal assertion (which he would not) only when the son agreed with his father—disagreement, on the other hand, was not to be expressed at all.

24   *Yoreh De'ah* 240:2. Cf. the Gaon of Vilna, *ad loc.*

25   *She'ilot,* 56. The interpretation of this text is that of R. Naftali Berlin, *Ha'amek She'alah*, note 5.

26   Maimonides lists specific bans on the striking and cursing of parents (*Sefer ha-Mitzvot,* Negative Commands 318–319) though he admits that these bans are derived from the more generalized bans which protect "all men" (319). Nahmanides comments, (*ad. loc.*): "I say that we are forbidden to strike or curse our parents because they are part of the community of Israel, . . . and though the striking or cursing of parents is specially punished, there is no unique ban to be counted in the list of commandments."

27   Cf. nn. 1 and 26, *supra.*

28   Maimonides, *Code, Mamrim,* Chapter V, section 15 (trans. A. Hershman, Yale Judaica Series, Vol. 3, p. 153). R. Ahai, *She'iltot,* 60, had already generalized that "it is forbidden for a man to pain his father or his mother."

29   *Mamrim,* Chapter VI, section 3 (Hershman, p. 154), derived from *Kiddushin* 31b.

30   *Pirke de-R. Eliezer,* Chapter 39. Cf. also *Sotah* 13b: "R. Judah said in the name of Rav: 'Why was Joseph called "bones" while he was yet alive (Genesis 50:25)? Because he did not object to the desecration of his father's honor when his brothers said, "Your servant, our father." ' "
31   *Baba Kamma* 94b; 111b.

32   P. *Pe'ah* 1:1;15c. See *Sefer Hassidim* (ed. R. Margoliot), sec. 337. An 18th-century halakhist speaks of a situation where "the mother and father are asleep, and the keys to the son's *store* are under their heads. . . ." (R. Abraham

Danzig, *Hayye Adam*, 67:12.)

33 "Rome" in rabbinic sources can mean any center of Roman-Hellenistic culture, cf. R. Moses Alsheikh as cited by R. Yehiel Heilperin "R. Jose b. Kismah," in *Seder ha-Dorot*, pt. 2 (repr. Jerusalem 1957), pp. 213–216, and the author's expansion of that discussion; P. Rieger, *JQR*, XVI (1925–1926), 229ff.

34 *Pesikta Rabbati*, p. 123b. The text states, "when the slipper fell from her hand." Elsewhere (see Jastrow, *Dictionary*, II, 1341), this slipper is used for striking, and were this not the case here why would the "slipper" have fallen from her hand? See also *Mo'ed Katon*, 25a, where R. Hisda similarly slapped his son; *Genesis Rabbah* 45:9.

35 This follows the emendation of M. Friedmann in his edition of *Pesikta Rabbati*. The manuscript reads: "He did not say to her, 'Enough, mother.'" The parallel text in *Deuteronomy Rabbah* reads: "He only said. . . ."

36 *Deuteronomy Rabbah* 1:15.

37 *Kiddushin* 32a. Cf. Chapter IV.

ff& *The Fathers According to Rabbi Nathan*, trans. J. Goldin, ch. 41, p. 173.

39 E. Cahn, *The Moral Decision*, pp. 40–42. Obviously, Jewish thought works out its own terminological and philosophical treatment of the areas denoted by Cahn as "morals" and "law." His discussion is, nonetheless, quite suggestive. S. Federbush, *Ha-Mussar veha-Mishpat be-Yisra'el*, 88ff, discusses the transformation of law into ethics and ethics into law in Jewish jurisprudence.

40 *Mamrim* 6:7 (Hershman, pp. 155–156). Note also R. David Halevi, *Turei Zahav, Yoreh De'ah* 240, n. 10.

41 Cf. n. 4.

42 In some tannaitic sources, the root *k-b-d* was in fact synonymous with service. See *Pesahim* 51a: "A man may wash with anyone [in the bathhouse], except his father, his father-in-law, his mother's husband, and his sister's husband. R. Judah permits washing with his father, because of the honor [*kevod*] of his father." It is clear that *kevod* here means the service the son can render his father.

43 *Tosefta, Kiddushin* 1:11 (ed. Zukermandel, p. 336).

44 *Pesikta Rabbati*, p. 122a. For the term *marbitz*, see Jastrow, *Dictionary*, II, 1445, and compare M. *Sanhedrin* 7:6 (where the entire routine should be compared with the list of filial duties) and *Shabbat* 40b.

45 It is not all impossible that the differences in these sources reflect disagreements as to how far the servant-son analogy ought to be pushed: it is more probable, however, that they merely derive from normal literary expansion and abbreviation.

46 *Kiddushin* 22b; cf. *Tosefta* 1:5 (Zukermandel, p. 335).

47 *Mekhilta, Nezikin*, 1 (ed. Horowitz-Rabin), p. 248; see the editor's notes to 1.9.

48   *Tanhuma, Noah,* sec. 19. Cf. *Tanhuma,* ed. Buber, 1, p. 29a, and L. Finkelstein, *Mavo le-Massekheth Avot,* pp. 32–5.

49   *Baba Batra* 127b: "If he served him in the manner of a son, and the master said, 'He is my son,' and then said, 'He is my slave,' he is not believed; if he served him in the manner of a slave, and the master said, 'He is my slave' and then said, 'He is my son,' he is not believed."

50   P. *Baba Batra* 8:8, 16b: "R. Mana said, 'Like those *Niftai,* who enslave their sons to excess!' " R. Mana is probably the 3rd-century Palestinian amora of that name, and not his later namesake; cf. Z. Frankel, *Mavo ha-Yerushalmi,* p. 114b. *Niftai* are generally Nabataeans, cf. A. Kohut, *Arukh ha-Shalem,* Vol. V, p. 370. But inasmuch as R. Manah is explicating a *baraita* that deals with Jewish behavior, he must refer to Jews who either copy the Nabataeans in this regard, or live in their vicinity and so are called Niftai themselves. P. *Kiddushin* 4:7; 66b reads, however, "Kutai," or Samaritans.

51   *Ketubot* 96a. See *Shabbat* 61a and p. *Shabbat* 6:2; 8a, where R. Yohanan is given his sandals by his disciple.

Interestingly, the *baraita* of "filial service" as found in the *Tosefta* and the printed texts of BT do not require this service of the son. The *baraita* as given in PT, *Pesikta Rabbati* (n. 47) and the *En Ya'akov* of R. Jacob ben Habib (d. 1516) does include it. Its absence in some versions may reflect the *Ketubot* material.

52   *Mamrim* 6:4. Maimonides is cited approvingly by R. Eleazer Azkari (16th century), who points to Exodus 4:23, which rendered literally reads, " . . . release my son so that he may serve me" *(Sefer Haredim,* Chapter 5 [Warsaw: 1879], p. 40).

53   Inasmuch as the rabbis contended (see Chapter 1, end) that "Esau" was a paragon of filial piety, it is to be expected that filial service, too, was not considered a uniquely Jewish institution (see *infra* on R. Gamliel and Esau), and, indeed, it is to be found in the traditional cultures of Greece and Rome (see Sachers, p. 1131, and the references in Chapter 3, n. 4).

This common ethos was assumed by Philo, who in describing the "Therapeutae" to his Alexandrian readers wrote: "They give their services (at meals) gladly and proudly like sons to their real fathers and mothers. . . . And they come in to do their office ungirt and with tunics hanging down, that in their appearance there may be no shadow of anything to suggest the slave" *(The Contemplative Life,* sec. 72 [trans. F. Colson, Loeb Classics, IX, p. 157]). Children, then, were expected to render "gladly and proudly" the services that would otherwise be done by a slave. On the need to distinguish this voluntary servant from the slave, compare the rabbinic sources cited in section III, part 1; the rabbis seem primarily concerned with the legal questions arising from such confusion, while the Therapeutae—as presented by Philo—seem anxious to avoid the suggestion that their service is anything but cheerfully and voluntarily given. But perhaps these sources ought to be interpreted in the light of each other. In his description of the Essene communities *(Every Good Man Is Free,* trans. F. Colson, sec. 87, p. 61), Philo writes, "To the elder men too is given the respect and care *(frontis)* which real children give to their parents."

54 See, e.g., *Kiddushin* 31a; see also *Sotah* 49a, *Sifre Deuteronomy*, sec. 218 ("light the candle"), and *Nedarim* 38b; *Mekhilta d'RSBI*, p. 47, 1, 21. Similarly, the Midrash states that Noah suffered in the Ark for want of a young son "to serve him" (*Genesis Rabbah*, 36:11).

55 Reuben is elsewhere seen by the Midrash as zealous in his mother's behalf; R. Simeon ben Eleazar and others (*Shabbat* 55b, cited in Rashi to Genesis 35:22) claim that Reuben did not actually lie with Bilhah, Jacob's concubine, after the death of Rachel, as the biblical text states (see Genesis 35:22), but rather "defended the honor of his mother [Leah], saying, 'Though my mother's sister shared my father with my mother, should the maid-servant of my mother's sister also do so?" And so he disarranged the bed."

56 *Genesis Rabbah* 84:13 (ed. Theodore-Albeck, II, pp. 1015–1016). The idea that Joseph's filial piety was evidenced by his willingness to comply with his father's demanding request is already found in tannaitic literature; see *Mekhilta Vayehi, Petihta*, 1 (ed. Horowitz-Rabin, p. 29).

57 Compare G. von Rad, *Genesis*, p. 347: "One is . . . surprised that Jacob so carelessly sent the defenseless youth to the camp of his brothers, whose hate, as just reported, had already reached such a menacing pitch. The way Joseph finally found his brothers . . . is told with strange minuteness. . . ."

58 *Yalkut Shim'oni*, sec. 153: " 'Joseph hitched his chariot and went to Goshen to meet his father Jacob' (Genesis 46:29): Joseph heard that his brothers had reached the Egyptian boundary, so he took his retinue and went to greet his father. Now people go to greet the king; the king does not go to greet others. Thus we are taught that a man's father is as his king." *Midrash ha-Gadol, Genesis* (ed. M. Margaliot, p. 785), concludes, "Scripture shows that Joseph did not go forth as ruler of Egypt, but as a son honoring his father."

59 *Menorat ha-Ma'or*, pp. 15–16. This medieval text exhibits certain post-talmudic developments in the norms of filial support of parents, which we treat in Chapter III.

60 *Menorat ha-Ma'or*, p. 16. *Sefer Haredim*, Chapter 4, p. 34 and Chapter 1 (p. 31).

61 *Kiddushin* 31a-b. We recall that Abimi was himself an exemplar of filial devotion.

62 P. *Kiddushin* 1:7

63 The Confucian sentiments are strikingly similar, even in style: "Tzu-yu asked about the treatment of parents. The Master said, 'Filial sons nowadays are people who see to it that their parents get enough to eat. But even dogs and horses are cared for to that extent. If there is no feeling of respect, wherein lies the difference?'

"Tzu-hsia asked about the treatment of parents. The Master said, 'It is the demeanor that is difficult. Filial piety does not consist merely in young people undertaking the hard work . . . or serving their elders first with wine and food. It is something much more than that.' " (*Analects*, II, pp. 7–8, trans. A. Waley, Vintage Books, p. 89.)

64   Rashi emphasizes the mean spirit in which the honor is rendered, while PT emphasizes here the more concrete and legally objectified irreverence of speech. Me'iri (p. 182–183) follows PT: ". . . . if he honors his parents in all (substantial) ways possible, yet insults them verbally, his good deed is outweighed by the bad. . . ." *Shulhan Arukh, Yoreh De'ah* 240:4 speaks, as does Rashi, of externalizations of a subtle nature: ". . . . he should perform these tasks cheerfully, for even if he feeds (his father) fattened fowl daily, yet betrays an angry countenance, he is punished." *Sefer Haredim* (Chapter 1) tells, "It happened in our days that a man who supported his mother *but considered her contemptible* because she married another husband after the death of his father, was killed at sea and thrown into the sea. . . ."

65   *Avot De-R. Nathan*, ed. Schechter, vers. B, Chapter 10, p. 13b. See L. Finkelstein, *Mavo le-Massekhtot Avot veAvot de-Rabbi Nathan*, pp. 32–34.

66   Maimonides, *Responsa*, ed. J. Blau, II, no. 448, p. 728. It should be noted, though, that Maimonides speaks here of the minimum possibility of reverence and honor; furthermore, his main desire is to stress the imperative of love for the proselyte, for which the filial situation is only a foil.

67   He doubtless relies on the fact that only love of God and love of the convert are phrased in the accusative (Deuteronomy 10:19, 6:5); the imperative to love one's fellow is in the dative (Leviticus 19:18). The latter can more aptly refer to loving acts, the former to feelings; see, for example, Buber, *Israel and the World*, p. 60; S. R. Hirsch, *Commentary to the Pentateuch*, III, pp. 527–528.

68   *Pirke de-R. Eliezer*, chapter 32.

69   *Genesis Rabbah*, Vatican ms., chap. XCVI (ed. Theodore-Albeck, III, p. 1239). Philo speaks of "bad sons" who honor their parents merely to comply with custom, in contrast with "good sons" who recognize the nobility of such conduct. (*Allegorical Interpretation*, I, sec. 99 [Loeb Classics, I, p. 213.]) And "Moses, estimating the claims of his real and adopted parents . . . requited the former with good feeling and affection, the latter with gratitude for their kind treatment of him." (*Moses*, I, 33 [L. C., VI, p. 293].)

70   Fromm notes the significance of obedience, but empties it of all emotional content: "It is perfectly true that the Hebrew Bible is permeated by an emphasis on obedience, but it must be noted that obedience is quite different from incestuous fixation. Obedience is a conscious act of submitting to authority; . . . obedience . . . is behavior rather than feeling, and it can occur also when the feelings toward the authority are hostile, and when the person obeys without agreeing with the authority's orders." (*You Shall Be As Gods*, p. 72.) Even the biblical *kabbed* goes far beyond obedience, as the rabbinic material makes clear.

71   The rabbis coin the phrase *gemillut hesed* for acts of love rather than use an

expression compounded from "love of neighbor." *Gemillut hesed* is apparently more immediately concrete and (as Glueck pointed out in *Hesed in the Bible*) the term *hesed* has the connotation of acts that are expected of a man.

72   Rashi, *Kiddushin* 32a, s.v. *podin u-ma'akhilin*. It is true that Rashi is defining the basis of support, specifically, and furthermore, that the talmudic context is most relevant to his comments. Yet the passage was explained by some (e.g., *Tosafot Ri ha-Zaken, ad loc.*) without mention of filial love.

73   *Sefer Haredim*, Chapter 1 (p. 31); *Hayye Adam*, 67:1.

74   Deuteronomy 6:5.

75   *Hayye Adam* does cite Maimonides verbatim on this point, though; see 67;11. *Sefer Haredim*, though, does not. Generally, *Hayye Adam* is slightly more reserved on this topic than *Sefer Haredim*.

76   The structure of *Sefer Haredim* differs, as love there follows service and reverence. Despite the general thrust of the passage, no unique halakhic basis for filial love is displayed. The love of a son for his parents continues to be expressed by *Hayye Adam* as an extension of "you shall love your neighbor as yourself."

NOTES FOR CHAPTER III

1   It seems that both Talmuds understood the *baraita* of "reverence and service" to refer to the physical services alone, and not to the question of expense. It is possible, though, that the view requiring the son to subsidize his parent supported its position by reading the *baraita* as obliging both the physical commitment and the necessary financial outlay.

2   The Talmuds do not attempt to harmonize these tannaitic teachings with Mishnah *Baba Mezia* 2:11, which allows the son to attend to his own loss in preference to that of his father. See *Tosafot Baba Mezia*, 33a, s.v. *'avedato*, who define *kibbud* as demanding financial sacrifice only where the father derives some positive benefit from the loss, as when money is spent to feed him.

3   See also *Halakhot Gedolot*, cited in Chapter II, n. 11, that requires that the son give his parent the first strike in business opportunities.

4   Both the expectation of filial support of parents and its legal enforcement were not rare in ancient Near Eastern and Mediterranean societies. King Lipit-Ishtar (19th century B.C.E., Mesopotamia) claims, "Verily, in accordance with . . . I made the father support his children and I made the children support their father" ("Prologue to Lipit-Ishtar Lawcode," trans. S. N. Dramer, in J. Pritchard, ed., *Ancient Near Eastern Texts*, p. 159); according to Dr. Jacob Klein, the connotations of the Sumerian "support," when that word is found in Akkadian, are clearly those of financial responsibility. The ancient "bills of adoption" guide us to a similar conclusion; see Chapter II, n. 3. W. K. Lacey (*The Family in Classical Greece*, pp. 116–117, and p. 290, nn. 115–116) marshals a host of sources indicating that there existed in classical Greece a "legal,

not merely moral obligation, for children to look after old parents. Maltreatment of parents ranks with maltreatment of orphans and *epikleroi* as a prosecution, . . . and 'do you treat your parents well?' was a question asked at the examination of all public officers . . . positive services were required, especially the provision of food supplies. . . . Hence, getting children in order to have someone to tend their old age is a frequently mentioned motive for parenthood, and especially for adoption." (See Chapter I, *supra*, n. 54.) In Roman law, as we have seen (see Chapter II, n. 3), filial property was for many centuries at the disposal of the father, and responsibility for parental well-being, if not legally codified, was a social more. Imperial times saw—perhaps as an outgrowth of the decline of these two factors—the legal codification of this responsibility (see Kaser, I, pp. 297–299). But as Taubenschlag (p. 107; also p. 114) notes, peregrine law apparently considered the responsibility of maintenance a moral, rather than a legal, obligation, analogous to the maintenance by parents of their children. (See *infra*, n. 26.) Thus, "local law permits parents to revoke gifts because of ingratitude; while Roman law . . . authorizes them to apply to the authorities for aid." See also John 19:27.

5   *PT Kiddushin* 1:7; 61b.

6   *Mekhilta Yitro, Bahodesh* 8 (ed. Horowitz-Rabin, p. 231).

7   *Kiddushin* 32a.

8   See Y. N. Epstein, *Mevo'ot Le-Sifrut ha-Tanna'im*, p. 662 and n. 235; D. Halivni, *Medorot u-Massorot*, pp. 653–4, and the citation of R. Me'ir Abulafia, n. 53 *infra*. Note, too, the citation of R. Simeon, *Tanhuma, Vayyigash*, 6.

9   The standard commentaries to this Mishnah (*Nedarim*) offer revealing illustrations of the "honor of one's parents": Rashi (*s.v. Rabbi*) comments, "For they (the judges) say to him (the son who has taken the vow), 'If you had known that people were saying of your father, "Woe to the father who has raised such a wicked son, a man who is free with vows!" would you have vowed?' " R. Nissim (*ad loc.*) adds to Rashi that parental honor is at stake because others no doubt will say that the son learned his bad habit from his parents' behavior; the tosafists present a subtle variation—at stake is not only parental reputation, but parental shame, for the son's behavior will be pointed out to the embarrassed parents. Maimonides (*Commentary to Mishnah, ad loc.*) notes, "R. Eliezer says that if his father or mother says, 'You have angered us by this vow, or we have been pained by it. . . .'" R. Menahem ha-Me'iri makes the same point about the scope of filial piety by citing (*Introduction to Bet ha-Behira* [Leghorn: 1795], p. 3) *Yoma* 86a: "If someone studies Scripture and Mishnah, and attends on disciples of the wise, is honest in business and speaks pleasantly to persons, what do people then say concerning him? 'Happy the father who taught him Torah, happy the teacher who taught him Torah.' But if someone studies Scripture and Mishnah but is dishonest in business and discourteous to others, what do people then say concerning him? 'Woe to the father who taught him Torah, woe to the teacher who taught him Torah.' (I was directed to this latter reference by Prof. I. Twersky.)

10   Mishnah *Nedarim* 9:1.

11   See the standard commentaries, and H. Albeck, *Mishnah, Nashim,* p. 174–5.

12   Considering both the vagueness of the Mishnah and the later talmudic conclusion that the son need not bear the expense of parental support, it is surprising to note how our Mishnah is embodied in the codes: ". . . . but they do give him an opening in matters concerning his parents, for example, if he has banned the use of his property by his parents, they say, 'If you had known that *you are obliged to support them,* surely you would not have vowed" (*Shulhan Arukh, Yoreh De'ah* 228:11, following *Tur*).

13   *Ketubot* 49b, p. *Ketubot* 4:8; 28d. The subsequent talmudic discussion of the validity of this legislation is irrelevant to our problem.

14   *Ben-Sira,* ed. Segal, 33:22–26, p. 213. See A. Buchler, *Studies in Jewish History,* pp. 15–45 (Hebrew).

15   See H. Mantel, *Studies in the History of the Sanhedrin,* pp. 153–174, especially p. 173.

16   A. M. H. Jones, *The Greek City,* p. 78. Jones speaks here of the attempts at evasion of those considered wealthy enough to hold office and undertake the financial responsibilities implied, but the same techniques may have been used for more general tax evasion, or our source may in fact be concerned with evasion of the former sort. See also G. Allon, *Toledot ha-Yehudim be-Eretz Israel be-Tekufat ha-Mishnah veha-Talmud,* II, p. 67; I. Horowitz, *Eretz Israel u-Shekhunoteha,* p. 33; S. Baron, *Social and Religious History, II,* pp. 183–185, 193; Allon, I, pp. 41–42; II, pp. 105–206. According to Jones, this phenomenon is already common in the second century. See also *Baba Mezia* 75b.

17   See R. Pinhas Horowitz, *Sefer ha-Makneh,* to *Kiddushin* 32a (Aufebach: 1800, p. 66b). Note also the recurrent discussions as to the widow's legal claim to subsistence—payments from the estate of her husband; this lien upon the estate was necessary even when the inheritors were her own children.

18   I am aware of no tannaitic precedent for such release of the son; all tannaitic material that deals with the question exhorts the son to filfill this responsibility. The disagreement between R. Simeon and other sages noted above relates to the extreme situation where the son is himself in need, but otherwise all agree that a son is normally expected to care for his parents. Is it merely curious that *Mekhilta de R. Ishmael* (ed. Horowitz-Rabin, p. 70) cites Joseph's readiness to obey his father's request (Genesis 37:13) as evidence of his filial piety, while *Mekhilta de R. Simeon* (ed. Epstein-Melamed, p. 46) cites Joseph's sustaining of his father (Genesis 47:12) to prove the same point?

19   In translating "gather the congregation," I follow *P'nei Mosheh.* R. Solomon b. Aderet (who reads *zor be kenishta* in *Responsa,* VII, 451) understood the phrase to mean, "close the synagogue," in reference to the medieval custom of interrupting the prayer for complaints of a social and ethical nature (*Responsa,*

IV, 56). Cf. L. Finkelstein, *Jewish Self-Government in the Middle Ages,* pp. 16–17, and n. 1; Rashba's reading, *bei kenishta,* probably is derived from his interpretation, rather than the reverse.

20   P. *Kiddushin, op. cit.*

21   The latter half of the passage ("Come and learn . . . .") is strewn with difficulties. One problem, in general, overshadows the others and has stimulated a large body of analytical discussion: the original question centered on the obligation of the son to contribute to the support of his parent, while the instance of R. Eliezer, and the succeeding give and take, center on the obligation of the son not to shame the parent even if it should cost him money (indeed, after the fact)! The literature on the subject can be traced through the talmudic and Maimonidean (*Mamrim* 6:7) commentators, down to *Shulhan Arukh (Yoreh De'ah* 240:8) and its annotators (note especially the Gaon of Vilna, *ad loc.,* who is forced to textual emendation).

The citation of the aphorism of R. Eliezer is, itself, both instructive and typical. For one might with good reason argue that the *sitz im leben* of both R. Eliezer and his questioners was the context of piety and *hasidut,* not that of legal requirement. Yet the Talmud easily exchanges one context for the other. Finally, we note the energetic and deliberate testing of Rabba by his father R. Hunna.

22   Though the two Talmuds reach different conclusions, the positions cannot be labeled "Babylonian" and "Palestinian." R. Judah, a native and lifelong Babylonian, held the position that was accepted in the Palestinian Talmud but rejected by the Babylonian.

23   Curiously, the Talmud never cites in this discussion that most dramatic instance of *kibbud av,* the devotion of Dama ben Netinah to his father. Dama, we remember, had suffered considerable loss by his refusal to disturb the rest of his father. The question is raised by R. Nissim, one of whose replies is that Dama sacrificed his profit, while our *sugya* discusses the filial obligation to make a direct contribution to the welfare of the parent and thus take a loss, as the Talmud itself concludes. What with the talmudic citation of R. Eliezer (*supra*) one cannot simply argue that only concretely legal rubrics—and not instances of exemplary piety—were valid sources of law.

24   *Hullin* 110b. The textual history and pragmatic application of this rule is of great interest, but is not our topic.

25   *Ketubot* 49b–50a: "R. Elai stated in the name of Resh Lakish: 'It was enacted at Usha that if a man assigned all his estate to his sons in writing, he and his wife are nevertheless to be maintained out of it. . . .' The question was raised: 'Is the law in agreement with his view or not?'—Come and hear. R. Haninah and R. Jonathan were once standing together when a man approached them and bending down, kissed R. Jonathan upon his foot. 'What is the meaning of this?' asked R. Haninah. 'This man,' the other replied, 'assigned his estate . . . and I compelled them to maintain him.' Now if it be conceded that this was not in accordance with strict law one can well understand why he had to

compel him, but if this was in accordance with strict law, why did he have to compel him?' " (I follow here the translation of W. Slotki in the Soncino translation of the Talmud, ed. I. Epstein. Many other interpretations of the last phrase have been suggested.) The incidents involving R. Jonathan were identified as one and the same (despite the variation in the name of his companion in the Talmuds, and the different record of parts of the conversation) by R. Asher, *Commentary to Kiddushin* 1:50, and more recently by Z. Frankel, *Mavo ha-Yerushalmi*, 99b.

26   The Midrash (*Numbers Rabbah* 17:1) assumes that a son ought to give his father gifts in recognition of his receipt of the parental estate, but that does not affect our discussion.

27   *She'iltot*, 56. Ironically, but in a more profound sense, deliberately, R. Ahai structures the financial responsibility of children to parents as identical with the financial responsibility of parents to children who are older than six: cf. *Ketubot* 49b and *Shulhan Arukh, Even ha-'Ezer* 71:1. Later exponents of this view (cf. nn. 33–34) were more explicit on the juridic assimilation of the parent's dilemma by *zedakah* structures. Cf. R. Naftali Berlin, *Ha'amek She'alah, ad loc.*, n. 6, especially end.

28   *Tosefta Ma'aser Sheni* 4:7, cited in *Kiddushin* 32a. R. Me'ir of Rothenberg (*Responsa and Decisions*, ed. I. Z. Cahana, II, pp. 118–119) cites *Nedarim* 65b: " 'He who falls does not fall first into the hands of the charity-wardens,' but into the hands of his relations." This is stated most explicitly in *Seder Eliyyahu* (Chapter 27, p. 135): "If a man has much food in his home and wishes to perform acts of *zedakah* so as to support others, what should he do? Let him first support his father and mother; if anything is left, let him support his brothers and sisters; if anything is left, let him support those in his house . . . his family . . . his neighbors, etc." The problem of supporting parents from the funds earmarked for one's charity tithe was not uncommon in medieval Europe; see R. Isaac of Vienna, *'Or Zarua, Zedaka*, sec. 26 (I, p. 17, Zhitomir: 1862), and R. Me'ir of Rothenberg, *Responsa*, Prague ed. M. Bloch, Budapest: 1895, 75 (p. 10b).

29   The problem of the use of force to compel adherence to *mitzvot* in general and *zedakah* in particular is quite complex, from the legal no less than the historical point of view. See M. Elon, *Freedom of the Debtor's Person in Jewish Law* (Hebrew), pp. 24–26, especially n. 64. While many talmudic sources bear implicitly upon the issue, a number of explicit *dicta* are recorded, and these become the matrix for subsequent decisions and codes. Thus we read:

(1)   " . . . in the case of a positive command, as when they tell him, 'build a *sukkah*,' and he refuses; 'make a *lulav*,' and he refuses, they beat the soul out of him" (*Ketubot*, 86a–b; cf. also *Baba Batra* 48a, for the approved compulsion of sacrifices and divorces).

(2)   " 'You must fulfull what has crossed your lips, and perform what you have voluntarily vowed to the Lord your God' (Deuteronomy 23:24) . . . 'And perform'—This is directed to the court, that they compel you" (*Rosh ha-Shannah* 6a).

(3) " 'You must have completely honest weights . . . if you are to endure long on the soil that the Lord your God is giving you' (Deuteronomy 25:15). 'If you are to endure long . . .'—Abba Hanin said in the name of R. Eliezer, 'The court is not forewarned about any *mitzvah* whose reward is written at its side' " (*Midrash Tanna'im* 69).

(4) "Meanwhile they brought in a man who did not honor his father and mother, and bound him. He (Rami B. Tamri) said to them, 'Leave him alone, for so it has been taught, "The earthly court is not forewarned concerning an affirmative commandment which carries its reward by its side" ' " (*Hullin* 110b).

(5) " . . . R. Bon b. Hiyya said, 'So reads the teaching: "The court is not punished for any *mitzvah* which carries its reward at its side" ' " (*p. Baba Batra;* Chapter 5, end).

(6) "(If a man is not affluent, he can be shamed into supporting his children) but if he is affluent he is compelled against his will. Just as Rava compelled R. Nathan b. Ammi, and extracted from him 400 *zuz* for charity" (*Ketubot* 49b).

(7) "The townspeople are also at liberty to fix weights and measures, prices, and wages, and to inflict penalties for the infringement of their rules [literally, 'to remove those who infringe their regulations']" (*Baba Batra* 8b).

Later legists attempted to reveal a consistent legal pattern in the citations above. Quite clearly, some *mitzvot* were beyond the jurisdiction of the court (3, 4) and others are clearly within it (1). Charity is apparently to be grouped with the latter (cf. 6). Yet gaonic opinion was taken to have rejected legal compulsion in charity assessments (cf. the interpretation given the statements of R. Hai by Rashba [cited in Lewin, *Ozar ha-Ge'onim,* VIII, pt. 1, p. 130, sec. 331–332] and R. Zerahiah ha-Levi, *Ba'al ha-Ma'or, Baba Kamma* 4 [Wilna ed. of R. Alfas, p. 18a]). Maimonides, on the other hand, ruled quite clearly that the courts can compel the payment of charity, and even attach the property of the recalcitrant donor (*Mattnot 'Aniyyim* 7:10; cf. also *Mamrim* 6:3); Nahmanides (*Milhamot, op. cit.*) understood the gaonim to allow all compulsion short of actual appropriation or the use of the ban.

The issue is more fully exposed, however, in the discussions of the tosafists. There, a new element is added to the problem: How could Rava compel R. Nathan to pay his charity assessment (6), when the charitable man is promised the blessings of God (Deuteronomy 15:10) and is therefore beyond the jurisdiction of earthly courts (3, 4)? Some tosafists interpreted (5) in the light of (3, 4), and thus allowed the court the *option* of compulsion; Ri rejected the question from Deuteronomy 15:10, arguing that the evasion of one's *zedakah* responsibilities was a violation of a negative command and is therefore quite properly the object of juridical compulsion. R. Tam, on the other hand, accepted the question and all its implications, ruling that no court could compel the payment of charity; the compulsion effected by Rava (6) must, he argued, have been limited to his bringing to bear strong communal pressures (*Tosafot Baba Batra* 8b, *s.v. yotzi*). He also allows that an individual may "enroll" in a community and give it the right to legislate for him (7); thus, for R. Tam the source of political authority is, in most instances, the consent of the governed, a conclusion he took to its logical limit in his discussion of minority rights (cf. *Mordekhai, Baba Batra ad loc;* and I. Agus, *R. Meir of Rothenberg*). R. Joseph Karo (*Even ha-'Ezer* 71:1 and *Yoreh De'ah* 248:1) took Maimonides as his guide, and ruled that the community can force the recalcitrant individual to pay his charity assessment. (My summary reflects, obviously, the juridical approach of the sources; a historical analysis would proceed quite differently and focus on different problems.)

30   Though a son is not obliged to support his wealthy parent, the pietistic *Sefer Hassidim* (ed. R. Margoliot, sec. 582, p. 381) writes: "There was a wealthy man, and his son was rich. The father was stingy in feeding himself. The sage said to the son, 'Though your father is wealthy, since he is stingy you ought to feed and clothe him from your own pocket.' "

31   See *Hiddushei ha-Ritba, ad loc.,* but see also R. Nissim.

32   I. Twersky, "Some Aspects of the Jewish Attitude Toward the Welfare State," *Tradition,* V (1963), p. 153.

33   Cited in *Ozar ha-Ge'onim* (ed. B. M. Lewin), VIII, pt. 1, p. 130. R. Hai states that parents have no lien or legal claim upon filial property other than that born of *zedakah,* which is not fully actionable (see n. 29).

34   Cited in *Ozar ha-Ge'onim,* IX, pt. 3, p. 24. R. Hanan'el does not explicitly state that the ground for compulsion is the *zedakah* structure, but this is assumed by R. Asher, who first cited this view. See also R. Asher, *op. cit.;* for the tosafists, see n. 47.

35   *Kiddushin, ad loc.*

36   *Shulhan Arukh, Yoreh De'ah* 240:5.

37   See note 19.

38   *Responsa,* IV, number 56. See also II, number 6.

39   A. Neumann, *The Jews in Spain,* II, p. 17, notes that "in all the responsa of the Spanish rabbis, there is only one case of a son who was hauled to court for the non-support of his father," citing the responsum of Rashba above. But see the responsum of Rashba cited by R. Joseph Karo, *Bet Yosef, Hoshen Mishpat,* 257, *mehudash* 2, which, while not directly concerned with filial support, does nonetheless touch on filial callousness in this area. In any case, the absence of court cases in this area is at least partially explained by the embarrassment of such a procedure, and the lack of quick and potent enforcement of the parental claim (as demonstrated in the responsum above).

40   See, e.g., R. Alexander Zusslein, *Sefer Aggudah, Pe'ah* sec. I. (Cracow: 1571), p. 185c; Ridbaz, *infra;* R. Me'ir Halevi Abulafia, as understood by the Gaon of Vilna, *Yoreh De'ah* 240, n. 14.

41   See, e.g., R. Asher, *op. cit.,* and n. 44.

42   *Sefer ha-Yashar, Hiddushim* (ed. Shlesinger), sec. 141, pp. 105-106; see also sec. 145, pp. 107-108.

43   R. Eliezer Halevi, *Sefer Rabiah,* IV (ed. A. Frishman and S. Cohen), sec. 915, pp. 239-243.

44   *Mamrim* 6:3: "We compel him to support his father and his mother as far as he is able to do so." (Hershman, p. 154–155, offers a slightly different rendering, but our contention is unaffected by it.) Much of the vocabulary is that of *She'iltot* and R. Alfas, but explicit mention of *zedakah* is absent; "as far as he is able" is tantalizingly ambiguous, but suggests a more extensive commitment than the charity levy. This understanding of Maimonides is rejected by most commentators (cf. R. Joel Sirkes, *Bayit Hadash* to *Tur, Yoreh De'ah* 240, and R. Shabbetai ha-Kohen *Siftei Kohen* to *Shulhan Arukh, Yoreh De'ah* 240, n. 6) but was apparently the reading of R. Moses Isserles, *op. cit.* See, however, *Mattnot 'Aniyyim,* 10:16: " . . . so, too, he who supports his father and mother has participated in an act of *zedakah,* and it is a great *zedakah,* for one is obliged first to aid those who are closest." However, this is a less narrowly halakhic statement than the quotation out of context might suggest, and the terminology ought to be understood flexibly. See also *Tur, Yoreh De'ah,* 251.

45   A close reading of R. Tam discloses this use of the *zedakah* precedent as analogue and precedent, but no more. This is also demonstrated by the fact that whereas R. Ahai had understood our *sugya* as ruling out filial expenditure in both situations of parental prosperity or filial poverty, R. Tam relates the *sugya* to the first of these possibilities only; filial piety demands financial sacrifice even from the son who has little himself. This is consistent with R. Tam's views on related questions; see n. 53.

46   See *Hiddushei ha-Ritba, op. cit;* R. Moses of Coucy (*Semag*) *'Asin* (Munkacs: 1905), no. 112-113, p. 116a; R. Levi b. Gershom, *op. cit.;* R. Bahya b. Asher, *Bi'ur la-Torah* (Amsterdam; 1734), p. 105d.

47   The contrast described in the text would not accurately reflect the views of all medieval scholars, however. Maimonides, for example, does allow juridical compulsion of the obligations of filial piety (see n. 44). R. Tam, on the other hand, disallows compulsion for *zedakah* levies as well (see n. 29, end), though his suggested conceptual alternative would doubtless function pragmatically to justify such action, and so let in by the back door almost—but not quite—everything he had barred at the front door. We recall that some tosafists equated filial responsibility and *zedakah:* in both situations, the court is not *required* to compel payment but has the option of so doing. The majority of medieval scholars treating the question, though, reflect the view later codified in the *Shulhan Arukh:* charity payment is to be compelled (see n. 29), but filial obligations are not (*Shulhan Arukh, Yoreh De'ah* 240:1).

The extent to which compulsion was actually practiced is unclear. The Jewish court in talmudic times (both in Palestine and Babylonia) possessed these powers for long periods in its history, and as the incidents cited show, used them. See J. Neusner, *A History of the Jews in Babylonia,* III, pp. 220ff, and IV, pp. 131ff, p. 140. Medieval codes speak of corporal compulsion (by flogging) but we do not know how often this power was used to collect charity levies. See S. Assaf, *Ha-*

'onshim Ahar Hatimat ha-Talmud. M. Elon discusses the functions and prevalence of imprisonment in classic Jewish law ("Imprisonment in Jewish Law," *Jubilee Volume* for *P. Rosen,* Heb., pp. 171–201); his materials—admittedly quite limited—indicate that imprisonment fulfilled a compulsory (as distinct from a punitive) function in matters of personal status, as when a husband refused to divorce his wife, but no example of imprisonment to compel payment of charity is cited.

48   *Seder Eliyyahu,* ed. Friedman, p. 134.

49   *Responsa,* II, p. 664. The responsum is much more complex than my brief citation would indicate.

Parental support of children offers an interesting comparison here. While a husband is expected to support his wife in grander style as he grows more prosperous, the extent of parental support of children does not increase with the increasing prosperity of the parent. The distinction—one applicable to filial support of parents too—is that husband and children owe wife and parents, respectively, *honor,* which is relative; parents owe children support of their needs, which is objective. See *Shulhan Arukh, Even ha-'Ezer* 73:6. (For an exception, see M. *Ketubot* VI, 5-6.) On the other hand, though parental support of children is a form of *zedakah,* different yardsticks will be used to decide a man's ability to support his children than are used to decide his ability to make a *zedakah* payment. See Y. Kister, "The Function of *Zedakah* in Israeli Law," *Papers of the Fourth World Congress of Jewish Studies,* I, Hebrew section, p. 170, n. 18.

50   *Responsa Hatam Sofer, Yoreh De'ah* 229. *Hatam Sofer* suggests, perhaps, that "public charity" might have adequately supported parents who were not "honored" and well-born.

51   See *Shulhan Arukh, Yoreh De'ah* 251:3.

52   S. Y. Zevin, *Ishim veShittot,* p. 61. Interestingly, R. Moses Isserles had ruled (*Yoreh De'ah* 240:8): "If a son is involved in litigation with his father, and the father is the plaintiff, the son must allow the case to be tried where the father desires though the son is the defendant and lives in a different town (generally, a case is heard in the locale of the defendant—*Hoshen Mishpat* 14:1) for this is the honor due his father. But the father must pay the son's expenses, for the son is not obliged to honor the father of his own funds." R. Joseph Kolon (Maharik), *Responsa* 58, is given as source for this ruling. Yet the responsum is somewhat ambivalent on this last detail: " . . . if you (the son) find that your coming to the court most convenient to your mother entails additional expenses, she shall pay this extra amount. *And though the law might not require this,* I so rule to forestall any complaint on your part. . . .[my italics]"

We have already noted that talmudic law (unlike Roman law) did not disadvantage the son in his legal relations with his parent or deprive him of his rights under law (see Chapter II, n. 3); in Jewish thought the child is not "in the power" of the parent. Hence we see that the son sues his father (as above, "there is no reason to prevent a son from forcing his father to take the oath"—an anonymous geonic responsum in *Teshuvot ha-Ge'onim,* ed. A. Harkavy, sec. 206, p.

96; *Shulhan Arukh, Yoreh De'ah* 240:8 and 241:6) though some adjustment is made in either the procedure or formula of any oath to be sworn by the father. (Obviously, a sensitive son might well refuse to become involved in litigation with his father—see *Sefer Hassidim,* ed. R. Margoliot, sec. 584, pp. 381–382, which shows, incidentally, that the son would be expected by all but the pious to sue his father in the circumstances described.) At the same time, however, the son is expected to be fully mindful of the norms of filial piety.

53 Discussions on congruent topics were derivative of the views analyzed in our text. This is seen in the varied medieval approaches to the statement of R. Simeon b. Yohai cited earlier: ". . . With regard to your father and mother, whether you have the means or not, 'Honor your father and your mother,' even if you must become a beggar at the door." Though the Palestinian Talmud itself declared that R. Simeon doubtless held a son responsible for his father's support—which would lead us to expect that his view would be rejected, as a consistent acceptance of the position of Babylonian Talmud would require—some decisors sought to harmonize his position with that of Babylonian Talmud. Others were able to integrate his view with that of Babylonian Talmud by limiting its impact. Finally, there were those who rejected his view *in toto.*

Thus, R. Asher, who reads the Babylonian conclusion as releasing the child from the obligation of support (except as required by *zedakah*), writes (*Kiddushin, op. cit.*), " . . . [it] does not mean that he is obliged to support him of his own substance, . . . but that he must honor him physically (i.e., do him service), losing working time, and thus be forced to beg at the door." R. Tam, whose general posture we have examined, is as one might expect more demanding. The son must reduce himself to poverty not only in the service of his parent, but he must also give of his substance even if he thereby condemns himself to poverty. Yet, a child who has nothing is not obliged to beg in order to provide for his parent (cited by R. Isaac of Corbeil, *Semak (Sefer Mitzvot Katan),* 50; given as the view of R. Isaac the Tosafist in *Sefer Aggudah, op. cit.*). R. Me'ir Abulafia (cited by R. Yeruham, *Sefer Adam veHavah, Adam,* 1:4) apparently rejected the position of R. Simeon because of its inconsistency with the posture of the Babylonian Talmud, maintaining—in deliberate contrast with the conceptual underpinnings of R. Simeon—that " . . . it is similar to what is expected in the honoring of God—one is not expected to stop work and become a beggar in order to visit the sick or comfort the mourner." R. Joseph Karo (*Yoreh De'ah* 240:5) reproduces the opinions of both R. Asher and R. Me'ir Abulafia, though one cannot help noting that, of necessity, a certain inconsistency arises.

However rare the situations described above may have been, their normative reflection is part of the Jewish ethos. And inasmuch as the devoted and intensive study and teaching of this ethos certainly contributed to the formation of the behavior patterns of the historical Jew, the most theoretical of discussions had its pragmatic impact upon Jewish living and values.

54 One can, perhaps, note a tendency in relatively recent times (post-*Shulhan Arukh*) to place filial property at parental disposal even where support is not an issue, by requiring a son to abide by parental deathbed wishes as an element of

kibbud av even when some financial loss must be borne. Thus, R. Ya'ir Hayyim Bachrach (17th century) obliged a son who had been commanded by his mother, before she died, that he not rent his house to anyone, to refuse to rent the house, despite the financial sacrifice involved. It is of course true that the son is sacrificing "profits," and is not actually spending money on his parent's behalf; nonetheless, considering the fact that the mother is dead and that the above distinction may be rendered quite theoretical by hard fact, it is a surprise that the respondent did not raise the question of financial loss at all (see *Responsa Havvot Ya'ir*, no. 214). The early 20th-century halakhist, R. Yehiel Epstein, does dissent from this ruling [*Arukh ha-Shulhan, Yoreh De'ah* 240:45], but on other grounds.) Another instance is afforded by R. Akiba Eiger (18th century), who considers the possibility that a son may be obliged to accede to parental desire with regard to the disposal of the estate he inherits from them as an expression of *kibbud av,* despite the fact that the estate is fully the property of the son. Both the question of financial loss and that of the many talmudic texts that discuss legal rubrics are raised, but neither factor is decisive enough to surmount R. Eiger's suspicion that the son is in fact obliged to accede to the parental wish (see *Responsa R. Akiba Eiger,* no. 68). Both the conceptual and pragmatic effects of such decisions (especially the former) are quire radical, and would give parents—not only posthumously, but even while alive—control over filial property to a degree unheard of in prior thought. It is, furthermore, to be noted that in neither instance does the parent actually derive any concrete enjoyment from the disposal of the property he requires of the son. See Chapter IV. The subject of filial responsibility for parental debts is quite complicated, and the rubric of filial piety is mobilized only with regard to inherited property; see *Ketubot* 86a-b, and 91b; *Tur, Hoshen Mishpat* 107, and especially Rashba, cited in *Bet Yosef, ad loc.,* and *Hagahot 'Asheri* to R. Asher, *Ketubot,* IX, sec. 14 (end).

55   *Midrash Aggadah* to Exodus 27:1, as translated in L. Ginzberg, *Legends,* III, p. 149. The 10th-century *Midrash Aseret ha-Dibrot* also assumes, in an attempt to fuse the claims of both createdness and gratitude, that children should support their parents: "Honor the parents from whom you came, as Myself. Said the Holy One, Blessed be He, 'Honor the womb in which you were born; provide for (*parneseim*) the breasts from which you sucked, for they were with Me when I created you'" *Bet ha-Midrash,* (edited by A. Yellinek), I/i, p. 76. Interestingly, attention is here focussed on the mother; cf. Chapter II, n. 14.

NOTES FOR CHAPTER IV

1   I follow the traditional commentators, who take *hamur* to mean "difficult" in this context; cf. also E. Urbach, *Hazal,* p. 304; M. *Avot* 2:1 and its explicators; L. Ginzberg, *Legends,* VI, 41, n. 223. R. Simeon's authorship of this statement is most apt; it was he who claimed that filial piety and service are required even where the service of God is not (see Chapter III). Maimonides (*Hilkhot Mamrim*

6:1) calls filial service and reverence a "great *mitzvah (mitzvah gedolah),*" a rather uncommon phrase, and points immediately to the analogies with the service of God.

2 Sa'adiah Gaon (*Sefer Emunot veDe'ot,* 5:4) understands *kibbud av* as a type, including the acceptance upon oneself not to miss his prayers, or to acquire wealth dishonestly, or to lie. He implies, in fact, that any single *mitzvah,* if singled out, can serve. The commandments specified by Sa'adiah all do possess a number of characteristics in common; they are central to the religious life and, more concretely, are especially challenging by virtue of their constancy.

3 *Menorat ha-Ma'or* (ed. H. G. Enelow), IV, pp. 17–18.

4 *Ketubot* 103a.

5 Reproduced in S. Assaf, *Mekorot le-Toledot ha-Hinukh be-Yisra'el,* IV, pp. 7–11. Of course, this document may well reflect an idiosyncratic personal situation. Curiously, the documents collected in I. Abrahams, *Hebrew Ethical Wills,* stress filial piety as a motive for obedience to the commands of the departing parent, but rarely is the child urged to filial regard for the surviving parent.

6 *Yalkut Shim'oni, Vayiggash,* sec. 164.

7 *Yalkut* to Proverbs 23:22. So too, "He who desires long life and wealth in this world, and long life in the next, which is endless—let him do the will of his father in heaven and the will of his father and mother" (*Seder Eliyyahu,* p. 134).

8 *Midrash Abkir,* cited in *Yalkut,* I, No. 276. Cf. also *Midrash Vayoshah,* in A. Jellinek, ed., *Bet ha-Midrash,* I/i, 36.

9 Clearly, the role of Isaac in the *Akedah* was stressed in Second Commonwealth and tannaitic liturgical texts, and in early tannaitic aggadah (see S. Spiegel, *The Last Trial;* and more specifically, E. E. Urbach, *Hazal,* pp. 445–449), in contrast to the biblical focus on Abraham alone; but this new stress is announced more than it is explored.

10 For the general development, see G. F. Moore, *Judaism: The Age of the Tannaim,* I, pp. 539–540.

11 Proverbs 10:1. See also 15:20, 17:21, 17:25, 19:13, 23:24-25, 29:15-17.

12 *Ibid.,* 28:7.

13 *Ben-Sira* (ed. Segal), 23:20. In a slightly different vein, a son will not fornicate because of his shame for his parents (14:22). And Tobit, in his instructions to Tobias, tells his son not to distress his mother (Tobit 4:3).

14 Tobit 3:10.

15 *Nedarim* 9:1; see Chapter III.

16 See Chapter II, n. 1. See also Chapter V, sec. I, pt. 4.

17 *Zohar* (Wilna: 1894), I, 164b. Similarly, Joseph's not disclosing his whereabouts to his father constitutes a major problem for Nahmanides: ". . . for were it not for what we have written above, Joseph would have sinned mightily

to cause his father anguish, and to leave him a mourner so many years . . . for one asks, since Joseph spent so many years in Egypt, and rose to such high office, how is it that he never sent even a single letter to his father, to tell him of his whereabouts and to console him, for Egypt is only a six-day journey from Hebron, and even were it a year's journey it were fit that he notify him, because of the honor due his father. . . ." (*Commentary* to Genesis 42:9.) Cf. *Midrash Tanhuma, Vayeshev* 8; *Sefer Hassidim* (ed. J. Wistinetzki), sec. 941.

18   R. Isaiah Horowitz, *Shenei Luhot Haberit* (Amsterdam: 1708), p. 303a.

19   *Sifra, Kedoshim,* Par. 1, sec. 10, p. 87a. The articulation of this idea—so patently necessary within any theocentric value scheme—can be documented to the period of the Second Temple. IV Maccabees, generally dated in the century preceding the destruction of the Temple (see Chapter 1, n. 115), declares: "Does not Torah rule over the love of parents, forbidding us to abandon virtue for their sake?" It is quite possible that he refers here to our rabbinic teaching (the author of this work was probably an Alexandrian!); Heinemann, *Philons . . . ,* p. 259, n. 2, notes this passage as well. But another source might be Deuteronomy 33:9: "And of Levi he said . . . Who said of his father and mother, 'I consider them not.' His brothers he disregarded, ignored his own children. Your precepts alone they observed, and kept your covenant." This passage was often taken (see Targums and Midrash) as referring to the tribe's willingness to defend virtue at all costs (see Exodus 32:27ff: " 'Each of you put sword on thigh, go back and forth from gate to gate, and slay brother, neighbor, and kin.' The Levites did as Moses had bidden. . . . And Moses said, ' . . . each of you has been against son and brother . . . ' ") The passage in Maccabees continues to enumerate wife, comrade, and brother along with parents, as persons whose claims are overridden by those of virtue. See also Deuteronomy 13:7-13.

20   *Yevamot* 5b.

21   *Responsa,* 15:5. Cf. R. Israel Joshua, *Responsa Yeshu'ot Malko,Yoreh De'ah,* 37. R. Ezekiel Katznellenbogen, *Resp. K'nesseth Yehezkel* (Altona, 1732), *Y. D.,* no. 35.

22   See Chapter V.

23   R. Me'ir of Rothenberg, *Responsa,* Prague edition, no. 717. See also the "Takkanot" (enactments) ascribed to R. Tam, as published and translated in L. Finkelstein, *Jewish Self-Government in the Middle Ages,* pp. 195, 202: "My master says, if a man hits a person who insulted his father, justice must be done for the person hurt, for we find no law permitting one to strike one who insulted one's father."

24   *Kiddushin* 32a.

25   The pietistic tendency to discount filial responsibility in favor of religious ritual fulfillment is rejected by *Seder Eliyyahu* (chapter 26, p. 134): "Let a man not say to himself, 'Since the command to honor God came first [i.e., the hallowing of the Sabbath is the fourth of the Ten Commandments, that to honor parents—the fifth] I shall not fulfill the will of my father and mother. . . . ' "

Probably as an inducement to just such sons, *Seder Eliyyahu* promises that he who fulfills his filial responsibility is forgiven his Sabbath transgressions. M. Zucker's claim (*Targum Rav Sa'adiah*, p. 215) that this represents an anti-Karaite position is supported by an anonymous gaonic epistle rebuking a community that refused its parents honor "because they wished to draw closer to God thereby" (S.Assaf, *MiSifrut HaGe'onim*, p. 173). Assaf notes, on the basis of other, internal, evidence, a Karaite provocation.

26   Interestingly, students of R. Simeon b. Yohai decided similarly in cases of conflict between the study of Torah and achievement of a *mitzvah:* if the *mitzvah* cannot be achieved by others, it takes priority over study of Torah; if it can be achieved by others, it does not—*Mo'ed Katon* 9a-b.

27   The former position is implied by Me'iri, *Bet ha-Behirah, Yevamot* (2nd ed.), p. 27, among others. The latter position is apparently maintained by the tosafists (Kiddushin 32a, *s.v. Rav;* R. Tam as cited by Ritba, *Yevamot, ad loc.*), Ramban and Ritba (in their commentaries to *Yevamot*), and others. Some later scholars maintain that the former position is endorsed by some of those I have listed as supporting the latter position; *cf. Bi'ur ha-Gra, Yoreh De'ah* 240, n. 36; *Hazon Ish, Nashim,* sec. 148, and others cited by S. Dickman, *Bet ha-Behirah, Yevamot,* p. 27, n. 258. Cf. R. Hayyim Heller, *Sefer ha-Mitzvot le-ha-Rambam,* p. 88, n. 5, for a presentation similar to ours. Discussion of these texts is beyond the scope of this inquiry; it is fair to note, however, that there is a tendency in the later sources generally to minimize the validity of filial independence, as we shall see. Thus, the late 18th-century *Sefer ha-Makneh* declares: "It appears that obedience to anything commanded by the father—even if the father derives no benefit from its fulfillment, and so that the obedience is not a form of *kibbud*—is, as long as no loss is caused the son, included in the rubric of *morah* ("reverence"), for if the son does not obey his father, it is the same as if he contradicted him" (p. 65c). Clearly, loss of autonomy is in itself not considered of much significance, as it does not warrant a clearly recognizable parental need to justify its sacrifice.

28   Though *Tosafot Kiddushin, op. cit.,* allows the father the "emotional pleasure of throwing a wallet into the sea in order to impress his authority upon his family." If generalized, the submission to any request can afford this type of pleasure, and its refusal—irritation and distress. Cf. Y. Perlow, *Sefer ha-Mitzvot le-Rav Sa'adiah Gaon,* I, pp. 202-203.

29   My translation follows the punctuation suggested by Y. Z. Kahane, *Teshuvot . . . Maharam,* II, p. 120, section 129. see Y. Shepanski, *Eretz-Yisrael be-Sifrut ha-Teshuvot,* I, p. 120; E. E. Urbach, *Ba'alei ha-Tosafot,* p. 423.

30   R. Moses of Trani (Mabit), *Responsa,* I, 139.

31   *Terumat ha-Deshen,* 40. See also *Pithei Teshuva, Yoreh De'ah* 240:22. Cf. also R. Judah Ayyas, *Responsa Bet David, Yoreh De'ah* 54.

Note the similar concern of the pietistic *Sefer Hassidim* (edited by R. Margaliot, section 575): "One who leaves a town . . . and goes to a dangerous place, and his parents are fasting or are worried over his safety, is obliged—if it is possible—to hire a messenger and notify his parents of his arrival at his final destination, so that they may be spared from further distress.'' See also section 340; the text is unclear, but it seems to say that despite the rule of filial freedom in areas of religious fulfillment, a son ought to forego voluntary ascetic exercises if they cause his parents to be concerned for his health.

32   *Pithei Teshuva, Yoreh De'ah* 240:22, citing R. Daniel of Horodna, *Hamudei Daniel* (ms.). Indirectly, R. David Ben Abu-Zimra *Responsa Ridbaz*, III, No. 910.

32a   R. Raphael Meldola, *Responsa Mayim Hayyim* (Amsterdam: 1737), 48. This was not the only factor in the 18th-century Italian rabbi's decision; the objective plight of the widow as well as the son's uncertainty that a new location spelled success at studies were also seen as significant issues. Compare his responsum 49 and n. 31 *supra*.

33   *Genesis Rabbah* 67:12, as given in ms. Leiden (Theodore-Albeck, II, p. 768, and notes). Other midrashic parallels cite Esau rather than Samson.

34   Robert de Vaux, *Ancient Israel* (trans. John McHugh, New York: 1965), pp. 26-30.

35   M. *Kiddushin* 2:1.

36   *Kiddushin* 41a.

37   A. H. Freimann, *Seder Kiddushin veNissu'im*, pp. 12–14. Freimann cites the regulations of Rav (*Kiddushin* 12b) and Samuel (p. *Kiddushin* 3:8) as directed against marriages hastily contracted without parental approval. But even if the major concern was the hasty or casual marriage, irrespective of parental approval, these regulations increased parental control.

38   *Kiddushin* 29a, and parallels, *Kiddushin* 30b and *Ketubot* 52b.

39   R. Pappa, in *Sanhedrin* 93a.

40   Cf. Raphael Patai, *Sex and Family in the Bible and the Middle East* (Anchor edition, N. Y.), pp. 46–47: ''romantic love . . . does . . . play a considerable role in the Middle East, even in the most restrictive tradition-bound sectors of society. . . . Side by side with the formalized aspect of marriage as a family affair, we find frequent manifestations of the power of love that break through barriers of custom.'' But (p. 48), ''. . . romantic love is more prevalent . . . in the nomadic tribes than in settled society.''

41   *Responsa*, I, 1219. The translation is largely that of Isidore Epstein, *The Responsa of Rabbi Solomon ben Aderet of Barcelona* (London: 1925), p. 82. The specific legal question concerns the marriage of a minor, but the generalization cited obviously refers to all maidens.

42   R. Moses Mintz, *Responsa*, 98.

43   Epstein, p. 84 (*Responsa of Rabbi Solomon*, I, 550).

44   Freimann, pp. 138–139, 79. See also pp. 66 ff.

45   *Ibid.*, p. 165.

46   *Ibid.*, pp. 214–215.

47   *Ibid.*, pp. 214–215. See also Salo W. Baron, *The Jewish Community* (Philadelphia: 1948), II, p. 310, and III, p. 203, n. 21.

48   A revealing pair of gaonic responsa discuss the validity of a betrothal entered into by a father for his mature (*boggeret*) daughter. The first responds as one would expect: the act of the father has no worth so long as the daughter did not delegate him as her agent (*Teshuvot ha-Ge'onim, Sha'arei Zedek, Sha'ar* 3, 1). In *Teshuvot ha-Ge'onim,* edited by Harkavy (section 194, p. 87), the respondent answers, however, to the contrary: the betrothal is valid, "for such is the wont of the daughters of Israel; though the daughter is mature—even if she be 20 years old—as long as her father lives, she is drawn after him. One does not find among the daughters of Israel such licentiousness or impunity that she expresses her own opinions and says, 'I desire so and so,' but she relies on her father. . . ." (On the identification of the respondents and the subsequent legal history of these opinions, cf. Harkavy, p. 358. The citation by this respondent, as well as by the respondent in *Sha'arei Zedek* 3:13, of *Kiddushin* 79a–b, is puzzling, and suggests a different approach to the Rav and Samuel *sugya* there; cf. *Sefer ha-'Ittur* (ed. R. Me'ir Yonah [Warsaw: 1874], part 1, p. 79d.) Subsequent opinion rejected this approach, as one might expect. Epstein, *Responsa of R. Solomon,* p. 82 and n. 28, enlists Rashba in support of this view, but *Responsa,* I, 549, which he cites, does not bear him out. See also Baron, *supra.*

49   Responsa Attributed to Ramban, 272; *Responsa of R. Joseph Kolon,* 164:3.

50   *Sotah* 2a.

51   Cited in *Responsa of Rabbi Joseph Kolon, loc. cit.*

52   I find this point somewhat difficult. While the son is not expected to spend his own money, he is expected to render personal service, which often implies physical discomfort or inconvenience.

53   *Responsa Attributed to Ramban,* 105. So too R. Abraham di Buton, *Responsa Lehem Rav,* 420.

54   See *supra,* notes 27–28.

55   Our respondent here enlarges upon R. Joseph Kolon's ambiguous requirement that the wife be a "proper" match. For the subsequent halakhic history of this open-ended phrase, see Ben-Sasson (p. 282, n. 7), who takes "blemish" to mean apostasy.

56   The responsum is found in the ms. work, *Me'ah She'arim,* and was published by H. H. Ben-Sasson, in *Sefer Zikkaron le-Gedaliah Allon* (1970), pp. 278–283. (My request to see the ms. was refused by the Jewish Theological Seminary.)

57   Given in Ben-Sasson, pp. 286–287. The custom described is found (though with some variation) elsewhere in Europe, too; cf. Ben-Sasson, p. 277, no. 5;

Israel Abrahams, *Jewish Life in the Middle Ages,* p. 33.

58   A partial listing would include, in addition to Rashba and Maharik, the following: *Responsa of Simeon b. Zemah Duran* (Tashbatz), pt. 3, 130, sec. 5; *Responsa of Samuel de Modena* (Rashdam), *Yoreh De'ah* 90, 95; *Responsa of Elijah b. Hayyim* (Ra'anah), pt. 1, 78; *Responsa Ya'akov le-Bet Levi,* 21; cf. also *Responsa of R. Isaac b. Sheshet,* 127. A secondary question was whether women had the same right to defy their parents; this problem derives from the fact that in rabbinic law only the male is considered commanded to "be fruitful and multiply." Thus, R. Shabbetai Ventura (cited in R. David Pardo, *Mikhtam le-David,* 32) ruled that only a son might reject parental opposition to his marriage but not a daughter. Most respondents, however, allowed both son and daughter equal rights: cf. Tashbatz *(supra);* R. David Pardo *(supra* 33) , who argues basing himself on *Responsa of R. Nissim* (Ran), 32—that the bearing of children by women, and hence their marriage, is a commanded act. The equality of sexes is also assumed by R. Ezekiel Landau, *Noda bi-Yehudah,* series II, *Even ha-'Ezer* 45; cf., too, *Responsa Give'at Pinhas,* 3.

The case of R. David Pardo is most instructive. Assuming that the couple concerned had explicitly rejected parental objections in their vow to marry, R. David argued that though parental honor was not involved *(per* Maharik), the couple may not marry. Firstly, the father stood to lose financially by the marriage; and inasmuch as the union was one of those banned in the will of R. Judah the Pious, "the woman is not a proper mate [*per* Maharik, again], though many do not abide by" the pietist's testament. "How brazen is this girl," he concludes, "for daughters of Israel do as their fathers direct." She must be forced to cancel her vow, "and if she will not do so, let her sit a spinster until her hair grays over."

Upon discovering, however, that the couple's vow to marry did not refer to parental objections at all (it being assumed that none existed), R. David changed his decision (though without re-arguing his earlier points, which he doubtless realized were rather weak anyway); "since the girl is not a minor . . . she may marry whomsoever she wishes, and her father has no power to prevent her doing so . . . indeed, so long as she loves the man and does not have a complete change of heart, the vow may not be cancelled." The court should urge her to change her mind but may not prevent the marriage. The rabbi's rage was apparently triggered by the impudence of a presumed vow to violate parental wishes; with this factor gone, his attitude changed. The reader is also left with the impression that other facts in the case had come to light, and that these too weakened the father's case.

59   *Sefer Hassidim,* section 564. See also R. Hayyim Yehudah Eliezer, *Simhat Yehudah,* sermon 4.

60   *Responsa,* II, *Yoreh De'ah* 27 (end). The question is put in responsum number 24, and the lengthy discussion is divided into three responsa. In *Responsa,* I, *Even ha-'Ezer* 46, R. Joseph argues that the disinheritance of a son conditional upon his marriage to a wife of whom his father disapproves is legally valid; he does not express any opinion there on the propriety of the behavior of

either father or son. Cf. also R. Yehiel Weinberg, *Responsa Seridei 'Esh*, III, 95, p. 300.

61   *Responsa Divrei Shemu'el*, 83.

62   R. Joseph of Trani does argue, though, that such behavior is improper and brazen.

63   Rabbi Yeruham F. Perlow, *Sefer ha-Mitzvot le-Rav Sa'adiah Ga'on*, I (*'Aseh* 9), p. 203. Cf. also n. 21.

64   See R. Hayyim Hezkiah Medini, *Sedeh Hemed* (Warsaw: 1937), I, 3, *kelal "Kaf,"* section 147, p. 65.

65   Maharik's idiom suggests *Ketubot* 28b, and Ritba and *Nimmuke Yosef* to *Baba Batra* 100a as sources; note R. Moses Isserles to *Even ha-'Ezer* 2:1.

66   Section 564. See sec. III, pt. 4, *infra*.

67   R. Naftali Z. Berlin, *Meshiv Davar*, pt. 1-2, 50. This short responsum focusses on *bizayyon* ("shame, disgrace") of the father as a virtual absolute in this context, emphasizing it above *za'ar* ("distress"). There is no discussion, however, of the criteria for such *bizayyon*—are they objective or subjective?

68   This distinction is found in other contexts, but not until the responsum before us was it utilized, to my knowledge, to compel filial obedience.

69   Cf. Paul, "Children, obey your parents. . . ." (Ephesians 6:1). This vocabulary is absent in both Talmud and early Midrash. In Ephesians it is part of a larger sequence on authority: "Wives be subject to your husbands . . . in everything (5:22, 24). . . . Children, obey your parents (6:1). . . . Slaves, obey your earthly masters with fear and trembling (6:5). . . ." In general, this structuring of filial responsibility resembles that of Philo; cf. Chapter I, note 46.

70   But why the stress on the "sleeping-place" as the area to be left? Surely the son did not occupy the parental bedroom till his nuptials! There are, I believe, three alternative readings of Onkelos: (a) "sleeping-place" stresses the sexual nature of the new bond; (b) the phrase is meant literally, stressing that the son is expected to be available for filial service of his parents, though he is no longer in the same intimate physical nearness—perhaps he is to live in the parental house with his bride; (c) the phrase is meant literally and contains the halakhic derivation of a ban on incest. Onkelos would then be saying: "Do not sleep [have sexual relations] with mother or father, but cleave to another for your wife." (S. Wertheimer, *Or ha-Targum*, p. 9.) Such an interpretation of the verse can be traced back at least as far as R. Akiba [*Sanhedrin* 58a] and is cited by Rashi *ad loc.*

71   See R. David Kimhi (Radak), *ad loc.*: "The meaning of the verse is close to its rendering by Onkelos; it is not said that a man shall leave his father and mother for his wife, so that he does not serve them or honor them as he is able, but that it is right that a man leave his father and mother . . . and no longer live with them, but live . . . with his wife." Radak reflects a reading of Onkelos from the perspective of *Pirke de-R. Eliezer*: cf. *infra*. Note also the transition from the

relatively descriptive terms of the Torah (see Cassutto, *Commentary on Genesis,* I, p. 137) for a more normative judgmental vocabulary.

72   See Cassutto, *op.cit.* whose comments derive—even verbally—from the midrashic material to be cited.

73   *Pirke de-R. Eliezer,* chapter 32.

74   One compares, for example, the comments of Abarbanel and R. Loewe (Maharal) of Prague. Abarbanel *(ad loc.)* states: "Just as Adam was left with no love for the earth, which was his mother, nor for the rains that fell upon him . . . that were like a father to him, but forsook his love for them and cleaved unto his wife, so too shall all his descendants leave their father and mother and cleave unto their wives. . . ." Clearly, a note of remoteness (deriving from the striking simile) has been introduced. Maharal, on the other hand, rejects a literal understanding of the verse, "for why should a man find it necessary to leave his parents for his wife?" (*Gur 'Aryeh* to Rashi, Genesis 2:24) Similar contrasting exegesis is found for Genesis 24:67: see Onkelos, *Pseudo-Jonathan,* and Nahmanides' implicit opposition of his interpretation *(infra)* to theirs.

75   *Sifra, Kedoshim,* 1:2–3 (ed. Weiss, 86c-d); *Tosefta Kiddushin* 1:11; *Kiddushin* 30b; p. *Kiddushin* 1:7; 61a-b. See Weiss (note 3) on the textual variation.

76   In p. *Kiddushin,* information *("if she is divorced. . . .")* is part of the *baraita* itself, and is given anonymously. See Weiss, *Mekorot,* p. 652.

77   This is the point of the *baraita* above, and is found in the Mishnah as well: ". . . all obligations of a son toward his father are incumbent both on men and on women" (p. *Kiddushin* 1:7).

78   This reservation is clearly more appropriate for positive acts of "honor" than for the avoidance of irreverent behavior; yet the verse from which the lesson is derived treats of reverence *(morah);* cf. Rashi, *Kiddushin* 30b, *s.v. ha-mutelet.* It would seem, then, that the terminological discrimination and hermeneutic consistency are of limited applicability; see Chapter II, note 3. The bulk of later commentators understand this passage as signifying a limitation of filial responsibility and not the release of the daughter from the norm, even from that of service where possible. See *Siftei Kohen, Yoreh De'ah* 240, n. 19; this view is already explicit in Maimonides, *Commentary to the Mishnah, Kiddushin, ad loc.* See, however, Ritba and Me'iri.

79   *Sifra,* section 9 (87a); *Kiddushin* 31a; M. *Keritot* 6:9.

80   See S. Belkin, p. 220, n. 6. The rabbinic sources do not—in contrast to Philo—state that the relation of a wife toward her husband is the same as that of a daughter to her parents.

81   See note 78, *supra.*

82   See M. *Ketubot* 7,4: "If a man vowed (to abstain from) his wife, should she go to her father's house, and he (the father) lives in the same town—if the vow was for one month he may keep her," but if for two she is entitled to a divorce

and payment of the marriage contract.

83   *Exodus Rabbah* 33:7: Before God could give Israel the Torah, Moses must ascend to God; after the Torah is given to Israel, God descends to Israel in His sanctuary. "This is like the groom who, before his marriage is a familiar visitor at the home of his father-inlaw. After the marriage, however, her father must come to visit her." The wife was—with certain exceptions—to follow her husband, who established the home where he desired: see M. *Ketubot* 13:10.

84   Normative requirements notwithstanding, it was generally assumed that a father was more secure in his daughter's house than in his son's, as a son-in-law would be more hospitable than a daughter-in-law. The Babylonian folk saying had it, "If the dog barks at you, enter; if the bitch barks at you, leave (*'Eruvin* 86a)."

85   A painful problem was raised when father and husband both demanded that their daughter and wife be buried next to their own future resting places. Most texts (see *Semahot* 14, [ed. Higger, pp. 205–6]; *Abel Rabbati*, p. 242) rule that the father's claim takes precedence. This stands in contrast to the talmudic attitudes outlined above where the wife owes her first allegiance to her husband; doubtless, a distinction was drawn between life and death—where the biological takes precedence. Nonetheless, a contrary version also exists; and both rulings are offered in *Shulhan Arukh, Yoreh De'ah* 361:3. All agree, though, that if the woman bore the husband's children, she was to be buried next to him. For the biblical parallel to all this, see Leviticus 22:12–13.

86   It is instructive, at this point, to contrast the *baraita* of filial honor and reverence (Chapter II) with the broader expectation that a man should "love his wife as himself, and honor her more than himself . . ." (*Yevamot* 63a).

87   M. *Sotah* 9:15.

88   See *Ketubot* 61b: a daughter-in-law is not obliged to serve her in-laws.

89   *Mo'ed Katon*, 20b.

90   *Ibid.*, 26b.

91   M. *Ketubot* 7:6, according to Abba Saul.

92   Edited by M. Friedmann, Chapter 24, p. 135.

93   *Massekhta de-'Amalek,* 1 (to Exodus 18:7); edited by Horowitz-Rabin, p. 193.

94   I Samuel 24:11, *Yalkut, ad loc.*

95   According to the sages (*Yalkut, ibid.*), David addressed Abner, who was "his father in Torah," as "father," and not Saul.

96   *Yoreh De'ah* 240:24, *Bah* and *Shakh* (note 22), *Arukh ha-Shulhan*, par. 44; *Sefer Haredim,* Chapter 5 (p. 40); R. Solomon Luria, *Yam Shel Shelomoh, Baba Kamma*, III, 9.

97   Cited by Ramban, *Hullin* 63a (S. Reichman, ed., p. 128, and n. 182). See

also note 83.

98   M. *Yevamot* 117a, 118a; p. *Yevamot* 15:8;, 15b.

99   M. *Yevamot* 15:7; the sages in *baraita Yevamot* 117a and R. Judah (who apparently understands her to be excluded by the mishnaic text); *Yevamot* 117a, 118a; p. *Yevamot* 15:8; 15b.

100   *Yevamot* 117a–b. The mother-in-law, according to the Talmud, "tells her son all that his wife does."

101   Talmudic law on the subject is summarized in Maimonides, *Code, 'Issurei Bi'ah* 22:1, 9, 12.

102   Louis Epstein, *Jewish Marriage Contract*, p. 276. A Palestinian *ketubah* of the 11th century stipulates, for example: "her mother Hisan has the right to dwell with them in the house"—M. Friedman, *Jewish Marriage Contracts in the Palestinian Tradition* (diss., U. of Pennsylvania, 1969),p.284.

103   See. R. Nissim of Gerona, *Responsa*, 15; see also S. Assaf, *Be-'Ohalei Ya'akov*, p. 105.

104   The basic gaonic responsum here is that of the 9th-century R. Paltoi (Pumbedita), given by R. Me'ir of Rothenberg, *Responsa*, Prague-Budapest (ed. M. Bloch), 81; Cremona, 291; and R. Menahem Recanati, *Piskei Halakhot*, section 511. "If the wife initiates the quarrels, she is like a 'rebellious wife,' and loses her marriage settlement *(ketubah)*, but if he initiates them, he must pay the settlement. And if the members of the household, such as her mother-in-law or her sister-in-law are responsible, he must remove her to another domicile, for no man can live with a serpent." R. Paltoi continues, that if the husband did not alleviate her plight and she flees to her father's home, he must support her there.

105   *Ketubot* 61a.

106   *Responsa*, no. 235 (ed. W. Leiter, p. 65a); see also *Teshuvot ha-Ge'onim*, no. 134, p. 292. A possible gaonic adumbration in cases of property disputes adapts M. Ketubot V, 8; see S. Assaf, *MiSifrut HaGe'onim*, p.111.

107   *Responsa*, no. 101 (Warsaw: 1870; p. 16a).

108   *Code, 'Ishut* 13:14.

108a   For an actual Maimonidean decision protecting the sick wife in this context, see *Responsa* (ed. J. Blau), II, no.234, p.428.

108b   Maimonides does know of the third-party device in connection with domestic quarrels, though: *Ishut*, 21:10. The use of this device in such circumstances goes back to the 10th-century, Spanish, R. Joseph ibn Abitur at least *(Teshuvot Sha'arei Zedek* IV.4.42 [Jerusalem, 1966, p. 141]).

109   The opinion of *Maggid Mishneh, ad loc.*, is a difficult one to defend; see R. Jacob Castro and R. Aaron Perahiah, *infra* and n. 108a *supra*. R. Benjamin b. Matityahu (18th-century Greece), *Responsa Binyamin Ze'ev*, no. 137, is a good illustration of how the Maimonidean doctrine functioned to allow the wife to compel her husband to exclude his mother from their domicile.

110   Note, also, that Maimonides does not include the wife's brother-in-law as an "objectionable" person, while he does so mention her brother. Mother-in-law and sister-in-law are the classic sources of certified antagonism in halakhic sources (see note 98). On the other hand, the variation may be casual. In general, the legal underpinning of this ruling is somewhat difficult to understand: Does the wife have property rights in her husband's house? It would appear, then, that considerations of domestic tranquility *(shelom bayyit)* do play a role. See *Derishah* and *Perishah*, to *Tur, Even ha-'Ezer* 74, and *infra*.

111   See R. Aaron Perahiah, *Responsa Perah Matteh Aharon*, I, 60.

112   R. Jacob Castro, *Responsa 'Ohalei Ya'akov* (Leghorn: 1783), 300.

113   R. Jacob Castro himself, and R. Abraham Cohen and R. Abraham Monson, who co-signed the responsum in question.

114   See, in addition to the material cited thus far, R. Aaron Perahiah, *op.cit.*, and R. Zemah Duran, *Responsa Yakhin u-Bo'az*, I, 122, where R. Isaac Barzeloni (Spain, 11th century), Rashba, and R. Solomon b. Simon Duran (Algiers, 15th century) are also cited as supporing the majority position.

115   *Responsa*, IV, 168. See also *Responsa Attributed to Ramban*, 103, where Rashba ruled that a wife who has fled her home, claiming that she was in reality fleeing not her husband but her mother-in-law, is entitled to support and is not considered a "rebellious wife"; cf. also note 103 *(supra)*, end.

116   *Shulhan Arukh, Even ha-'Ezer* 74:10. R. Moses Isserles, by appending material taken from a responsum concerning quarrels within an already common domicile to a ruling on the wife's right to stop her mother-in-law from moving in, inclines to the opinion that the common household must be tried before it is found wanting. Despite the authority of Rama, the 19th-century *Bet Me'ir* (R. Me'ir Posner), *ad loc.*, argued that the wife is believed if she accuses her mother-in-law of provoking strife, as suggested by Maimonides and Rashba. R. Moses Isserles introduces the Alfasian third party in cases of direct husband-wife altercations, too: *Shulhan Arukh, Even ha-'Ezer* 154:3. Note, also, that the female third party of R. Alfas now includes a male possibility, too. It must be remembered, finally, that even in the absence of the third-party device, cases of this latter sort were not simply decided "by the book"; rather, the court was always expected to inquire into the circumstances of conflict: see *Responsa Attributed to Ramban*, 102; *Responsa Binyamin Ze'ev*, 98.

117   *Sefer Hassidim*, sec. 564, p. 371.

118   *Ibid.*, sec. 562, p. 370.

119   *Ibid.*, sec. 563. This paragraph continues, "And if his father or mother are contentious people who bicker with his wife, and he knows that his wife is in the right, he should not rebuke his wife so as to please his parents." The need to restrain the son in this fashion itself speaks volumes.

120   R. Eliezer Pappo, *Peleh Yo'etz*, part I, "*Kaph,*" pp. 170–172.

121   Ben-Sira 3:12, p. 13.

122   Tobit 4:3, p. 321.

123   *Ketubot* 103a. The Talmud claims that this behest referred, actually, to the honor of their stepmother.

   The version of R. Judah's testament given in the Palestinian Talmud (*Kil'ayyim* 9:4; 32a) reads, ". . . do not move my widow from my house," which is less an aspect of "honor" than a privilege that was binding in civil law (see M. *Ketubot* 12:13–14). The fact that the two testaments are otherwise different in all respects suggests that the former was spoken to the patriarch's sons, the latter to his colleagues.

124   See Chapter II.

125   M. *Baba Batra* 6:4. The talmudic discussion strongly implies that this "house" is adjacent to the parental home. L. Finkelstein, *The Pharisees,* I, 46, argues that this represents the practice of "rich homes and rural districts."

126   See *Baba Batra* 98b, *Pesahim* 113a, *Kiddushin* 12b, p. *Kiddushin* 3:8; 64b. Different situations and motives are reflected in these sources, as they are in the later commentaries and codes as well, but a full exploration of this topic is beyond the scope of this monograph.

127   M. *Ketubot* 1:5, *Tosefta Ketubot* 1:4. The sources cited in the previous note doubtless reflect the fact that many young couples were living in the homes of maternal parents.

   See also *Genesis Rabbah* 74:10 (II, 867): "Can a son-in-law living in the home of his father-in-law avoid enjoying even a single utensil, even a single knife, of his father-in-law?"

128   *Megillah* 16b, and *Dikduke Soferim, ad loc.*

129   *Genesis Rabbah* (II, p. 369).

130   *Jubilees* 12:28–31. Similarly, when Jacob left his father's home so as to put himself beyond Esau's vengeance, *Jubilees* (27:6–8) stresses that the son gained permission from his aged father before he left; filial abandonment was definitely not a proper line of conduct for the Patriarchs.

131   The first comment ("the wicked are called dead") is primarily concerned with the contradiction between Genesis 11:32 and the fact that Terah continued to live another sixty-five years, and not with the substantive question of Abraham's unfilial behavior.

132   The textual matrix is the seemingly superfluous *lekha.*

133   See *supra,* note 12 and Chapter VI.

134   ". . . a proselyte . . . is not culpable if he strikes or curses his father . . . [but] a proselyte is forbidden to curse or strike his heathen father, nor is he to treat him desrespectfully, lest it be said that [in embracing the Jewish religion] he descended from a higher degree of holiness to a lower degree, seeing that he slights his father. It is his duty to show him some respect" (*Code,*

Mamrim 5:9–10; Hershman, p. 152).

135   *Megillah* 17a.

136a   *Yam Shel Shelomoh, Kiddushin,* 1:72.

136   *Seder 'Olam,* Chapter 2 (ed. Neubauer, *Medieval Jewish Chronicles,* II, p. 28, especially n. 23). See also *Genesis Rabbah* 76:2 (II, pp. 897–898), where Jacob "fears" (Genesis 32:8) the merits of Esau, who has engaged in the honor of his parents while Jacob was away from home.

137   *Exodus Rabbah* 34 (end).

138   P. *Berakhot* 2:8; 5c. One would suspect that R. Yohanan saw quite through the parable were it not for the explicit continuation: "They went and told R. Yohanan that Kahana had departed for Babylon. He said, 'How did he leave without asking permission?' They answered, 'His parable was his permission.' " Or was the master deliberately ingenuous to both Kahana and his own pupils?

139   *Kiddushin* 31b.

140   Cited by R. Bahya b. Asher, *op. cit.*

141   R. Yehiel M. Epstein, *Arukh ha-Shulhan, Yoreh De'ah* 240:11.

142   *Supra,* note 112.

143   *Supra,* note 117. See also R. Judah Ayyas, *Responsa Bet Yehudah,* no. 54, who allows a son to override parental objections and leave them to study Torah in the Holy Land, but suggests that such permission should possibly be given only for the *mitzvah of talmud torah* (of which it is said specifically—*Megillah* 16b—that it overrides filial piety). See n. 31, *supra.*

144   *Sefer Hassidim,* section 343, p. 257.

145   *Peleh Yo'etz, loc. cit.*

145a   *Midrash Ha Gadol, Genesis* (ed. M. Margaliyyot), p.597. In the version of *Pirkei Derekh Eretz* (ed. M. Friedman), p.15, the sons are even less generous: "theywould place them outside the city walls and they would die."

146   My translation follows the comment of Segal, p. 15. Segal also cites *Derekh Tovim* (ed. Edelman, p. 25): "Be careful . . . lest you shame your parents in their old age, saying to yourself, 'They lack sense.' "

147   *Wisdom of Ben-Sira,* 3:12, p. 13.

148   *Seder Eliyyahu,* Chapter (27) 25 (ed. M. Friedmann, p. 136). Drooling is probably a sign of mental incompetence, as in I Samuel 21:14. It might merely reflect old age, however. See also Proverbs 23:21.

149   *Deut. Rabbah,* 1:14

150   *Tosafot Kiddushin* 31a, *s.v. 'u-ba'at* cite the midrash that describes the mother of Dama as unbalanced. This might reflect their general position that one need not honor the wicked parent at all; had Dama's mother been merely malicious, his restraint would have been uncalled for.

151   Segal, *op. cit.*

152   See Chapter III, section I, part 2. Needless to say, the behavior of R. Hunna cannot determine the meaning of the other, earlier statement.

153   See Chapter V, section II.

154   Cf. R. Solomon Luria, *Yam Shel Shelomoh, Kiddushin,* I, 64.

155   Cf. R. Samuel Strashon (Rashash) *ad loc.*

156   *Mamrim* 6:10.

157   See R. Joseph Karo, *Kessef Mishneh, ad loc.,* and the other standard commentaries. Ra'abad, incidentally, argued for maximal protection of the sick *wife* too: *Maggid Mishneh, Ishut* 14:17.

158   *Mamrim* 6:3. See Chapter III, n. 42.

159   *Tosafot Ri,* in contrast, writes: ''. . . and he (the son) could not fulfill the duty laid upon him by heaven. . . .''

160   R. Shem Tov ben Abraham, *Migdal 'Oz;* R. David ben Abu-Zimra, Ridbaz, *ad loc.*

161   See *Derishah* to *Tur, Yoreh De'ah* 240, n. 2, and R. David Halevi, *Turei Zahav, Shulhan Arukh, Yoreh De'ah* 240, n. 14: Rabad agrees with Maimonides that the son may sometimes be forced to leave his parent; however, if the condition of the parent is such that he does respond to care (and hence the Maimonidean insistence that the son arrange for such care before he departs) then the son is himself obliged to remain and tender it. In effect, though, the son would never actually be entitled to leave. (The ''solution'' of *Derishah* is thus self-defeating.) A simpler explanation for the stricture of Rabad (and one that reflects the understanding of the gloss by *Migdal 'Oz, ad loc.*) is: With the son gone, there is no responsible supervision of the care given the parent, who is by all accounts difficult to treat. Moreover, who would undertake to perform that which a man's own son refuses to do?

162   *Yoreh De'ah* 240:10.

163   R. David Halevi, n. 14. *Derishah, Tur,* 240, n. 2, expounds the view of Rabad, but does not necessarily espouse it.

164   *Midrash ha-Gadol, Exodus,* p. 8.

165   Another expression of this centrality can be found in *Eliyyahu Rabbah,* Chapter 27: ''A man should not allow his parents to be dressed in worn clothing, but should see that they are dressed well. If a man spends five *maneh* on his own clothing, he should spend ten on that of [each of] his parents.''

166   The 1962 Jewish Publication Society translation, *The Torah,* here reads: ''And Jacob said to his kinsmen . . .'' My translation reflects the midrashic teaching.

167   *Genesis Rabbah* 74:13 (II, pp. 871–876).

168   *Midrash ha-Gadol, Genesis,* p. 553.

1   *Kiddushin* 29a. In *Mekhilta* (*Pasha* 18; ed. Horowitz-Rabin, p. 73) to Exodus 13:13, R. Akiba is given as the author of the added requirement that he teach him "how to swim," and R. Judah the Patriarch adds "practical citizenship" (*yishuv medinah*) to the list. (Perhaps R. Akiba's insistence upon instruction in swimming was due to his own near-drowning at sea: *Yevamot,* 121a).

2   *Yevamot* 62b.

3   While the Talmud may have been merely playful in its suggestion (see Chapter I, n. 33) of such a correspondence, its existence is a fact.

4   A similar story is told of a teacher and a maid-servant: "A maid-servant of Bar Pedah passed before a synagogue, and saw a teacher striking a child more than was necessary. She said. 'Let that man be under the ban . . . ' " (p. *Mo'ed Katon,* 3:1; 81c).

5   Two classic instances should illustrate the teaching: " ' . . . the blind'—that means he who is blind in a particular matter . . . do not advise a man to sell his field and buy a donkey, because you want to buy the field from him (and he is uninformed in the matter)" (*Sifra, ad loc.*). "R. Nathan says, 'How do I know that one should not give wine to the Nazarite, or flesh torn from a living animal to a Noahide?' Scripture says, 'You shall not place a stumbling block before the blind.' " (*Pesahim* 22b). The first instance describes blindness to commercial realities; the second, weakness of will.

6   The implications of this passage for halakhic discussions of the degree of presumption necessary to establish a criminal nexus between the act of him who "places the stumbling block" and "who stumbles" is not our concern. See R. Hanan'el and Rashi, *ad loc.,* and R. Reuben Margaliot, *Mekor Hesed,* in his edition of *Sefer Hassidim,* p. 373, n. 1 (end).

7   *Mamrim* 6:8–9; Hershman, p. 156. See R. Joseph Karo, *Kessef Mishneh, ad loc.,* and *Bi'ur ha-G'ra, Yoreh De'ah* 240, n. 30, for the relationship of Maimonides to his talmudic sources. It is clear, though, that he went beyond the letter of these sources.

8   A number of talmudic sources stress that a man should not "put excessive fear into his household" (*Gittin* 6b), and R. Zera attributed his longevity to the fact that, among other wise habits, he "was not overly rigorous in his home" (*Megillah* 28a). But these probably refer to domestic affairs generally, specifically the relations between husband and wife (see the continuation of *Gittin* 6b).

9   *Sefer Hassidim,* sec. 565, p. 372.

10 *Tanhuma,* Exodus, 1; see also *Exodus Rabbah* 1:1.

11 Actually, the rabbinic attitude was not monochromatic but varied. Mishnah

Makkot 2:2 states, "Abba Saul says . . . the law of the unwitting murder applies to every act of free choice; this excludes the father who smites his son, or the teacher who chastises his pupil, or the agent of the court," who are commanded to strike. Yet the sources found in *Tosefta Baba Kamma* 9:8–11 discourage the striking of one's own children, and even ban it. Thus, the father who beats his child is liable to suit for assault, and must compensate even the minor. Furthermore, although the teacher or father who injures the child (in the process of educating him) cannot be sued, "if they struck him beyond what is proper, they are liable." Such a regulation, leaving the final evaluation to the court, would tend to discourage the use of the rod. Cf. also *Tosefta Makkot* 2:5, and *Baba Kamma*, 6:17; *Makkot* 8a.

The following stories also bear on the rabbinic attitude toward physical punishment, making the point that the threat of parental discipline can have more injurious effect upon the child than the actual blows: "It happened that the son of Gorgos ran away from school. His father threatened to box his ears. In terror of his father, the boy went off and cast himself into a cistern [thereby killing himself]. . . . Another incident is that of a child from Bene Berak who broke a flask. His father threatened to box his ears. In terror of his father, the child went off and cast himself into a cistern. . . . As a result of this, the sages said: 'A man shoud not threaten his child. He should spank him at once, or else hold his peace and say nothing'" (*Semahot* 2:4–5; trans. D. Zlotnick, pp. 33–34).

Most typical of the disapproval of excessive punishment, and yet the willingness to tolerate it, is the story told (*Gittin* 36a) of ". . . the teacher of children whom R. Aha bound by a vow . . . [to give up teaching] because he maltreated the children; but Rabina reinstated him because no other teacher as thorough as he could be found."

12 See especially Rashi to *Kiddushin* 30a, *s.v. meshitsar.*

13 *Mo'ed Katon, ad loc.*

14 Ramah bases himself on the talmudic statement (*Kiddushin* 30a) that "one's hand is on the neck of one's son" most effectively between the ages of 16 and 22 or 18 and 24, which Rashi interprets as sanctioning—indeed, recommending—corporal discipline till those ages. Thus, while as readers of a legal text we note that Ramah merely rejects the applicability of the ban to a man who struck his "immature" son, and does not say anything about the propriety of such behavior, his specification of 22 or 24 as the crucial years of transition clearly identifies his point of view with that of Rashi.

15 *Yam Shel Shelomoh, Kiddushin.* I, sec. 68. The statement found in the 20th-century *Arukh ha-Shulhan* (section 42) that Maharshal disapproved in general of the striking of younger sons is a misquote, and betrays the discomfort of R. Yehiel Epstein with the ruling of Ramah. It is true, though, that Maharshal introduces an element of socially conditioned relativity to the discussion, but accepting as he does the implications of Rashi's exegesis, he only applies this new standard to the situation of a married son.

16 *Bet Yosef, Yoreh De'ah* 334.

17   Cf. *Baba Mezia* 12a–b and parallels cited by *Yefe 'Enayyim, ad loc.*

18   *Baba Kamma* 87b. Obviously, I am concerned with the talmudic treatment which was authoritative for the medieval jurists, not with the actual scope of R. Yohanan's statement *per se. Baba Kamma* 87b does indicate, of course, that *gadol* need not always be taken in R. Yohanan's sense. For further discussion, see R. Hezkiah Medini, *Sedeh Hemed, vav,* section 26, n. 14 (vol. I, part II, pp. 32–33).

19   *Kiddushin* 32a.

20   *Sifre* Deuteronomy 218 and parallels; the teaching is given by R. Josiah in the name of R. Ze'irah, who heard it on the authority of "the men of Jerusalem."

21   *Kiddushin* 31b.

22   P. *Pe'ah* 1:1; 15c–d.

23   *She'iltot,* 60 (end). For further discussion, see S. Y. Zevin, *L'or ha-Halakhah,* pp. 319–320.

24   Cited by *Neziv, ad loc.,* n. 14. *Neziv* himself supports this position, and cf. Chapter II, n. 1.

25   *Responsa,* no. 220. See also Ridbaz, *Responsa,* I, no. 524. The talmudic sources, particularly the incident involving R. Ishmael and his mother, would seem to disallow this distinction. Presumably Rabad distinguished between the positive pleasure of the mother of R. Ishmael and the mere waiving of irritation denoted by *mehila.* But see R. Aryeh Leib of Metz, *Turei Even, Megillah* 28a.

26   *Sefer Hassidim,* section 152, p. 153.

27   *Ibid.,* section 570, p. 374. See also section 574, p. 376, which states that the parent feels more pain at watching his sons hit each other than in being struck himself, but does not allow the father to accept such blows.

28   *Ibid.,* section 573, p. 375.

29   *Ibid.,* see Chapter IV.

30   *Ibid.,* see Chapter II, section II, part 1, and section III, part 1; Chapter IV, section III, part 4.

31   The point, obviously, is not that God cannot also be inflexible and unforgiving, but that this aspect of His power is not described as a function of His fatherhood. An instructive contrast is Aeschylus's utilization of the fatherhood of Zeus in *Prometheus Bound* to assert the nature and source of the god's stern punitive quality.

32   *Enchiridion,* section 30.

33   *Kiddushin* 32a. The teaching that a son who corrects his father for the latter's violation of a command of the Torah must take care lest he be irreverent in the process may be construed as referring to deliberate violations of the Torah and not only inadvertent ones. Thus, filial reverence is to be maintained in the

very confrontation with parental wrongdoing. Of course, our text refers to an incident, rather than a status. But Maimonides integrates this ruling into his treatment of the "wicked parent" (*Mamrim* 6:11 and *infra*).

34   *Yevamot* 22a–b.

35   *Baba Kamma* 94b.

36   *Sanhedrin* 85a–b.

37   Though often translated "bastard," *mamzer* in rabbinic usage is not a child born out of wedlock, but a child born of incestuous or adulterous relations. "Illegitimacy" is a category alien to rabbinic thought on filiation.

38   See *Tosefta Yevamot* 3:1, where R. Eliezer does not commit himself on the right of a *mamzer* to inherit his father or perform the act of *halizah* as his brother's levir. It is possible that inheritance and the levirate posed special problems, asserting as they do the principle of continuity. The Mishnah, in any case, asserts that the *mamzer* is his father's son for all purposes.

39   See Heinemann, *Philons . . .* , pp. 313–314: Belkin, *Philo,* p. 234, n. 59; Lacey, p. 290, n. 116; Kaser and Sachers, *op. cit.*

40   For a survey of rabbinic law and opinion, see R. Mordekhai ha-Kohen, "Adoption of Children in Jewish Law" (Heb.), in *Torah She-Be-'al Peh,* III, pp. 64–84.

41   Similar conclusions were reached by R. Me'ir Simha of Dvinsk (*Or Sameah, Mamrim* 6:11) on the basis of *Sanhedrin* 71a; though if the crucial statement of R. Judah means that only the children of licit marriages can be judged "rebellious sons" (cf. H. Albeck, *Mishnah, Nezikin,* p. 451), the liability of the son is in fact predicated upon parental virtue. In any case, that case is a specialized one, and one cannot generalize from it. The divergent tannaitic views on the ability of a son to act as blood avenger against his father (*Sifre Deuteronomy* 181; p. *Makkot* 2:5, 31d; *Makkot* 12a) also contain specialized elements (cf. *Enzyklopedia Talmudit,* V, pp. 229–231).

42   R. Judah ben Batra, *Mekhilta* to Exodus 22:27 (*Kaspa,* 19; ed. Horowitz-Rabin, p. 318).

43   *Mekhilta, ad loc.,* 11:7–8. Clearly, this exegesis conflicts with that of R. Judah ben Batra, as a comparison of the anonymous view of the *Mekhilta* (ll. 1–5) and the teaching of the latter tanna indicates.

44   *Mekhilta* to Exodus 21:17 (*Nezikin* 5; Horowitz-Rabin, p. 268). Cf. also Maimonides, *Sefer ha-Mitzvot,* Negative Precept 318, and Nahmanides, *ad loc.*

45   The application and scope of "those who do not do the deeds of your people" is a fascinating topic, but would take us far afield. May the wicked be cursed, or even physically set upon? Is an assaulter then free of stripes, or even of liability for damages? These questions are discussed in the Talmud and *rishonim.*

46   *Sanhedrin* 47a, *s.v. 'al; Berakhot* 10b, *s.v. girer.* The context—Hezekiah's

public display of the bones of his father—is not one of wanton insult, but rather that of a punitive object-lesson for others. See note 47, *infra*.

47   *Tosafot Yevamot* 22b, *s.v. ke-she-'asah; Mordekhai, Yevamot,* sec. 13. Here too—the question is whether a son may act as an official of the court to inflict corporal punishment upon his father (*Sanhedrin* 85a-b)—there is normative value in the act by which filial piety is set aside. The position of both Rashi (see n. 46, *supra*) and the tosafists may not, therefore, be as different from that of Maimonides as is commonly assumed. The polarization of views, presented in my text, derives from later *rishonim:* R. Nissim, *Hiddushei Sanhedrin ad loc.; Hagahot Maimoniyyot, Mamrim,* Chapter 6, n. 7.

The tosafist interpretation of *Sanhedrin* 85b, end (C), is in any case forced; it is clear that the school of R. Ishmael (and R. Yoshiyya: *Midrash Tanna'im,* p. 66) forbids a son to punish his father as agent of the court. Note Rashi, *Makkot* 12b.

48   *Yevamot, ad loc.*

49   *Mamrim* 5:12; see also Ibn Ezra to Deuteronomy 21:18, *Mamrim* 6:11.

50   The tosafists take Exodus 20:12 ("Honor your father and mother. . . .") and Exodus 21:15, 17 ("He who strikes his father or mother shall be put to death," "He who reviles his father or mother shall be put to death") as one conceptual unit: release from the penalties of Exodus 21:15,17 (as in *Yevamot* 22b) implies the prior lapse of Exodus 20:12. Maimonides, on the other hand, sees the command to honor (Exodus 20:12) as independent of the penalties spelled out in Exodus 21:15, 17.

51   Chapter II, note 66.

52   See note 41.

53   Cf. Shakh, Taz, and *Bi'ur ha-Gra to Yoreh De'ah,* 240:18.

54   Cf. Taz, *op. cit.*; R. Moses Isserles had rejected this distinction, 240:8.

55   The talmudic range is, at first glance, rather broad: even a usurer can forfeit his son's honor (*Baba Kamma* 94b), and not only the criminal condemned to death. This also holds true for the more generalized talmudic discussions where a variety of offenses qualify to enlist one in the ranks of "those who do not do the deeds of your people"; R. Eliezer of Metz, *Sefer Yera'im ha-Shalem,* no. 217, speaks of him "who violates a single command." But two facts ought to be stressed: most talmudic discussions are concerned with the lapsing of protection only in that precise area in which the wicked themselves sin: a man who stole, for example, cannot expect his sons to protect his reputation by returning the stolen goods. Second, there is a clear tendency on the part of some medieval jurists to require total wickedness of the parent before he forfeits filial respect; others apparently use criteria that evaluate parents no differently from other people.

Maimonides *(supra)* writes of "completely wicked" parents, who "violate the commands"; *Sefer ha-Hinukh* (48): ". . . he whose parents were notorious for being completely wicked . . ."; R. Moses of Coucey, *Semag,* Negative

219: "... a wicked man"; *Hagahot Maimoniyyot (supra)*: "... if he has not repented, one need not honor or revere him, since he violates the command deliberately and he has been rebuked but has not turned from his wickedness." The first three citations all demand a rather total devotion to evil on the part of the parent before his son is not liable under the law for improper behavior toward him. It is of interest that these thinkers both reject the idea of a lapse of the *duty* of filial responsibility, and peg their criteria for the lapse of filial *liability* very high. It may be inferred from *Malveh veLoveh* 4, 4 that Maimonides (following *Baba Mezia* 62a) distinguishes (a) between the total rejection of a parent, and dishonoring him in the single area of his own moral delinquency; and (b) between a positive act of dishonor, as against passive acquiescence to dishonor of his own making and the omission of an act to correct it (as do *Tosafot Ketubot* 86a, *s.v. peri'at*). It is also of interest that Maimonides does not explicitly cite or generalize from the rubric of "he who does the deeds of this people."

At the other extreme we find R. Eliezer of Metz (a 12th-century disciple of R. Tam), who accepts the tosafist position generally, and concludes, "If the father is a [habitual] violator of the Torah, even of one command therein, and does not repent, the son is not commanded concerning him" (*Sefer Yera'im ha-Shalem*, sec. 174 [ed. Schiff, p. 166]); similarly *Hagahot Maimoniyyot (supra)*, that generalizes the father's status on the basis of his being an unregenerate thief or usurer. Other specific issues mooted include the question of whether a parent could be considered "wicked" for what he said: R. Asher thought he could (*Responsa* XV, 5), while *Hagahot Maimoniyyot (Mamrim* 6, n. 8) thought he could not, in both instances the "statement" in question was a command to the son to violate a law of the Torah, and the status of "wicked" would presumably have extended to that area only (this is less true of *Hagahot Maimoniyyot* than of R. Asher).

56 Thus, though it is agreed that an unduly severe parent places a "stumbling-block" before his son and violates a law of the Torah in so doing, there is no suggestion that he thereby becomes a "wicked parent." On the contrary, the logic of that structure presupposes the continued fealty of the son, as we have seen.

This included religious as well as moral degeneracy. Thus, R. David ha-Kohen (16th-century Greece) assumed that a convert was a "wicked parent" (*Responsa of Radakh, bayit* XI, 1–2). The twentieth-century *Arukh ha-Shulhan* (par. 39) includes in this category "those who sin in a spirit of defiance (*lehakh'is*), such as heretics (*minim* and *apikorsim*). (Many contemporary halakhists consider the last of these categories inapplicable to current phenomena; see A. Kirshenbaum, "Crisis Halachah and Heterodoxy Today," *Judaism*, XIV, 1 [Winter, 1965], pp. 88–91.)

57 *Leviticus Rabbah* 12:1. In some manuscripts of this midrash (cited by M. Margoliot in his edition of *Leviticus Rabbah*, II, pp. 245–7) the sons leave their father in the cemetery to die, and are thus doubly astonished at finding him alive and drunk when they return.

1   The Bible will also use *av* for the founder of a community, or a figure of authority (see *IDB*, II, p. 245; this usage persists in rabbinic literature—see M. *Eduyyot* I:4, for example), but it is unlikely that this derives from the position of the biological father in the family. It is possible that Elisha's "My father . . ." refers to the title of authority, but Jewish literature—at least from the Midrash on—took the phrase in its filial sense. This may have been due to the familiarity reflected by the personal pronoun.

2   Examples are given in E. Ben-Yehudah, *Dictionary of the Hebrew Language* (Heb.), I, p. 560–561.

3   In the verse cited, Hezekiah is actually addressing the priests and Levites (" . . . and he brought in the priests and the Levites . . . and said unto them . . ."). Perhaps the *Sifre* is to be understood as saying that Hezekiah could call all the priests and Levites "sons" because he had taught them—as indeed he had taught all the children of Israel—Torah. This view of Hezekiah is common elsewhere in rabbinic literature (see for example, *Yalkut Chronicles* II, sec. 1085, to II Chronicles 32:33); it dovetails with the biblical accounts of the religious reforms undertaken by that king. That Hezekiah taught the people "the entire Torah" is more fully developed in the amoraic aggadah (see *Sanhedrin* 94b), and may be implied in the tannaitic assertion that he was worthy to have been King Messiah.

4   See Brown, Driver, Briggs, *Lexicon of the Old Testament*, p. 561 (4); W. F. Albright, *From the Stone Age to Christianity* (Anchor edition, 1957), p. 306, and Genesis 4:20–21. Nonetheless it is significant that the language utilized *av* and *ben* for this broader field of meanings. See also Y. Kaufmann, *Toledot ha-'Emunah ha-Yisra'elit*, II, part 4, pp. 243–244.

5   See W. R. Smith, *The Religion of the Semites*, 2nd ed., p. 41.

6   *Tosefta Horayyot* 2:7.

7   *Sifre Deuteronomy*, section 305 (end) (ed. Finkelstein, p. 327).

8   P. *Berakhot* 2:5; 5c.

9   P. *Sanhedrin* 10:2; 28b (bottom).

10   *Sanhedrin* 105b.

11   Maimonides, *Code, Talmud Torah* 5:12. There is no such explicit talmudic imperative to my knowledge, though the Palestinian material cited above obviously considers such love a virtue, and we read that a master ought to be pleasant to his disciple and not impatient with him: *Avot* 2:6 and *Ta'anit* 8a. The broad source for Maimonides is of course M. *Baba Mezia* II:11, to which we shall shortly turn. One wonders if the section immediately following explains how the disciple benefits the master in the world to come: "The students increase the wisdom of the master, and broaden his understanding. The sages have said: 'Much Torah have I learned from my companions, and more from my masters, but most

of all—from my students.' And just as a small piece of wood can ignite a great one, so can a simple student sharpen a master, until his questions draw from his teacher glorious wisdom.'' It is noteworthy that the disciple is not loved for what he is, but for his stimulating effect upon the master.

12 'Eruvin 72b–73a. It should be noted that our source reflects, not the economic situation alone (in which son and disciple shared the board of father and master), but the personal one as well. See Rashba, ad loc. (Warsaw: 1895, p. 68, top), and Y. N. Epstein, Mavo le-Nusah ha-Mishnah, pp. 1097—1098.

13 See, e.g., M. Horayyot 3:8.

14 Sanhedrin 101a.

15 Betzah 15b.

16 Mishnah Baba Mezia II:11 (33a). The text as given is that of the standard printed editions of the Mishnah. The latter half of the Mishnah, from "If his father and his teacher were each carrying a burden," was apparently added to the Mishnah text after its publication by R. Judah the Prince from a baraita (Epstein, Mavo le-Nusah, pp. 956–957). This is of no immediate significance for our inquiry, however.

Of much greater significance are the variations in the text itself. According to the text found in our printed Mishnah editions, the father takes precedence over the master if he is himself a sage in both the former (the "lost article" problem) and the latter ("burden-carrying," "redemption from captivity") instances. There is no stipulation that the father be the master's equal, or for that matter any suggestion that the father should have taught his son. The Mishnah text in the printed editions of the Babylonian Talmud duplicates that of the printed editions of the Mishnah.

The Munich ms. of the Mishnah stipulates in its text, however, that in the former instance (the Munich ms. omits from the Mishnah text the latter instances, see supra), "if the father is a sage equal in weight" to the son's master, then— and apparently only then—is the father given preference. This reading is found in other manuscripts as well, and is also the view of a baraita (Tosefta Baba Mezia 2:30).

Yet a third, and in its own way most perplexing, version is found in the Mishnah text printed in the Palestinian Talmud; this version is reproduced by some medievals, among them R. Alfas. It states in the former instance, that the father need be the equal of the master to rate preference; but in the latter instances, he need only be a sage of indeterminate rank (see note 22 infra). Thus this version resembles the Munich ms. tradition in the former case, and that of the printed Mishnah text in the latter.

From the narrow perspective of textual history, one might explain the genesis of these texts in the following way: There are two original traditions—according to the first, the father need be only a "sage" to merit priority (our printed texts); according to the second, he should be the equal of the master (Munich ms.; it is possible that this tradition arose as a comment to the earlier and undefined "if his father is a sage"). The Mishnah, in both traditions, only contained the first problem of the "lost article." When the Mishnah was enlarged to include the latter instances (see *supra*), this material was added only in the texts represented by the printed editions, and naturally was cited in consonance with the view of that tradition ("a sage"). Copyists of the Palestinian Talmud (and subsequently those of R. Alfas) had before them a Mishnah identical in both brevity and tradition with that of the Munich ms. This Mishnah they undertook to supplement with the additional material in the BT Mishnah before them (which was that now represented by our printed texts), not realizing that the norm of this material demanded that the father be only "a sage," and did not stipulate that he be "equal to the master."

The weakness of this approach is, as always, the need to posit a copyist who was a half-scholar—knowledgeable about certain differences in Mishnah texts, but ignorant of others. Furthermore, we are thus able, sometimes all too easily, to consign conceptual probing of the cases and their charateristics to the "casuistical pilpulists." The strength of this method lies in the fact that copyists, according to contemporary testimony, were just the sort of half scholars necessary to produce the jumble before us. Thus the suspicion grows that an oversight such as the one I described was in fact the way it happened.

These texts became the subject of extended medieval discussion in large part because of the *Code* of Maimonides and its inconsistency on these points. In *Talmud Torah* 5:1, Maimonides rules in accordance with our printed Mishnah text, stipulating expressly that the father who is a sage be given preference "even if he is not the equal of his master." But in *Gezelah ve'Avedah* 12:2, he states that one prefers the lost article of one's father to that of one's teacher only when the former is the teacher's equal. Attempts to resolve this inconsistency have ranged from the assertion that the first text is corrupt (*Hagahot Maimoniyyot, ad loc.*), that Maimonides was working from different talmudic texts during the writing of the parts of the *Code* in question (Ridbaz, cited by R. Bezalel Ashkenazi, *Shittah Mekubezet, ad loc.; Tosafot Yom-Tov, ad loc.*) One must point out, however, that the express stipulation in *Talmud Torah* indicates that at that point Maimonides knew of both traditions, and so it must represent the later recension, or that there was adequate conceptual and contextual cause for the differing rulings— that the law grants priority to one's parent more quickly in cases of physical discomfort and danger than in situations where property-damage is at issue, etc. (See R. Joseph Karo, *Kessef Mishneh, ad loc.*). See also *Mattanot 'Aniyim* 8:18.

Of more significance than the reconciliation of these divergent rulings and texts is the inquiry into the values represented by each.

The pragmatic differential, and the value-judgment emerging therefrom, is obvious. According to our printed texts, there is no adequate ground for linking the growth of the individual and his shifting filial loyalties and attachments. The individual may indeed have matured under the tutelage of his master, but so long as his father is a sage, he owes the latter the primacy in filial loyalty. The rationale behind this posture is somewhat difficult to grasp;: biological paternity and a minimum of Torah attainments outweigh mastership, which would otherwise be more significant than biological paternity alone. It would seem to be a case of adding apples and pears. Is the father assumed to have taught his son, in whatever measure, and thus to have "brought him into the world-to-come"? However this dilemma is resolved, the axiological upshot is that any father, so long as he is something of a sage (no mean achievement, to be sure) remains the object of his son's filial loyalty.

The other tradition requires that the father be the equal of the master if he would retain his son's primary loyalty in conflict-situations. It has been pointed out (see R. Joseph Karo, *Bet Yosef, Yoreh De'ah* 242; H. Albeck, *Mishnah Kodashim,* p. 268) that this view is in accordance with Mishnah *Keritot* VI:9, which predicates the master's priority upon the honor owed him by both father and son, a duty that can be eclipsed only when the father is the master's equal. Yet even here the nexus between filial loyalty and the nature of the father-son relationship is not spelled out; the explicit demand is that the father equal the master in Torah, not that he have taught his son as much as the master did. Thus even here it is difficult to dovetail intellectual and spiritual maturation with a shift in filial loyalties.

This difficulty is recognized most explicitly by the Palestinian Talmud *(Horayyot* 48:2): " 'If the father is the equal of his master, he takes preference'—Of what significance is his eminence? R. Jose b. R. Bon said, 'This ruling speaks of a situation where the son has acquired half his education from his father.' " See also *Yoma* 86a; *Kiddushin* 31a, and *Tosafot Pesahim* 108a, *s.v. bifne.*

This understanding would restore the absolute nexus between filial loyalty and maturation. But it is better adapted to the Mishnah version found in the Palestinian Talmud and the Munich ms. than to the Babylonian version; furthermore, many authorities do not accept this as the plain sense of the text being interpreted. One might further probe the meaning of "a sage equal to his master": if maturation is the key, the lesser sage may nonetheless have the more crucial role in the development of the younger man! It would seem, in a sense, that the stress is not being placed upon the personal relationships or upon the specific contribution of each man to the development of the son and disciple, but perhaps upon the struggle of the scholar-class to claim the primal loyalty normally given to the parent. This understanding would, of course, require that we put a different construction upon many of the sources that we are to cite than they are normally granted.

17   Mishnah *Keritot* VI:9. It has been noted that "So too, in the study of the law . . ." is probably not part of the original Mishnah (see R. Solomon Adeni, *Melekhet Shelomoh, ad loc.;* Y. N. Epstein, *Mavo le-Nusah,* p. 951).

18   This text—which, as we note, is probably not part of the Mishnah (see n. 17, *supra)*—presents one glaring difficulty: its rationale justifies according any master of the law preference over one's father, and not one's personal master alone.

19   Compare and contrast Hebrews 12:5–11, especially 9.

20   Jesus' attitude toward family distorts the Jewish ethos on this point. The crucial text reads: "Then his mother and his brothers arrived, and remaining outside sent in a message asking him to come out to them. A crowd was sitting round and word was brought to him: 'Your mother and your brothers are outside asking for you.' He replied, 'Who is my mother? Who are my brothers?' And looking round at those who were sitting in the circle around him he said, 'Here are my mother and my brothers. Whoever does the will of God is my brother, my sister, my mother'" (Mark 3:31–35). Whatever the motivations for coupling his affirmation of the fraternity of those who do God's will with his rejection of his mother and brothers—who were apparently left standing outside—the Jewish ethos would find Jesus' total orientation harsh because of its needless exclusion of kin. This incident was noted by medieval Jewish polemicists: see S. Krauss, "Un Fragment Polemique de la Gueniza," *Révue des Études Juives*, LXI (1912), pp. 63ff, especially pp. 69, 72. Curiously, Jesus' famous "Let the dead bury their dead" (Matthew 8:22) was spoken to a disciple who wished to bury his *father;* a conflict was seen between immediate attendance upon the master, or delay in order properly to honor one's parent. A more complex situation is created by John 19:26–27, where Jesus, about to die, "saw his mother, with the disciple whom he loved standing beside her. He said to her, 'Mother, there is your son,' and to the disciple, 'There is your mother'; and from that moment the disciple took her into his home." Here we find both tender regard for his mother and her needs typical of the native Jewish ethos, as well as a restructuring that deliberately rejects the biological definition.

21   See note 16.

22   See H. Mantel, *Studies in the History of the Sanhedrin,* pp. 132–135. The problem, of course, is whether the word is used here as a technical term, or merely descriptively. The Palestinian Talmud's version of the latter half of the Mishnah merely requires the father to be a *talmid hakham* ("a student of a sage").

23   E. Fromm, *You Shall Be As Gods,* p. 75.

24   *She'iltot,* 131 (III, p. 82). Maimonides (*Code, Talmud Torah* 5:1) uses the same phrase, but it is unclear whether he thereby sums up the instances of conflict or provides a general evaluation. So too ben Aknin, in S. Eppenstein, *Sefer ha-Yovel le-Sokolow* (Warsaw:1904), p. 385.

25   Both *Tosefta Baba Mezia* (2:30) and *Horayyot* (2:5) give "he who illumined his eyes in the Mishnah," which could conceivably mean something other than "even if he enlightened his eyes in a single Mishnah," as the *baraita* quoted in the Talmud reads. But the Palestinian Talmud (*Horayyot* 3:8; 48b), which presents the text as found in the Tosefta, nonetheless cites the same incident of Samuel as does the Babylonian Talmud, and thus understands its text as though illumination of a single Mishnah alone earns for its author the title "master," in the opinion of R. Jose. The text of p. *Mo'ed Katon* (3:7; 83a) is most revealing. "R. Jose says: Whoever enlightened his eyes in the Mishnah, even in one matter." Here we perhaps see a more original version, "even in one matter"

appearing as an interpretative element, only later to be integrated with the basic definition.

26   *Avot* 6:3. See especially Maimonides, *Code, Talmud Torah* 5:9, and *Migdal 'Oz ad loc.*

27   Interestingly, the Talmud understands the plain sense of the mishnaic, "he who has taught him widsom," to support R. Jose, and, only on second thought, claims that this clause means, "he who taught him the greater part of his knowledge." Yet this latter understanding surely better reflects the mishnaic rationale, "for his teacher brought him to the life of the world-to-come." I follow R. Hanan'el in his reading of the talmudic give-and-take at this point, rather than Rashi (who sees here an expression of support for R. Me'ir), *s.v. u-tenan.*

28   The description of the master in Mishnah *Horayyot* (cited above) as one from whom "the son gained much wisdom while sitting before" him surely best suits the view of R. Judah, though the two are not identical, to be sure.

29   Needless to say, the critical question is very much in place in discussion of our passage. Were R. Judah and R. Jose in fact concerned with the question of priority, or did their debate center on another situation—say, the question of mourning—only to be cited later in our context? Indeed, many medievals raise the problem in one fashion or another. Yet the fact that merits overriding consideration is the passage as it stands in its present context; the fact that the talmudic *sugya* considers the debate on the definition of "master" within the context of master-parent priorities is decisive for our purposes. Furthermore, even a critical analysis of the sources (motivated, as we must recognize, not by textual or logical difficulties, but by our surprise at the extreme view of R. Jose and its pragmatic application alone) does not in fact lend any support to the idea that the debate of R. Judah and R. Jose centered only on mourning ritual and not on the more sensitive question of parental as against magisterial priority. If we examine the passage cited above, we see it is composed of four sections:

(a)   the tannaitic debate as to the definition of master ("Our rabbis taught . . . he is his master");

(b)   the statement of Samuel's behavior, which implies support of R. Jose's definition at least within the context of mourning ritual;

(c)   the statement of Ulla that the scholars of Babylon accepted—and, as in the case of Samuel above, slightly broadened—the definition of R. Jose for purposes of mourning, but the definition of R. Judah in questions of parental-magisterial priority;

(d)   a generalized debate as to a general decision on the original tannaitic debate.

Both (a) and (d) are generalized fragments, neither of them indicating the context for which the definition of "master" is being sought. Given the radical posture of R. Jose, one immediately (and preconceivedly!) suspects that his broad definition of "master" should function in the narrower context of mourning alone; some medievals do raise this possibility, as we shall see.

But there is no adequate reason—textual or conceptual—for understanding our source in this way. The *baraita* (a) is cited in three separate texts: (1) the passage in *Baba Mezia* before us and its parallel in *Tosefta Baba Mezia* 2:30; (2) *Tosefta Horayyot* 2:5, following upon the rubric of priority to be accorded a master in the ransoming of captives; (3) p. *Mo'ed Katon* 3:7; 83b, following upon the requirement of extended mourning procedures for one's master. Thus, two of the three (or three of four, inasmuch as (a) comprehends two passages) passages in which the *baraita* is cited deal with the question of priority.

The medievals did, in fact, sense the difficulty in R. Jose's view (a difficulty heightened by the 'compromise' of Ulla), or to be more precise, they sensed its extreme quality. Thus we read in Ritba, *ad loc.*: "R. Jose's definition of 'master' applies to all instances where the term is used, even to questions of priority; the other views (of R. Me'ir and R. Judah) disagree only in regard to the question of priority, for they consider that one should not refuse to honor one's parent for an insignificant reason but only in the case of one's teacher *par excellence*; they agree with R. Jose in the instances of mourning and other gestures of respect. . . ." Thus Ritba finds it necessary to underscore the uncomprising extent of R. Jose's own view. R. Joseph Kolon (*New Responsa of Maharik*, ed. A. Pines, Jerusalem: 5730, pp. 18–19), goes even further when he argues that R. Jose is concerned with the definition of "master" only in the context of mourning, etc., and accepts the definition suggested by R. Judah for use in the context of priority. See also R. Naftali Z. Berlin, *Ha'amek She'alah* to *She'iltot*, 131, n. 4. But the primary *baraita*, and especially its utilization by both Tosefta and Talmud, offer no support for this discrimination, as we have seen.

30   *She'iltot*, p. 131; Maimonides, *op. cit.* (n. 5); *Shulhan Arukh, Hoshen Mishpat* 264:1. The notable exception to this consensus is R. Hanan'el, who decides in favor of R. Jose; see his commentary *ad loc.*

31   *Sefer Hassidim*, sec. 585, 579 (pp. 382, 380); R. Moses Isserles, gloss to *Shulhan Arukh, Yoreh De'ah* 242:34 ("some say . . . and this appears to me correct"; interestingly, the last provision of *Sefer Hassidim* concerning strangers who engage the teacher is omitted by the gloss, but is supplied by most commentators), and *Responsa*, 118 (discussing the rights of a grandfather to aspects of filial loyalty). It is reasonable to speculate on the shift in social milieu suggested by *Sefer Hassidim*, but unfair to consider *Sefer Hassidim* simply interested in enlarging paternal right: in sec. 579 *Sefer Hassidim* also teaches that "if your father has taught you more Torah [than your teacher], though he should be given priority—give priority to your teacher if you know he will (otherwise) become angry."

32   *Tosefta Horayyot* 2:5; *Horayyot* 13a.

33   In the later Middle Ages, scholars asked whether "all (*kulam*)" might not include even himself! See *Shulhan Arukh, Yoreh De'ah* 252, *Shakh*, n. 10.

34   *Kiddushin* 32a. The scope of *mehila* was discussed in tannaitic times: see *Sifre Deuteronomy* 218 (to Deuteronomy 21:18) and *Kiddushin* 32b. The tannaitic discussion is much more restricted, however, and more concrete.

35   *Pesahim* 108a.

36   For additional discussion, see *She'iltot*, 77, and *Ha'amek She'alah*; R. Loewe (*Maharal*) of Prague, *Gevurot Ha-Shem*, Chapter 40.

37   For data on mourning and bereavement, see both Talmuds, *Mo'ed Katon*, Chapter III; *The Tractate 'Mourning,'* translated with notes by D. Zlotnick (Yale Judaica Series, III); M. Lamm, *The Jewish Way in Death and Mourning*.

38   Mo'ed Katon 22b, 26a; Maimonides, *Code*, *Avelut* 9:2–3, and *Ta'aniyyot* 5:17. Maimonides is disputed by many others—among them, Ra'abad and Ramban—on this last point.

39   *Mo'ed Katon* 25b.

40   See the sources cited in note 37.

41   The distinction between *keriah* (rending of garments) and other gestures of bereavement is made explicit by a number of talmudic sources:

(1)   "Does one rend his garment (in a case of 'far tiding,' i.e., when he hears of the death only 30 days after its occurence) or does he not? . . . Said R. Mani to R. Hanina: 'My view that he does not rend his garment is consistent with the fact that there is no observance of the seven days of mourning. But according to your view that he should rend his garment, tell me, is there a rending of the garment without the observance of the seven days of mourning?' But is there not? . . . In the case of one's mother or father one always rends one's garment!—What you cited refers to the deference (*kavod*) to be shown to one's father or mother."
—*Mo'ed Katon* 20b (I follow the reading of Ramban, *Torat ha-Adam* [*Works*, ed. Chavel, II, p. 237] as against *Tosafot, ad loc., s. v. kore'ah*.)

(2)   "Is there rending of garments without mourning (*ibbul*)? Yes, for one rends one's garments for one's father or mother even after a great while (has passed since their death)."
—p. *Mo'ed Katon* 3:5

(3)   " . . . the observance of mourning comes under one category and the act of rending under another category."
—*Mo'ed Katon* 26b.

(4   "For no relatives does he rend to expose his heart, only for his father and mother. . . . R. Samuel in the name of R. Abdimi b. Tanhum said, 'This is because he now loses the *mitzvah* (imperative) of honor (*kibbud*).' "
—p. *Mo'ed Katon* 3:8, 83d.

Clearly, *keriah* operates under different rubrics from the gestures of mourning in effect during the seven-day period (*shiv'ah*). A possible reason for this is that it occurs normally, before the burial, which is when *shiv'ah* and mourning begin (*Nimmuke Yosef* and others). It seems to express a more intense and immediate response than do the gestures of *shiv'ah*. Furthermore, not being totally integrated into the rubrics of mourning, *keriah* can be modified by the imperative of reverence. Therefore, perhaps, one performs it for a master though one does not make the gestures of mourning for him. Thus, Ra'abad points to the *keriah* for a master as another example of the general distinctions between *keriah* and *avelut* (cited in *Sefer ha-Mikhtam,* ed. A. Schreiber, p. 315), and Ritba (Commentary to *M. K.* 26b) insists that one rend one's garment upon the 'far tiding' of a master's death much as one would upon that of a parent: *"keriah* is different (from *avelut*), and it is not right that a man should hear of the death of his master and not rend a garment." See Y. Denari, "Ha-Minhag veha-Halakha . . . ," *Memorial Volume for B. de Vries* (Heb.), p. 188, and especially n. 157 for the citation of R. Isaac ben Giat.

42 *Mo'ed Katon* 25b. Both the behavior of R. Ammi and the statement of R. Yohanan indicate that the denial of mourning ritual upon the death of a master seemed to some inconsistent with the general proposition that he was to be honored in greater measure than a parent. See R. Solomon b. Ha-Yatom, *Commentary to M. K.* (ed. Z. H. Chayyot), p. 119. It is not at all improbable that the actions of R. Ammi reflected a general tendency among disciples. Further discussion of the extent or nature of mourning upon the death of a master in talmudic and medieval times would take us far afield. See p. *Berakhot* 3:1, 6a, which indicates that one could render oneself impure (*tame*) upon the death of one's master, in which case one ought not to drink wine or eat meat at that time; *Perush mi-Ba-'al Sefer Haredim, ad loc.; Sefer Ra'abiah* (ed. A. Aptowitzer), III, p. 529, which does understand the text in question to speak of a generalized *avelut; Tur, Yoreh De'ah* 374 (end); R. Yehiel Epstein, *Arukh ha-Shulhan, Yoreh De'ah* 374:19.

One parallel between the mourning of son and disciple should be noted however. As we have seen, the disciple is required to (a) rend his garment for his master, and (b) observe a one-day period of mourning. This dual movement is analogous to the structure imposed by some medievals (see especially Ramban, *Torat ha-Adam* [pp. 236–239]) upon a son who receives 'far tidings' of the death of his father, even after a year. Clearly, the filial structure reflects filial respect, and not a generalized rubric of *avelut;* perhaps this accounts for the parallel here of son and disciple. (But see *Shulhan Arukh, Yoreh De'ah* 402:2; 242:25, and their sources; I believe that Ramban would allow the rule of "part of the day is the equivalent of the whole" and the other relaxations stated in 402:2 to apply with regard to a master as well.)

43 *Tractate on Mourning (Semahot),* ed. D. Zlotnick, Chapter IX, par. 2, p. 67. For exposure of the shoulder and arm during the funeral procession, see p. 144; "'money-changer'—to determine the value of each coin," see p. 145. See also R. Me'ir Abulafia, *Yad Ramah* to *Sanhedrin* 68a.

44 *Ibid.,* IX, 3, p. 67. Zlotnick translates the preceding, "For all other dead, the mourner need not bare his arm; for his father and mother, he should do so. But even for his father and mother he need not bare his arm, if he does not wish to do so. Now it happened that when R. Akiba's father died . . ." The rendering, "if he does not wish to do so," is, as the translator himself admits (p. 145) difficult. The variant texts (and the medievals) give, "if it is not proper." See n. 39. For the view of the Babylonian Talmud, see *infra.*

45 Ramban, *Torat ha-Adam* (pp. 56–57). Inasmuch as the father of R. Akiba

was honored by the disciples it would not appear that he was considered personally unworthy.

46   Contrast the view of *Semahot* (according to Zlotnick's rendering, n. 44 *supra*).

47   *Mo'ed Katon* 22b.

48   "If you ask . . . why is the divine command violated and parental honor slighted . . . the answer is that the honor of the Torah takes precedence. The Talmud asks, 'Ought a son who is his father's master to rise before his father?' and gives no answer. Certainly, then, a disciple ought not to demean himself in the service of his father."—Ramban, *op. cit.*

49   P. *Hagigah* 2:1;77c.

50   *Kohellet Rabbah* 7:8.

51   The continuation of the story is better suited to the former version too. On the other hand, the former version might be an emendation aimed at bringing R. Me'ir's reply into harmony with M. *Keritot,* end.

52   This reflects the narrative as found in *Avot de-R. Nathan,* version B, ed. Schecter, Chapter 13, pp. 30–33. An account of the initiation of R. Eliezer is found in four other sources, with significant variations. See Z. Kagan, "Divergent Tendencies and Their Literary Molding in the Aggadah," *Scripta Hierosolymitana,* XXII (Jerusalem: 1971), pp. 151–170; J. Neusner, *Development of a Legend* (Leiden: 1970), index, "R. Eliezer, beginnings."

53   *Berakhot* 17a.

54   *Kiddushin* 33b.

55   "The son of R. Joshua ben Levi married into the Patriarchal house." —Rashi. R. Hanan'el (cited in B. M. Lewin, *Ozar ha-Geonim,* IX, pt. 2, p. 25) read *bat ha-Nasi* ("the daughter of the Patriarch") in the talmudic passage cited, rather than *bet ha-Nasi* ("the house of the Patriarch") as in our texts.

56   In other words: the Patriarchal connection is decisive only because I am my son's teacher, but if he were my teacher I should rise before him on that score alone, though I am his father.

57   The talmudic assumption—for which there is no specific prescriptive statement—is that a son should rise before his father. "You shall rise before the aged and show deference to the old" (Leviticus 19:32). Note also Maimonides, *Mamrim* 6:3; " . . . and the son rises before him as he does before his master," and *Kessef Mishneh, ad loc.* Certainly, this gesture is most consonant with the pattern of behavior explicitly required. See also *Ketubot* 62b: "Is there a father who rises before his son?"

58   The ascending order of the two questions is noteworthy; the second query seems to presuppose a negative answer to the first, which, of course, is not given.

59   " . . . R. Judah, his son, said to him: 'Father, don't teach that the Mish-

nah text reads, etc.' Said Samuel to R. Judah: 'Keen scholar! Don't speak to your father so. . . . ' ''—*Kiddushin* 32a.

60 R. Ezekial, father of R. Judah, was in fact known as an extremely pious man, whose prayers were noted and preserved by his son: see p. *Berakhot* 9:2.

61 A more explicit expression of such feelings is that of the midrashic explanation of Jacob's obeisance before his son (Genesis 47:31—" . . . then Israel bowed at the head of the bed," if understood to mean that Jacob bowed to Joseph): "One bows even to a jackal in power." (*Megillah* 16b). I. H. Weiss *Dor Dor*, III, pp. 56–57 posits a tense relationship between R. Joshua b. Levi (though he claims there were two figures of that name) and the Patriarch, but there is little evidence to support this.

While we do know that the leading families of Sepphoris, and even the scholars, were wont to pay their daily respects to the Patriarch in the third century (see p. *Shabbat* 12:3; 13c). and that marriage into the Patriarchal family was of advantage, there is no other indication that men would rise in the presence of the Patriarch's son-in-law. Indeed, the earlier *baraita* requires signal respect only for the *Nasi* himself (*Horayyot* 13b); so, too, R. Yohanan in the 3rd century (*M. K.* 27b). But in the 4th century there is an attempt—rejected by some of the rabbis— to have priests participate in the funeral of the sister of the Patriarch; see p. *Berakhot* 3:1;6a.

62 This is narrated in the Vatican ms. of *Genesis Rabbah* (ed. Theodore-Albeck, III, 1242), and *Midrash ha-Gadol, Genesis,* ed. Margaliot, p. 817. Inasmuch as other incidents concerning R. Meyasha were sometimes erroneously attributed to the "son" of R. Joshua b. Levi (see A. Hyman, *Toledot Tanna'im ve'Amora'im,* III, p. 881), and that "son" and "grandson" will often interchange, it is quite possible that R. Meyasha is the subject of R. Joshua's comment in *Kiddushin* 32b, and that the grandfather had double reason for rising before his grandson. In any case, the entire nexus of relationships provides an interesting insight into the workings of the Patriarchate at this time, and indicates the growth of nepotism.

63 *Yam Shel Shelomoh Kiddushin* 1:57.

64 Uncertainties in law of rabbinic origin would be decided in the direction of leniency.

65 The problem of reciprocal honor is assumed by R. Asher (and by the halakhists who subsequently discuss the matter) to have been the motivation for R. Me'ir's behavior; speculation on the accuracy of this assumption, while relevant to the immediate biographical question, is not relevant to the halakhic development. Cf. also I. Agus, *R. Me'ir of Rothenberg,* I, p. 40, n. 4: "This statement needs no apology. R. Me'ir's conduct in this matter was a direct result of his great piety and his general attitude to the Halakha; it fits in perfectly with his consistent avoidance of a situation of doubt," and the bibliography given there. My presentation reflects Urbach. But even the halakhically oriented exposition of R. Me'ir's conduct that is offered by R. Solomon Luria (see *infra*) presupposes that

this separation did not present personal difficulties. It is also told of R. Barukh, father of R. Shene'ur Zalman of Lida (the 18th-century founder of *Habad Hasidism*), that he left the town in which his son lived because the latter insisted on rising before his father, and R. Barukh—conscious of his son's greatness—considered his acceptance of this honor an offense to the Torah (S. Y. Zevin, *Sippurei Hassidim*, I, p. 85; I was directed to this incident by Rabbi Dr. A. B. Z. Metzger).

66   *Darkhei Mosheh Tur, Yoreh De'ah* 240:2.

67   *Yoreh De'ah* 240:7.

68   *Yam Shel Shelomoh, Kiddushin*, 1:72. For the problem of *mehila*, see also *Bah, Tur, ad loc.*

69   *Mamrim* 6:4 (Hershmann, p. 155). So too R. Menahem ha-Me'iri, *Commentary to Kiddushin*, p. 187.

70   R. Joel Sirkes, *Bayyit Hadash* to *Tur, ad loc.*; R. Menahem Azariah di Fano, *Responsa*, 71.

71   See I. H. Weiss, *Dor Dor*, III, pp. 198ff; Y. Levinger, *Ha-Mahashava Ha-hilkhatit shel ha-Rambam*, pp. 155ff.

72   The discussion of this topic by E. Fromm, *You Shall Be As Gods*, pp. 68ff., is flawed by his insistence that the true thrust in these sources is toward "full independence," with God serving primarily "to guarantee man's independence from human authority." In this modern explication of rabbinic thought, God becomes the radical device by which culture propels itself beyond human fixations.

Post Talmudic Authorities
and Responsa Cited

R. Aaron Perahiah (17th century, Greece)
  She'elot u-Teshuvot (S. uT.) Perah Matteh Aharon (Amsterdam, 1703)

R. Abraham di Buton (16th century, Greece-Turkey)
  S. uT. Lehem Rav (Izmir, 1660)

R. Abraham Danzig (c. 1747–1820, Prussia-Lithuania)

R. Abraham b. David—Ra'abad—(c. 1120–1198, Provence)

R. Abraham b. Ezra (1092–1167, Spain)

R. Abraham Isaiah Karelitz (1878–1953, Lithuania-Israel)

R. Aha of Shabha (8th century Babylon-Israel)

R. Akiba Eiger (1761–1837, Hungary-Poland)
  S. uT. R. Akiba Eiger (Warsaw, 1884)

R. Alexander Zusslein (d. 1349, Germany)

R. Aryeh Leib (c. 1695–1785, Russia)

R. Asher b. Yehiel (c. 1250–1327, Germany-Spain)
  S. uT. Ha-Rosh (Wilna, 1881)

R. Bahya b. Asher (d. 1340, Spain)

R. Bahya b. Pequdah (11th century, Spain)

R. Bezalel Ashkenazi (d. 1592, Israel)

R. Benjamin b. Matityahu (18th century, Greece)
  S. uT. Binyamin Ze'eb (Venice, 1739)

R. David Ha-Kohen (d. 1530, Greece-Turkey)
  S. uT. Radakh (Constantinople, 1537)

R. David Ha-Levi (c. 1586–1667, Poland)

R. David Kimhi (c. 1160–1235, Spain)

R. David Pardo (1710–1792, Italy-Israel)
  S. uT. Mikhtam Le-David (Salonica, 1769)

R. David b. Abu-Zimra (c. 1480–1574, Spain-Israel)
  S. uT. Ridbaz (Warsaw, 1882)

R. Eliezer Pappo (d. 1824, Bulgaria)

R. Eliezer b. Joel Ha-Levi (c. 1140–c. 1225, Germany)

R. Elijah, Gaon of Vilna (1720–1797, Lithuania)

R. Elijah b. Hayyim (1530–1610, Turkey)
  S. uT. Ra'anah (Constantinople, 1600)

R. Ephraim b. Jacob (1133–1196, Germany)

R. Ezekial Katznellenbogen (1670–1750, Poland-Germany)
S. uT. Knesset Ezekial (Altona, 1732)

R. Ezekiel Landau (1713–1793, Poland-Prague)
S. uT. Nodah bi-Yehudah (Wilna, 1904)

R. Hai Gaon (939–1038, Babylonia)

R. Hanan'el b. Hushiel (990–c. 1055, N. Africa)

R. Hayyim Benveniste 1603–1673, Turkey)

R. Hayyim Heller (1879–1960, Poland-U.S.A.)

R. Hayyim Soloveitchick (1853–1918, Russia)

R. Hezkiah Medini (1833–1905, Turkey-Israel)

R. Isaac Abarbanel (1437–1509, Spain-Italy)

R. Isaac Barceloni (11th century, Spain)

R. Isaac of Corbeil (d. 1280, France)

R. Isaac al-Fasi (1013–1103, N. Africa-Spain)
S. uT. Ha-Rif (Pittsburgh, 1954)

R. Isaac of Vienna (c. 1180–c. 1260, Austria)

R. Isaac b. Samuel (12th century, France)

R. Isaac b. Sheshet (1326–1407, Spain)
S. uT. Ribash (Wilna, 1878)

R. Isaiah Horowitz (c. 1556–c. 1630, Germany-Israel)

R. Israel b. Joseph Alnakawa (d. 1391, Spain)

R. Israel Brunna (15th century, Germany)
S. uT. Mahari Brunna (Jerusalem, 1960)

R. Israel Isserlein (1390–1460, Germany)
S. uT. Terumat ha-Deshen (Warsaw, 1882)

R. Jacob b. Asher (fl. 1300, Spain)

R. Jacob Castro (1525–1610, Egypt)
S. uT. 'Ohalei Ya'akov (Leghorn, 1783)

R. Jacob Emden (c. 1697–1776, Germany)
S. uT. She'elat Ya'abetz (Lemberg, 1884)

R. Jacob Tam (c. 1100–1171, France)

R. Joel Sirkes (d. 1640, Poland)

R. Jonah Gerondi (d. 1263, France-Spain)

R. Joseph Albo (c. 1380–c. 1435, Spain)

R. Joseph Babad (d. 1874, Galicia)

R. Joseph Kolon (c. 1420–1480, Italy)
S. uT. Maharik (Warsaw, 1884)

R. Joseph Habiba (16th century, Spain)

R. Joseph Herz (1872–1946, Great Britain)

R. Joseph Karo (1488–1575, Spain-Israel)

R. Joseph b. Megas (1077–1141, Spain)
S. uT. Ri Megas (Warsaw, 1870)

R. Joseph of Trani (1568–1639, Israel-Turkey)
S. uT. Maharit (Lemberg, 1861)

R. Joshua Falk Katz (d. 1614, Poland)

R. Judah Ayyas (c. 1690–1760, N. Africa-Israel)
S. uT. Bet Yehudah (Leghorn, 1746)

R. Judah Ha-Hasid (d. 1217, Germany)

R. Levi b. Gershom (1288–1344, Provence)

R. (Yehudah) Loewe (d. 1609, Prague)

R. Me'ir Abulafia (c. 1170–1244, Spain)

R. Me'ir Simha of Dvinsk (1843–1926, Latvia)

R. Me'ir of Rothenberg (c. 1220–1293, Germany)
S. uT. Maharam (Budapest, 1895; Berlin, 1891–2; Cremona, 1557)
Teshuvot, Pesakim, u-Minhagim, ed. I. Kahana, vol. 2 (Jerusalem, 1960)

R. Menahem Azariah di Fano (1548–1620, Italy)
S. uT. R. Azariah Menahem (Sziget, 1892)

R. Menahem Ha-Me'iri (1249–1306, Provence)

R. Moses of Coucey (13th century, Spain-France)

R. Moses Isserles (c. 1525–1572, Poland)
S. uT. Ramah (Warsaw, 1883)

R. Moses b. Maimon (1135–1204, Spain-Egypt)
S. uT. Ha-Rambam, ed. J. Blau (Jerusalem, 1958–1961)

R. Moses Mintz (15th century, Germany-Poland)

R. Moses b. Nahman (1194–c. 1270, Spain-Israel)

R. Moses Sofer (1762–1839, Hungary)
S. uT. Hatam Sofer (Vienna, 1895)

R. Naftali Z. Y. Berlin (1817–1893, Russia)
S. uT. Meshiv Davar (Warsaw, 1895)

R. Nissim Gerondi (14th century, Spain)
S. uT. Ha-Ran (Lemberg, 1860)

R. Paltoi Gaon (9th century, Babylonia)

R. Pinhas Horowitz (1730–1805, Poland-Germany)

R. Raphael Meldola (1685–1748, Italy)
S. uT. Mayyim Hayyim (Amsterdam, 1737)

R. Sa'adiah Gaon (882–942, Egypt-Babylon)

R. Samson R. Hirsch (1808–1888, Germany)

R. Samson of Sens (c. 1150–c. 1215, France)

R. Samuel Abohab (1610–1694, Italy)
S. uT. Devar Shemu'el (Venice, 1702)

R. Samuel di Modena (1506–1589, Turkey)
S. uT. Rashdam (Lemberg, 1862)

R. Samuel Strashon—Rashash—(1794–1872, Lithuania)

R. Shabbetai Ha-Kohen—Shakh—(1621–1662, Moravia)

R. Shem-Tov b. Abraham—*Migdal 'Oz*—(14th century, Spain)

R. Simeon b. Zemah Duran (1361–1444, N. Africa)
S. uT. Tashbatz (Lemberg, 1891)

R. Solomon b. Aderet (1235–1310, Spain)
S. uT. Rashba, pt. I (Hanover, 1610); pt. III (Lvov, 1812);
pt. IV (Pietrkov, 1883); pt. VI VII (Warsaw, 1868); *Meyuhasot*
(attributed) *la-Ramban* (Warsaw, 1883)

R. Solomon b. Ha-Yatom (11th–12th century, Italy)

R. Solomon b. Isaac—Rashi—(1040–1105, France)

R. Solomon b. Simon Duran—Rashbash—(c. 1400–1467, N. Africa)

R. Solomon Luria —*Rashal*—(1510–1573, Poland)

R. Vidal of Tolosa—*Maggid Mishneh*—(14th century, Spain)

R. Ya'ir Hayyim Bachrach (1638–1701, Germany)
S. uT. Havvot Ya'ir (Lemberg, 1896)

R. Yehiel Epstein—*Arukh Ha-Shulhan*—(1835–1905, Lithuania)

R. Yehiel Weinberg (1884–1967, Germany)
S. uT. S'ridei 'Esh (Jerusalem, 1965–1969)

R. Yeruham b. Meshullam (14th century, Provence)

R. Yeruham Perla (1846–1934, Poland-Israel)

R. Yom-Tov b. Ashbilli—Ritba—(d. c. 1330, Spain)

R. Zemah Duran (15th century, N. Africa)
S. uT. Yakhin u-Bo'az (Leghorn, 1782)

R. Zerahiah Halevi—*Ba'al Ha-Ma'or*—(12th century, Provence)

Index

Note: This index does not, by and large, duplicate the topic headings of the Table of Contents. Also, it refers to the notes only when these contain independent discussion.

I. Sources

II. Subjects and persons